The Rule of Law in Britain from the Roman Occupation to the Present Day

The Rule of Law in Britain from the Roman Occupation to the Present Day

The only Liberty

By

Anthony Babington

THIRD EDITION

A Short History of the Rule of Law in Britain

43 AD
From the Roman Occupation to the Present Day

BARRY ROSE

CHICHESTER

1995

First published 1978 by Barry Rose (Publishers) Ltd.
Little London, Chichester,
West Sussex, England.

Second Edition published 1985

Babington, Anthony
The rule of law in Britain from the
Roman occupation to the present day.
1. Law – Great Britain – History
I. Title
340'.0941 KD532

ISBN 1-872328-07-5

Printed in Great Britain by BPC Wheatons Ltd, Exeter

Also by Anthony Babington

Autobiographical

NO MEMORIAL

Historical

THE POWER TO SILENCE
A History of Punishment in Britain

A HOUSE IN BOW STREET
Crime and the Magistracy,
London, 1740–1881

THE ENGLISH BASTILLE
A History of Newgate Gaol and
Prison Conditions in Britain 1188–1902

FOR THE SAKE OF EXAMPLE
Capital Courts-Martial 1914–1920

MILITARY INTERVENTION IN BRITAIN
From the Gordon Riots to the Gibraltar Incident

THE DEVIL TO PAY
The Mutiny of the Connaught Rangers,
India, July, 1920

The only liberty I mean, is a
liberty connected with order;
that not only exists along with
order and virtue, but which
cannot exist at all without them.

EDMUND BURKE, 1774

PREFACE TO THE THIRD EDITION

Since this book was first published in 1978 the stability of the Rule of Law in Britain has been repeatedly placed in jeopardy.

The I.R.A.'s campaign of bombing, murder and maiming has continued unabated. Their outrages have been committed with the object of terrorizing the whole nation. No person and no building had been immune from attack: the victims have even included a number of elderly people and small children.

The existence of civil order in our cities and our towns had also been endangered in recent years by the re-emergence of the rampaging mob. Some of the occurrences during the urban riots which erupted in the 1980's were reminiscent of the violence of the rabble in bygone centuries.

Apart from terrorism and public disorder, the incidence of crime in Britain is escalating every year. In 1965 there were 1,133,882 recorded offences: by 1992 the figure had gradually increased to 5,592,000. According to a MORI opinion poll carried out in January 1994 in various parts of Britain, 77 per cent of the people interviewed were afraid of their homes being burgled and 52 per cent were afraid of getting mugged in the street. Over 50 per cent of the interviewees admitted that they are afraid of going out at night.

Unless we can find an effective way of mastering the criminal, the belief that we are living under Thee Rule of Law may soon become exposed as a fanciful myth.

ANTHONY BABINGTON

1994

THE RULE OF LAW IN BRITAIN

by

ANTHONY BABINGTON

Since this book was first published a little over five years ago there have been many happenings, not only in Britain but throughout the world, which have been wholly inimical to the advancement of the Rule of Law. Britain is no longer an island otherwise than in the strictly geographical sense. The ease and the speed of intercontinental travel, the ever-increasing number of our people who journey abroad, and the ability of the news-media to place before us in an instant the events in distant corners of the globe – all these have served to break down our traditional insularity and to make us more conscious of the places and the people beyond our own shores; they have also brought us more closely into contact with the methods of administration employed by foreign governments.

Historians of the future might well regard the present era as being the age of the terrorist. It is an age of hijacking, shoot-outs, kidnaps and indiscriminate bombings in which the inhumanity and ruthlessness of politically motivated gangsters have known no bounds. Their outlook was epitomized by a member of the German Baader-Meinhof gang who, when asked if they were at all troubled about the carnage occasioned to innocent bystanders by their outrages replied, "We do not believe that there is any such person as an innocent bystander".

In recent years terrorist organizations have become aware of the comparative simplicity of hijacking, or in modern terminology skyjacking, an aircraft on an ordinary schedule flight. The usual routine is for the armed hijackers to seize control of the plane when it is airborne and then to hold the occupants as hostages while they demand either a huge ransom or the release of some of their colleagues who are serving lawfully imposed sentences of imprisonment for their crimes. Often they add a warning that if their claims are not satisfied by a stated time they will proceed to blow up the aircraft together with all those inside her. This creates an appalling dilemma for the Government concerned, which is faced with the alternatives of succumbing to a most brutal form of blackmail or of jeopardizing the lives of the captive passengers and crew. A number of countries now have specially trained squads of anti-terrorist troops. These have achieved several notable successes against skyjackers in operations in which they have stormed a hijacked aircraft killing or capturing the gunmen and rescuing the surviving hostages. There can be little doubt that skyjacking has been actively encouraged by a few nations which have always offered a ready asylum to any escaping terrorists with whose aims they sympathize.

Even young children are not considered to be "innocent bystanders" by the average extremist terrorist organization, as has been amply demonstrated by the recent activities of the Provisional I.R.A. In the spring of 1977 a group of South Moluccan gunmen in Holland simultaneously seized a village school and an express train in furtherance of their grievances against the Dutch Government. Six teachers and 105 pupils at the school, and 50 of the passengers in the train were held by them as hostages. After some days Dutch troops freed the train in a dawn attack in which six of the terrorists and two of the passengers were killed. The occupation of the school was ended on the same day without any additional casualties.

No persons and no places are immune from the barbarity of the terrorists. In March 1979 Airey Neave M.P., the Conservative Shadow Northern Ireland Secretary, was killed by a bomb which exploded in his car as he was driving out of the underground car park at the House of Commons. An organization calling itself the Irish National Liberation Army claimed responsibility. Five months later the revered wartime leader and statesman, Admiral of the Fleet Earl Mountbatten of Burma, aged 79, was cruelly murdered by the Provisional I.R.A. when a remote-controlled bomb destroyed his 30-foot boat moored in a cove in Co. Sligo. His 14 year old grandson and another young boy also perished and three other members of Lord Mountbatten's family, one of whom died later, were severely injured. Any public figure is regarded as a justifiable target for assassination by the political gangsters. In September 1978 Georgi Markov, an *emigre* Bulgarian writer and broadcaster with known anti-communist views, died painfully after being jabbed in the thigh with the point of an umbrella as he waited for a bus outside the studios of the B.B.C. overseas broadcasting services in London. A post mortem examination revealed that he had been killed by a metal pellet containing poison twice as deadly as cobra venom. Then, in June 1982, the Israeli Ambassador to London was shot and critically injured by a Palestinian gunman as he was leaving a function at the Dorchester Hotel in Park Lane.

Nowadays Embassy buildings are particularly vulnerable to terrorist attacks. In the spring of 1975 the West German Embassy in Stockholm was beset by members of the Baader-Meinhof gang demanding the immediate release of some of their associates from prisons in West Germany. They had murdered the military attache and one other hostage before they themselves were killed or captured by the Swedish police. The following summer a terrorist squad belonging to the Japanese Red Army forcibly took over the consular section of the American Embassy in Kuala Lumpur. They offered to spare the lives of the 50 staff they were holding as hostages if, and only if, seven Red Army members were freed from prisons in Tokyo. The Japanese Government submitted to their terms. In a much publicized incident in April 1980 six gunmen who described themselves as belonging to the Mahealdin Al Nasser Martyr group burst into and occupied the Iranian Embassy in London. They seized 26 hostages, including a police constable and two employees of the B.B.C., whom they threatened to murder unless 91 Arab prisoners in Iran were unconditionally released. During the six day siege which followed two of the hostages were murdered. The terrorists were finally overpowered, five of them being killed, in a skilful rescue operation conducted by the Special Air Service in conjunction with the Metropolitan Police.

Terrorism can be a costly business when exercised on an elaborate scale; murder squads must be financed; sophisticated weapons must be purchased and gunmen trained in their use; the components of bombs must be bought and places arranged for their manufacture. There can be no doubt that without the money, support and encouragement the terrorist gangs are receiving from certain revolutionary governments they would be hard put to it to continue their campaigns of violence on anything like the present level. In addition there are other malicious or tragically misguided individuals who are regularly donating funds to subsidize the killings and the mutilations. It has been estimated that over the past decade the Provisional I.R.A. has needed about £2m a year to keep up its programme of systematic outrages. Their front organization in the U.S.A. is a society called Noraid whose members are mostly Americans of Irish origin. The U.S. Justice Department in a recent report disclosed that Noraid was providing approximately three-quarters of the Provisional I.R.A.'s entire income. The remaining quarter comes mainly from armed robberies committed in England and Ireland.

The terrorist gangsters occasionally attempt to obtain money by kidnapping a prominent citizen and then demanding a large ransom for the release of their captive unharmed. This form of terrorism was once more common on the continent than in the British Isles. In September 1977 the President of the West German Employers' Federation was kidnapped in Cologne by a dissident communist group after his chauffeur and his three bodyguards had been killed. Six weeks later his dead body was discovered in the boot of an abandoned car. In October of the same year a Dutch millionaire businessman was kidnapped in the centre of Amsterdam. He was only freed when a ransom of over £2m had been handed over to his kidnappers. A French industrialist abducted by hooded gunmen outside his home in Paris early in 1978 escaped two months later after a shoot-out between his kidnappers and French police in the vicinity of the Paris Opera House. The Provisional I.R.A., desperate to increase its finances has now added this form of sadistic extortion to its well-established repertoire of barbarity. Even at the moment of writing, Mr. Don Tidey, a chain stores executive, has just been rescued by the Irish security forces after a three week ordeal in captivity. Mr. Tidey had been kidnapped in Eire as he drove his daughter to school. The I.R.A. demanded a ransom of £5m from his company and made it clear that he would be murdered unless the money was paid. Whilst negotiations were still proceeding a joint operation was carried out by the Irish Army and the Garda in Co. Leitrim during which members of the kidnap gang were tracked down with their captive in an area of thick woodland. During the ensuing battle an Irish soldier and a police officer were killed. At the end the I.R.A. kidnappers tried to shoot Mr. Tidey, whose life was probably saved by the gallantry of a detective who was wounded in shielding him from the gangsters' bullets.

There is no weapon more favoured by terrorist organizations than the high-explosive bomb. It is comparatively easy to assemble in almost any size. It can be planted with the minimum fear of detection in a letter, a car, a package, a public building or a doorway, and those responsible can be at a safe distance before it is detonated. Above all, it inflicts the most terrible havoc and injury and causes the greatest consternation amongst the law-abiding public. England and Northern Ireland have in recent years suffered more grievously than any other country from indiscriminate terrorist bombing attacks; these have nearly always been perpetrated by the Provisional I.R.A. or the Irish National Liberation Army. On the British mainland alone approximately 80 people, most of them civilians, have been murdered by acts of Irish terrorism since 1972. Each outrage, far from bowing the national will, has merely served to increase the loathing and contempt in which the terrorists are held.

In 1973 one person was killed and 238 injured, including 44 children, by car bombs planted by the Provisional I.R.A. outside the Old Bailey and Great Scotland Yard in London. The casualties inflicted by the Irish bombers during 1974 made it the worst single year which England had endured at their hands. In February 12 men were killed when a an Army coach was blown up in Lancashire; in July a woman was killed and 44 people were injured in a bomb explosion in the Tower of London; in October five were killed and 65 injured by terrorists' bombs planted in two public houses at Guildford; in early November two were killed and over 30 injured when a bomb was hurled at random through the window of a public house in Woolwich – two young men and a girl each had to have a leg amputated as a result of this attack. The worst outrage of the year, as regards fatalities, took place on November 21, when as a result of bombs exploding in two crowded public houses in Birmingham 21 people died and close on 200 were injured. Even that was not the end of it for the year. The I.R.A. have always taken a sadistic pleasure from inflicting casualties upon civilians around the time of Christmas, and they were true to their custom in 1974 when a man was killed and 10 persons sustained injuries by various bomb explosions in central London during the middle period of December.

The indiscriminate bombing in England went on after 1974 and has continued ever since. In 1975 more people were killed and wounded in London, Manchester and Caterham. In 1976, apart from a bomb which injured 50 in the crowd at the Ideal Home Exhibition at Earls Court, the I.R.A. endeavoured to blow up a London underground train and a crowded commuter train in Kent. In 1978 bomb attacks took place at Bristol, Coventry, Liverpool, Manchester, Southampton and in central London. In 1979 casualties due to bombing occurred in Birmingham and at Yeovil in Somerset. In 1980 it was the turn of the Irish National Liberation Army who injured two soldiers and a civilian by bomb explosions at an Army barracks and a weapon camp on Salisbury Plain. The Provisional I.R.A. followed up a few months later by causing a bomb explosion in Catford police station in which a 19-year old probationer police constable had his right hand blown off and suffered permanent damage to his eyesight; four other police constables were injured by the blast.

The following year the I.R.A. resorted to a new instrument of terror – the nail bomb. The first of these went off outside Chelsea Barracks in London killing a woman shopper and an 18-year old youth; a total of 40 people were injured including 25 Irish Guardsmen who were passing at the time in a coach. Nail bombs were employed again in a double atrocity on a day in July 1982. As a detachment of the Household Cavalry was riding through Hyde Park on their way to the guard-changing ceremony at Horse Guards Parade a remotely controlled car bomb was exploded beside them. A lieutenant and three troopers were killed and 21 people, soldiers, police and civilians, were injured; in addittion seven cavalry horses were either killed by blast or were so badly hurt they had to be destroyed. Two hours later a bomb with a timing mechanism was exploded underneath a bandstand in Regents Park while the regimental band of the Royal Green Jackets was giving a lunchtime concert. Seven bandsmen were killed and 27 people were injured, some of them very seriously.

The latest act of devilry committed by the Provisional I.R.A. was one, perhaps, that has occasioned more horror than any of their previous atrocities both for its timing and its location. On Saturday December 17, 1983, early in the afternoon, a car bomb was detonated outside Harrods in the West End of London. It happened on a day and at an hour when it was quite obvious that the precincts of the famous store would be crowded with family parties intent on their Christmas shopping. On December 18, *The Sunday Times* gave some eyewitness accounts by people who had been close at hand. One man, who had thrown himself down in the street when the explosion occurred, recounted the scene when he stood up again:

> "I could see bodies lying on the pavement, people stumbling around so completely shocked they didn't know what was happening. I saw a little girl clinging to her mother, who was trying to hold her stomach, where blood was gushing from a wound".

A visitor to London from Paris said that he noticed wounded children blown on to a traffic island from a zebra crossing outside the store. He added, "I saw mostly women and children with injuries caused by the blast". A total of three police officers and three civilians were killed in this outrage; 77 members of the public, including nine children under 16, were injured.

It is a truism that the Rule of Law cannot exist in any country where the fundamental liberties of the subject are not protected in the courts of justice. Many of these liberties have ceased to exist only a few hours flying time from the shores of Britain in the communist states of eastern Europe.

Under their governments it is customary for a citizen to be deprived even of the right to travel abroad or to emigrate without official authorization, which is seldom granted to anyone below retirement age except for a holiday in another communist state. For example, in the German Democratic Republic it is an offence under Article 213 of the penal code to cross the border without having a permit to do so. Those caught in the act are liable to a sentence of up to eight years' imprisonment. According to the latest report of Amnesty International[1] large numbers of would-be emigrants who sought to leave the G.D.R. lawfully during 1982 were also imprisoned.

An Albanian who crosses the border without permission or who attempts to do so can be sent to prison for five years under art. 127 of the criminal code. If he leaves Albania with permission but declines to return again he can be tried for an offence under art. 47(1) which carries a penalty of 10 years' imprisonment or death. Bulgaria and Romania have similar prohibitions on what is called "illegal" or "fraudulent" crossing of the border. In the case of Romania the Amnesty International report gives details of two would-be emigrants who were forcibly confined in psychiatric hospitals.

The laws of all these socialist republics are drafted in wide and general terms so as to give their governments an absolute power in suppressing freedom of thought and expression. Among the offences listed by the criminal code of the U.S.S.R. are "words or actions" which are termed "anti-soviet agitation and propaganda" and "anti-soviet slander". In the G.D.R. a person can receive a substantial term of imprisonment for "anti-social behaviour", and likewise in Romania for "propaganda against the socialist state". The Albanian and Bulgarian codes both include the offence of "anti-state agitation". In Poland any persons can be arrested and indefinitely detained where there is a "justified suspicion" that if they remained at liberty they would engage in activities "endangering the interests of the security or defence of the state".

The sweeping powers of oppression possessed by these governments have not only been used by them to subdue their political opponents, but have also been employed against religious orders, academics, writers, intellectuals and, indeed, against anyone whose viewpoint might differ from their own. In Czechoslovakia a number of people were convicted during 1982 for distributing unauthorized religious literature and several Roman Catholic priests were imprisoned for saying Mass or for holding theological discussions without state approval. Religious worship is illegal in Albania, which was officially proclaimed in 1967 to be an atheist state. The leaders of the various denominations have been persecuted ever since. Amnesty has reported that a Jesuit priest was imprisoned in 1980 for baptizing the children of one of his relations. Eight members of a Christian group, most of them Baptists, were convicted in Romania in 1982 for distributing Bibles which had been smuggled into the country; they were all sent to prison for terms of either five years or six years. In the U.S.S.R. religious worship is allowed under stringent restrictions; for instance, it is forbidden for parents to bring up their children according to their own theology or to profess their beliefs in public. The Russian Orthodox Church and the Islamic and Jewish faiths have all suffered their share of persecution in recent times. At least eight Jews were tried in 1982 for campaigning for the right to emigrate to Israel or for the preservation of Jewish culture.

The latest survey prepared by the Writers in Prison Committee of International P.E.N. has stated that "the Soviet Union continues to have the largest number of writers and journalists in prison, labour camps and psychiatric hospitals of any country in Europe, and there is no sign of any easing of the repression of intellectual life there".[2] Authors who criticize the existing regime are dealt with savagely. It is known that in May 1983 Leonid Borodin was sentenced to 10 years' imprisonment to be followed by five years internal exile for alleged "anti-soviet agitation", a charge founded principally on his book, "Tale of a Strange Time" which was published outside the U.S.S.R. The written word can be anathema to a despotic government. In September 1981 a Turkish citizen visiting some of his relatives in Bulgaria was arrested by the secret police and charged with possessing "anti-soviet literature" relating to the Turkish minority in Bulgaria. He received a sentence of 41 years' imprisonment. The authorities in the G.D.R. are particularly sensitive to criticism by their own people. In 1980 an author was imprisoned for five years for "hostile propaganda" contained in an unpublished book about the East German political order. During the summer of 1982 two members of a dissenting Marxist-Leninist group were both sent to prison for eight years for distributing literature critical of socialism as practised in the G.D.R. When martial law was suspended in Poland in December 1982 a new amendment to the criminal code made it an offence, punishable with up to five years' imprisonment, to produce, possess or distribute what were described as "anti-state publications".

Freedom of speech in the east European communist republics is virtually confined to the expression of opinions which happen to accord with the party line. Amnesty International has received unofficial reports that during the last few years a number of people have been imprisoned in Albania for asserting views of which the authorities disapproved. In 1981 a young Albanian conscript soldier was given a sentence of eight years' imprisonment for criticizing government ministers in private conversations with his army friends. There is evidence that Czechoslovak courts have consistently punished people for making what are considered to be "anti-socialist" statements. On January 13, 1982 a former political prisoner was tried by a military court in Romania on a charge that he had "disparaged the central organs of the party and the social order of our country". He was convicted and sentenced to eight years' imprisonment. In the

U.S.S.R. it is quite customary for men and women to be charged with "the circulation of fabrications known to be false which defame the Soviet state and social system"; conviction for this offence usually attracts a severe sentence.

Human Rights organizations have expressed grave concern about the conditions in which the east European communist countries sometimes keep political prisoners and at their methods of trial. There is evidence that political detainees in Albania have been held in solitary confinement for as long as six months whilst the cases against them were being investigated; during this time they have been denied contact with their families or with defence lawyers and frequently have been beaten in an effort to extract confessions from them. It is known that solitary confinement is widely used throughout the communist bloc and the beating of political prisoners occurs there as a matter of routine. Political trials are often heard in camera and there is seldom an effective appeal procedure from the decisions of the courts. A large number of prisoners in the U.S.S.R. are kept in psychiatric hospitals – for reasons which are ideological rather than medical. When these so-called patients are considered to represent "a special danger to society" they are sent to a punitive mental institution for an indefinite period. Very recently Viktor Artsimovich, a Russian historian, was accused of writing a critical essay on the works of Karl Marx which had displeased the Soviet authorities. After he had been arrested he was diagnosed by state doctors to be suffering from schizophrenia and "philosophical intoxication" and he was ordered to undergo forcible treatment at a special psychiatric hospital.

The communist states in the east are not the only countries in Europe which are deprived of the benefits of the Rule of Law. Allegations of beatings and torture have been made by foreign subjects who have been detained at police stations in Greece or have served sentences on criminal charges in Greek prisons. In Spain, where the authorities are permitted under the anti-terrorist legislation to keep a suspect incommunicado for up to 10 days without access to family, friends or legal advisors, prisoners have complained that they were subjected to physical assaults and electric shock treatment; one man asserted that his face had been plunged repeatedly into a pail of water while he was being interrogated. A very credible testimony has come from a former Mother Superior of a Spanish convent of the Roman Catholic order of the Missionary Mothers of Mercy who had become a well known writer for a Basque newspaper. She was arrested in Bilbao in April 1982 on suspicion that she was associating with an armed band of terrorists. She afterwards complained that she had been severely beaten up by her interrogators, and when she was transferred to Madrid she was examined by police doctors who found she had injuries which fully confirmed her allegations. The following November she was acquitted of all the original charges brought against her but she was given a short suspended sentence for resisting arrest and for using insulting language. Martial law was proclaimed in Turkey when a military coup took place in September 1980 and since that time all political offences have been tried by military courts. Certain provisions of the penal code at present in use are drafted to curb the free expression of opinion. A prominent sociologist recently received a sentence of 10 years' imprisonment on his conviction under art. 140 which forbids the publishing abroad of any information which damages the Turkish state. Two other arts., 141 and 142, which prohibit the spreading of left-wing propaganda inside Turkey have been used extensively to prosecute authors, journalists, publishers and academics. The editors of two socialist newspapers were sentenced during 1982 to 31 years' and 14 years' imprisonment respectively for the dissemination of communist ideology.

The 1983 reports of Amnesty International and the Writers in Prison Committee have not confined their attentions to Europe, but have carried out investigations in every part of the world. In the continent of Africa, in Latin America, in Asia and in the Middle East there are certain countries in which the governance of tyranny has usurped the Rule of Law; where the ill-treatment and torture of political prisoners is commonplace, where the inhabitants can be arrested on specious charges and imprisoned indefinitely without trial, where the military courts have jurisdiction over civilians, where prisoners disappear without explanation and where the most elemental human rights are treated with contempt. There are many examples; they are, however, only examples of practices which have now become widespread.

Under the military dictatorship in Chile there are doctors who specialize in the treatment and rehabilitation of released torture victims. Ex-detainees have complained of repeated beatings and the application of electric shocks to various parts of their bodies including their genitals; others have been subjected to sadistic psychological pressures such as deprivation of sleep, mock executions, and threats against the lives of their families. A 19-year-old girl, arrested in 1981, reported that in addition to the more customary forms of torture she had been raped four times by members of the secret police and had been made to lie down beside a decomposing corpse. Although there is no accurate information about the number of writers who are imprisoned in Chile the names are known of 15 authors and journalists who were originally arrested but have now disappeared without trace. The state security police in Cuba are empowered to arrest anyone suspected of "illegal" political activities. The prisoners can then be kept incommunicado for indefinite periods during which time they are subjected to perpetual intimidations to force them to confess. Many Cubans are punished by the courts for belonging to proscribed societies and cults; last year two men were sentenced to long terms of imprisonment for fulfilling their religious observances as Jehovah's Witnesses. Now that Argentina has adopted a democratic constitution there are more writers imprisoned in Cuba for expressing their opinions than in any other Latin American country.

Turning to the Middle East, Iran has achieved an especial notoriety for state-inspired babarity and injustice. In August, 1982, Ayatollah Khomeini issued a proclamation in which he said, "I hereby declare to all the Judges across the country and all those engaged in judicial affairs that all the laws in practice during the former regime were contrary to Islam and should be discarded". Since then a system of law known to the Ayatollah's supporters as "Islamic Law" has been administered by newly-established Islamic Revolutionary Tribunals. Whipping, the amputation of limbs, and even stoning to death have become recognized punishments for certain offences. Drug and alcohol offenders can be executed, as can adulterers and homosexuals; there have been numerous authenticated reports of the execution of pregnant women and of young people below the age of 18. Prisoners in Iranian gaols have complained of habitual ill-treatment. They have told how they were starved and blindfolded for many hours at a time, how they were beaten with cables all over their bodies, how they were given repeated electric shocks and how their heads were held under water at intervals while they were being interrogated. Many prisoners have been detained in close custody without ever being charged with an offence, whilst others have been punished, sometimes they have been executed, without being convicted at any sort of trial.

In Asia another Islamic republic, Pakistan, has abandoned all pretentions to the existence of a Rule of Law. In October 1979 the military government of the country prohibited further activities by its political opponents, and since then all critics of governmental policies have risked arrest for being what are described as "criminal anti-social elements". Many of those detained in this category have been lawyers, journalists, trade unionists, doctors, teachers and students. Civilian defendants can now be tried for political offences by military courts in accordance with military regulations. Many of the procedures at such trials cannot be said to accord with the accepted standards of justice of today. A martial law regulation which came into force in September 1982 shifted the burden of proof from the prosecution to the defence. The courts can, and do, order political offenders to be flogged. The death sentence can be imposed for acts of sabotage and terrorism causing damage to property, as well as for various offences which may be considered as "likely to cause insecurity, fear or despondency among the public" – a sufficiently wide definition to allow an infinite discretion to the court of trial. In Pakistan, as in other Asian countries, people detained at police stations and in prisons have alleged that they have been subjected to beatings and torture. In this respect the re-education camps for political prisoners in the People's Democratic Republic of Laos and in the Socialist Republic of Vietnam are especially notorious.

In every part of Africa there are states where human rights are trampled, divided and annulled. Political opponents are often branded as counter-revolutionaries, a category of criminal which receives no mercy. Frequent proclamations in Libya call for the "liquidation of the enemies of the revolution", and sometimes for the pursuit and murder of Libyans who have escaped abroad. Arrests are wholesale under legislation framed for "the protection of the revolution". The proceedings at the revolutionary courts are summary and there is no appeal from their decisions. The basement of the Military Intelligence Headquarters in Tripoli is said to be the centre for political interrogations during which all forms of torture, the sophisticated and the crude, are practised as a matter of routine. The sombre clouds of tyranny have also cast their shadows over Ethiopia to the east. Here too there is arbitrary arrest, detention without trial and torture and ill-treatment of prisoners. The authorities have carried out a studied programme of religious persecutions. At the beginning of 1982 the Foreign Minister asserted that some of the churches had indulged in "anti-revolution, anti-government and anti-people activities". He blamed in particular the Ethiopian Evangelical Mekane Yesus sect; several of their leaders were imprisoned, their churches were closed and their church property confiscated. Thirty members of an Ethiopian Jewish community were arrested during the year for "betraying the revolution" by attempting to leave the country without permission.

And so it goes on whether one turns one's attentions in a westerly or a southerly direction throughout the length and breadth of the African continent. In Guinea about 2,900 prisoners, detained for opposing the Government, have disappeared without any explanation being offered by the authorities. In the Congo there have been arrests on spurious charges, interrogations and torture by the secret police and indefinite imprisonment without trial. Last June in Ghana three High Court Judges and a retired

Army Major were seized at their homes one night by the security forces and were taken away for summary execution. In 1979 the Government of Mozambique set up the Revolutionary Military Tribunal with jurisdiction to try all offences against the security of the state, and empowered to pass sentence of death to offenders. Trials before this court can be held in camera; prisoners are not legally represented and there is no right of appeal from its judgments. In South Africa, apart from the continuing obscenity of apartheid, the Terrorism Act of the Internal Security Act permits the authorities to detain suspects indefinitely without trial and to withhold all information about them; to ban individuals and organizations arbitrarily; and to prosecute for purely political offences. There are frequent complaints about the ill-treatment of prisoners, several of whom have died in custody under highly suspicious circumstances. In Zimbabwe, a nation still within the British Commonwealth, there occurred last year the disgraceful episode of the air officers' trial. It started with the blowing-up of a number of fighter aircraft at the principal Zimbabwean air force base in July 1982. By all accounts the security police carried out their inquiries into this act of sabotage with utter incompetence and decided, upon no evidence whatsoever, that it had been carried out by a small group of senior white officers, six of whom were arrested and tortured into making "confessions". In August 1983 the six were tried and acquitted by a High Court Judge who found that the charge against them had no foundation and that the alleged confessions were utterly worthless. On the day of their acquittal the officers were taken back into custody under the new detention orders, members of the Zimbabwean government expressing the view quite openly that they disagreed with the verdict at the trial. All six were released at intervals on the condition that they left Zimbabwe immediately, the last three only being freed at the end of the following December after spending 17 months in gaol. On his return to England one of the officers told how he had been tortured for a fortnight before he had agreed to "confess". He said:[3]

"I was connected to an electric generator by electrodes

placed all over my body, including my genitals. I suffered convulsions. The torture lasted about two and a half hours". After this experience, he went on, he had suffered nightmares for a good five months.

It is against such a background that this book might well be read. Not because we have any cause to imagine that the Rule of Law in Britain is without imperfection, but because we have every cause to be thankful that over the years we have established in this land a policy in which the dignity and freedom of the individual are recognized as being the very essence of our social order. Towards the end of the 19th century William Sacheverell, the Whig politician, declared, "The foundation of Government is in People's hearts". His words are still true today. The foundation of Government should rest within the hearts of all the people, whatever their creed and whatever their colour, who make up the citizenship of a nation. It should not rest solely within the rarefied hearts of the despotic few, whether they be the masters of the ruling party or the leaders of the latest successful revolution.

The persistence of the surging level of crime is one of the least satisfactory aspects of law and order in Britain today. This applies particularly in the towns and cities. A recent independent survey carried out by the Political Studies Institute revealed that many Londoners believed that the Metropolitan Police were losing the battle against muggers and burglars and considered the streets of the capital had become unsafe to use at night. During the last few years the British public has also witnessed a spate of rioting the extent and ferocity of which have not been matched in this country during the present century. Professor Asa Briggs has attributed this violent eruption to an unprecedented change which had occurred in English society. He says:[4]

> "Until 1948 there had been only a trickle of black and coloured immigrants into England, and it was in the 1950's that they first became "visible" ethnic minorities. Travel agencies, backed by advertising, actively developed the traffic, particularly from the West Indies. Low wages and heavy unemployment were one spur: relative prosperity in Britain was another".

In the prevailing conditions of affluent living and over-employment a considerable portion of this immigrant labour force took on the type of jobs which were shunned by native-born workers. "There was little general knowledge among English people", writes Professor Briggs "of the different backgrounds from which these newcomers came or of their way of life".

During the 60's and 70's the West Indian population in England continued to increase. There was also an influx of Kenyan Asians with British passports in 1967 and of Ugandan Asians in 1972. The second and third generations of these immigrant families were mostly born here and naturally grew up regarding this country as their own. Professor Briggs has observed, "English social history takes a new turn when children of people of different backgrounds live in England in large enough numbers for their presence to be felt". The moment had been reached when it was necessary for every section of the community to adapt themselves to the recognition that Britain had become a multi-racial nation. Unfortunately, before the mental and emotional adjustments had been fully made tensions, recriminations and allegations of colour-prejudice arose, mainly in the urban areas where large numbers of coloured immigrants had settled. The matter came to a head with the riots and disorders of 1981.

The worst of the violence occurred at Brixton in South London during the weekend of April 10-12. In his subsequent report on the disorders Lord Scarman commented:[5]

> "The British people watched with horror and incredulity an instant audio-visual presentation on their television sets of violence and disorder in their capital city the like of which had not previously been seen in this century in Britain. In the centre of Brixton, a few hundred young people – most, but not all of them, black – attacked the police on the streets with stones, bricks, iron bars and petrol bombs, demonstrating to millions of their fellow citizens the fragile basis of the Queen's peace. The petrol bomb was now used for the first time on the streets of Britain (the idea, no doubt, copied from the disturbances in Northern Ireland).

These young people, by their criminal behaviour – for such, whatever their grievances and frustrations, it was – brought about a temporary collapse of law and order in the centre of an inner suburb of London".

The Report analyses with meticulous detail the background of the disorders, the course of their development and their aftermath. It tells of widespread looting and arson, of police cars and private vehicles being wrecked and set on fire, and of wilful attacks on members of the ambulance and fire services to prevent them from carrying out their duties. Lord Scarman says:

"In one of the most disturbing aspects of the disorders, ambulances and fire engines responding to calls for help in this area were attacked and an ambulanceman and several fire officers were injured. Altogether on Saturday evening one ambulanceman and 14 fire officers were reported injured and four ambulances and nine fire appliances were damaged. Four fire appliances were temporarily abandoned by their crews in the face of the hostility of the crowd, a turntable ladder was stolen and set alight, and a considerable quantity of fire brigade equipment was stolen or damaged".

The worst rioting occurred on the Saturday evening. When the police eventually restored the locality to order, Lord Scarman goes on,

"the toll of human injury and property damage was such that one observer described the scene as comparable with the aftermath of an air raid".

Altogether 279 policemen were injured during the evening, as well as at least 45 members of the public. Twenty-eight buildings were damaged or destroyed by fire, and numerous motor vehicles were wrecked or burnt.

Serious disturbances involving the immigrant population also occurred during 1981 in Southall, Toxteth, Moss Side and the West Midlands. The pattern was always the same; confrontations with the police, looting, arson, missiles, and attacks on vehicles. Lord Scarman comments:

"The common strands in many of the major disorders, for which there is much evidence, are to be found in shared social conditions, in economic insecurity and perceived deprivation, in enforced idleness because of unemployment, and in the hostility of at least a section of young people to the police."

In the light of recent happenings, those with long memories could look back and reflect sadly that we in Britain had travelled far from the days of the smiling copper on the beat who had the occasional task of controlling unruly crowds. But they could take comfort, none the less, that even now we do not have, like so many other countries, armed police at the street-corner and para-military riot squads ever ready for use against civilian demonstrators.

FOOTNOTES

[1]All the facts relating to alleged offences in the next few pages are taken from Amnesty International Report 1983, unless otherwise stated.

[2]Report of the Writers in Prison Committee presented to the International P.E.N. Congress at Caracas in September 1983.

[3]*The Times,* December 31, 1983.

[4]A Social History of England by Asa Briggs.

[5]The Brixton Disorders April 11-12, 1981. Report of an inquiry by the Rt. Hon. The Lord Scarman O.B.E.

CONTENTS

CHRONOLOGICAL TABLE OF EVENTS

Part I	*THE ROMAN OCCUPATION*	BC
First invasion of Britain by the Romans under Julius Caesar		55
Second invasion of Britain by Julius Caesar		54
		AD
Invasion of Britain by Roman forces under Aulus Plautius		43
Defeat of Caratacus		51
Boadicea's insurrection		61
Agricola, Governor of Britain		78–84
Britain incorporated into Prefecture of Gaul		292
Invasion of Britain by Picts and Scots		367
Constantine withdrew majority of Roman garrison from Britain to fight in Gaul		407
Roman occupation of Britain officially ended		410

Part II	*THE ANGLO-SAXON PERIOD*	
Anglo-Saxon invaders drove the Britons into the west of their island		449–455
Britain divided into seven or eight petty Teutonic Kingdoms		457
Smaller kingdoms become merged into four principal independent kingdoms of Northumbria, Mercia, Wessex and Kent		550–600
St Augustine arrived in Britain to convert Anglo-Saxons to Christianity		597

Viking invasions of Britain commenced	800
Kings of Wessex reigned as Bretwalda of Britain	825–1013
Alfred of Wessex defeated the Danes	870
Alfred became King of Wessex	871
Alfred framed Code of laws	890
Death of Alfred	899
Danes resumed raids on British coast	980
King Swein of Denmark invaded Britain and King Aethelred of Wessex, Bretwalda of Britain, fled to Normandy	1013
Swein died. Aethelred returned to Britain	1014
Death of Aethelred	1016
Canute of Denmark crowned King of England ..	1017
Death of Canute. His sons Harold and Harthacnut became joint Kings of England	1035
Harold became sole King of England as Harold I ..	1037
Death of Harold I. Harthacnut became King of England	1040
Death of Harthacnut. Saxon dynasty restored when Edward, son of Aethelred became King of England	1042
Death of Edward	1066

Part III *THE NORMAN PERIOD*

Harold II crowned. William of Normandy invaded England. Harold defeated and killed at Battle of Hastings. William I crowned	1066
Norman Conquest of England and Wales completed ..	1070
Domesday survey completed	1086
Death of William I. Accession of William II	1087
Death of William II. Accession of Henry I. Old Anglo-Saxon laws restored	1100
First comprehensive English law book, *The Laws of Henry* compiled	1115
Death of Henry I. Accession of Stephen	1135
Death of Stephen	1154

Part IV *THE PLANTAGENET PERIOD*

Henry of Anjou crowned as Henry II	1154
Thomas à Becket became Chancellor	1155
Thomas à Becket appointed Archbishop of Canterbury	1162
Constitutions of Clarendon	1164
Murder of Thomas à Becket	1170
England divided into circuits for the administration of justice	1176
Henry II appointed five officials from his household to exercise a permanent judicial function in the curia regis	1178
Death of Henry II. Accession of Richard I	1189
Certain knights appointed as 'keepers of the peace' ..	1195
Death of Richard I. Accession of John	1199
Normandy lost of England	1204
England placed under an interdict by the Pope ..	1208
Lateran Council condemned trial by ordeal and trial by battle. Trial by petty jury generally adopted in England	1215
Magna Carta	1215
Death of John. Accession of Henry III	1216
Counties invited to send specified number of knights as delegates to meeting of National Council ..	1224, 1254 & 1258
National Council first known as 'parliament' met	*circa* 1246
Henry III forced to agree to Provisions of Oxford ..	1258
The Barons' War	1262–1268
Simon de Montfort summoned first regular national parliament	1265
Death of Henry III. Accession of Edward I	1272
Statute classified offences as 'bailable' and 'non-bailable'	1275
Wales United to England	1283
Inns of Court established in proximity to the courts of law at Westminster	*circa* 1292

Knights, citizens and burgesses summoned to attend at meeting of the Great Parliament	1295
Edward I accepted constitutional axiom that the king could not impose taxes without the consent of Parliament	1297
Scotland regained her independence	1297–1298
Death of Edward I. Accession of Edward II	1307
Queen Isabella's revolt	1326
Murder of Edward II. Accession of Edward III	1327
Statutory recognition given to office of 'keeper of the peace'	1327
Keepers of the peace accorded certain judicial powers	1328 & 1330
Outbreak of Hundred Years War between England and France	1338
House of Commons separated from House of Lords	1344
Black Death reached England	1348
Statute of Labourers	1349
Justices of the Peace created	1361
Justices of the Peace ordered to hold their sessions four times a year	1363
Decision that petty juries' verdicts must be unanimous	1367
Death of Edward III. Accession of Richard II	1377
Peasants' Revolt led by Wat Tyler	1381
Richard II forced to abdicate. Accession of Henry IV	1399

Part V THE PERIOD OF THE HOUSES OF LANCASTER AND YORK

Death of Henry IV. Accession of Henry V	1413
France invaded by Henry V	1415
Death of Henry V. Accession of Henry VI	1422
Property qualification for County Justices of the Peace set at £20 per annum	1439

Hundred Years War ended	1453
Wars of the Roses	1455–1471
Sheriffs deprived of powers of arresting and fining offenders	1461
Henry VI deposed. Accession of Edward IV	1461
Printing introduced by Caxton	1471
Birth of the Court of Chancery	1474
Death of Edward IV. Accession of Edward V	1483
Edward V murdered in the Tower. Accession of Richard III	1483
Richard III defeated and killed at Battle of Bosworth by Henry Tudor	1485

Part VI *THE TUDOR PERIOD*

Accession of Henry VII	1485
Court of Star Chamber instituted	1487
Court of Requests founded	1493
Death of Henry VII. Accession of Henry VIII	1509
First of statutes for the punishment of vagrancy	1530
Fall from power and death of Cardinal Wolsey	1530
Establishment of national English church	1531–1536
Catherine of Aragon divorced	1533
Henry VIII became 'Head of Church'	1534
Abolition of Pope's authority in England	1534
Anne Boleyn beheaded	1536
Suppression of the Monasteries	1536–1539
Jane Seymour died	1537
Anne of Cleves divorced	1540
Thomas Cromwell beheaded	1540
Catherine Howard beheaded	1542
Death of Henry VIII. Accession of Edward VI	1547
English Prayer-Book introduced	1548

Promulgation of the Forty-Two Articles	1551
Death of Edward VI. Lady Jane Grey proclaimed Queen	1553
Accession of Mary. Re-introduction of Roman Catholicism	1553
Execution of Lady Jane Grey	1554
Justices of the Peace authorized to hold preliminary enquiries into indictable offences	1554–1555
Mary married Philip of Spain	1554
Burning of Protestants	1555–1556
Calais re-taken by French	1558
Death of Mary. Accession of Elizabeth. Church of England restored	1558
Court of High Commission established	1559
Lay courts empowered to punish prisoners who had been granted Benefit of Clergy	1576
Barons of Court of Exchequer elevated to status of judges of courts of Queen's Bench and Common Pleas	1579
Mary, Queen of Scots beheaded	1587
Inauguration of Poor Law system	1601
Death of Elizabeth	1603

Part VII *THE STUART PERIOD*

Accession of James I	1603
Dynastic Union of England and Scotland	1603
James I styled as 'King of Great Britain'	1604
Small debts courts set up in London	1606
Chief Justice Coke dismissed from the bench	1616
James I asserted superiority of equity over common law	1616
Women allowed to claim Benefit of Clergy for some offences	1622

Statute of Monopolies	1624
Death of James I. Accession of Charles I	1625
Darnel imprisoned for refusing to pay a forced loan	1627
Petition of Right	1628
Charles I governed without a parliament	1629–1640
John Hampden's trial for refusing to pay 'ship money'	1637
First meeting of the Long Parliament	1640
Impeachment and Execution of the Earl of Strafford	1641
Abolition of courts of Star Chamber, High Commission and Requests	1641
Attempted arrest by Charles I of five members of the House of Commons	1642
Civil War began	1642
Charles I defeated at the Battle of Naseby	1645
Charles I surrendered to the Scots	1646
Charles I handed over to Parliament	1647
Pride's Purge	1648
House of Lords abolished	1648
Charles I tried before 'High Court of Justice', condemned and executed	1649
Oliver Cromwell dismissed the Council and the House of Commons	1653
Cromwell invested as 'Lord Protector'	1654
Death of Oliver Cromwell	1658
Richard Cromwell appointed Protector	1658
Richard Cromwell resigned	1660
Restoration of monarchy. Accession of Charles II	1660
House of Lords re-established	1660
Principle of 'settlement' introduced to Poor Law system	1662
The Great Plague	1665
The Fire of London	1666
'Tyburn Tickets' introduced to combat crime	1669

The Secret Treaties of Dover	1670
Bushell's case established the independence of juries	1671
Charles II's Declaration of Indulgence	1672
The Test Act	1672
The Popish Plot	1678
Persecution of Roman Catholics	1678–1679
Habeas Corpus Act	1679
Death of Charles II. Accession of James II	1685
Duke of Monmouth's rebellion	1685
Lord Chief Justice Jeffreys' 'bloody assize'	1685
James II's Declarations of Indulgence	1687 & 1688
Acquittal of the seven bishops	1688
Abdication of James II	1688
Bloodless Revolution. Declaration of Rights. Bill of Rights. William III and Mary accepted the throne jointly from the Convention Parliament	1689
Women's right to Benefit of Clergy extended	1692
Act to combat crime by offering rewards, and free pardons for turning 'Kings Evidence'	1692
Triennial Act limiting duration of every Parliament to maximum of three years	1694
End of official system for licensing books	1694
Death of Mary. William III reigned on as sole monarch	1694
Defendants charged with treason allowed to have defence counsel, to call witnesses on oath, and to see indictments	1695
Defendants charged with felony allowed to call witnesses on oath	1702
Act of Settlement	1702
Death of William III. Accession of Anne	1702
Defendants claiming Benefit of Clergy allowed to memorise words of 'neck verse'	1705
Copyright of books introduced	1710
Death of Anne	1714

Part VIII *THE HANOVER PERIOD*

Accession of George I	1714
Riot Act	1715
The South Sea Bubble	1715
Robert Walpole's Ministries	1715–1717 & 1721–1742
Septennial Act extended maximum duration of Parliament to seven years	1716
Act permitting prisoners convicted of certain clergyable offences to be transported to the American plantations	1717
The Bubble Act	1720
Act offering financial recompense to those injured, or dependants of those killed in detaining criminals	1722
Jonathan Wild, the sham thief-taker, convicted at the Old Bailey and executed	1725
Death of George I. Accession of George II	1727
Property qualification for County Justices of the Peace raised to £100	1732
Artists Copyright Act gave statutory copyright to makers of prints and engravings	1735
Lord Hardwicke's term as Lord Chancellor	1737–1756
Justices of the Peace given jurisdiction to settle disputes between masters and servants	1746
Henry Fielding took up residence in Bow Street	1748
Henry Fielding published his treatise *An Enquiry into the causes of the Late Increase of Robbers* etc	1751
Henry Fielding commissioned by the Government to clear up the outbreak of crime in London	1753
Lord Hardwicke's Act to make the grant of a licence or the publication of banns essential to a valid marriage	1753
Henry Fielding resigned from the Bow Street Office and was succeeded by his half-brother (Sir) John Fielding	1754
Death of Henry Fielding	1754

Duke of Newcastle's Ministries	1754–1756 & 1757–1762
First regular payment by Government for upkeep of the Bow Street thief-takers	1755
Earl of Mansfield's term as Lord Chief Justice ..	1756–1788
Death of George II. Accession of George III	1760
John Wilkes obtained damages against a Home Secretary who had authorized the illegal entry of his house	1763
Sir John Fielding's small horse patrol operated from the Bow Street Office	1763–1764
Cesare Beccaria published his *Essay on Crimes and Punishments*	1764
Publication of Sir William Blackstone's *Commentaries on the Laws of England*	1765–1769
Death of the Duke of Newcastle	1768
American colonies declared their independence ..	1776
Publication of John Howard's book on the state of the prisons in England and Wales	1777
Death of William Pitt the Elder, first Earl of Chatham	1778
Gordon Riots	1780
Death of Sir William Blackstone	1780
Death of Sir John Fielding	1780
Introduction of transportation to New South Wales ..	1787
Commencement of the French Revolution	1789
Death of John Howard	1790
Formation of Bow Street foot patrol	1790
Fox's Libel Act gave a jury the right to return a general verdict in criminal libel cases	1792
Middlesex Justices Act created stipendiary magistrates in London	1792
Right of judges to adjourn over-night in cases of treason and felony established	1794
Death of Edmund Burke	1797
Combination Acts	1799 & 1800
Union of Britain with Ireland	1801

First Act for protection of children in factories ..	1802
Penal Colony established in Van Diemen's Land (Tasmania)	1803
Para-military Bow Street horse patrol formed	1805
Last impeachment by House of Commons (Lord Melville)	1805
Death of William Pitt the Younger	1806
Death of Charles James Fox	1806
Abolition of the Slave Trade by Parliament	1807
Copyright introduced for works of sculpture	1814
Sentence of 'Hanging, Drawing and Quartering' modified	1814
Battle of Waterloo	1815
'Blood-Money' system abolished	1818
Act to prevent exploitation of children in cotton mills	1819
Trial by Battle formally abolished	1819
Corporal punishment abolished for women	1820
Death of George III. Accession of George IV	1820
(Sir) Robert Peel's periods as Home Secretary	1822–1827 & 1828–1830
Peel's Prison Act forbade use of irons for prisoners ..	1823
Combination Acts repealed	1825
Fee system for payment of judges abolished	1826
Tyburn Tickets abolished	1826
Benefit of Clergy abolished	1827
'Pressing' of prisoners who refused to plead abolished	1827
Formation of Metropolitan Police	1829
Catholic Emancipation Act	1829
Death of George IV. Accession of William IV	1830
Reform Act substantially reformed the House of Commons	1832
Death of Jeremy Bentham	1832
The Metropolitan Police dealt with their first large-scale riot at Coldbath Fields	1833

Act to prevent exploitation of children in mills and factories 1833

Quakers allowed to become members of the House of Commons 1833

Poor Law Amendment Act creating Poor Law Commissioners 1834

Trading Companies Act 1834

Sir Robert Peel's first government 1834–1835

Gibbeting of murderers abolished 1834

First Prison Inspectors appointed 1835

Bow Street horse patrol became mounted section of Metropolitan Police 1836

Prisoner's Counsel Act allowed defendants charged with felonies to be fully represented 1836

Copyright introduced for plays 1836

Wills Act 1837

Pillory abolished 1837

Death of William IV 1837

Part IX *THE VICTORIAN PERIOD*

Accession of Victoria 1837

'People's Charter' drawn up the Chartists 1838

Bow Street Runners disbanded 1839

Justices of the Peace empowered to form professional police forces and to appoint Chief Constables .. 1839

Metropolitan Police Courts Act required all Police Magistrates to be appointed from practising barristers 1839

Prison Act required all prisoners to undergo 'separate confinement' 1839

Transportation to New South Wales suspended .. 1840

Sir Robert Peel's second cabinet 1841–1846

The Chartists presented their grievances to Parliament 1842

Copyright Act extended copyright for book and musical compositions	1842
Quarter Sessions deprived of jurisdiction to try cases of treason, murder and felonies punishable with prison for life	1842
Examinations for qualifying as a solicitor became a statutory requirement	1843
Creation of new County Courts	1846
Lord Campbell's Act gave a right of action to the relatives of a person killed by negligence	1846
Transportation to Van Diemen's Land discontinued	1846
Powers of the Poor Law Commission were transferred to a Poor Law Board	1848
Public Health Act created the Board of Health	1848
Civil Servants first paid by regular salaries instead of by fees	1848
Creation of the Court of Crown Cases Reserved	1848
Creation of regularized Magistrates Courts	1848–1849
Death of Sir Robert Peel	1850
Death of the Duke of Wellington	1852
The Earl of Derby's Cabinets	1852, 1858–1859 & 1866–1868
Creation of the Council of Legal Education by the Benchers of the four Inns of Court	1852
Common Law Procedure Act terminated many unnecessary technicalities	1854
Jews allowed to belong to the House of Commons	1855
Palmerston's Cabinets	1855–1858 & 1859–1865
Extension of limited liability from shareholders	1855
Formation of police forces by the Justices of the Peace became mandatory	1856
Creation of the Court for Divorce and Matrimonial Causes	1857
Creation of the Court of Probate	1857

Board of Health disbanded: its powers taken over by the Privy Council and the Home Secretary ..	1858
Death of Lord Macaulay	1859
Major part of criminal law codified by seven statutes ..	1861
Bankruptcy became available to non-traders	1861
Introduction of Highway Boards	1862
First Merchandise Marks Acts	1862 & 1887
Whipping Act abolished public floggings	1862
Copyright extended to paintings, drawings and photographs	1862
Carnavon Committee advocated harsher treatment for prisoners	1863
Death of Palmerston	1865
Prison Act implementing proposals of Carnavon Committee	1865
Sheffield and Manchester Outrages	1865–1866
Sanitary Act compelling local authorities to appoint Sanitary Inspectors	1866
New Reform Act increased the electorate and introduced household suffrage in the boroughs	1867
Abolition of the Hundred Courts	1867
Master and Servant Act ended punishment of imprisonment for workmen guilty breaches of contracts of employment	1867
Transportation ended	1867
Disraeli's Governments	1868, 1874–1880
Gladstone's Governments	1868–1874, 1880–1885, 1892–1894
Parishes deprived of the right to levy church rates ..	1868
Abolition of public executions	1868
First meeting of the Trades Union Congress	1868
Creation of a detective branch in every division of the Metropolitan Police	1869
Office of High Constable abolished	1869
Imprisonment for debt abolished	1869
Court of Bankruptcy established	1869

Open, competitive examinations introduced for entry to the Civil Service	1870
Education Act to ensure there were sufficient school places available	1870
Responsibilities for hygiene transferred to the Local Government Board	1871
Compulsory examinations introduced as a qualification for being called to the Bar	1871
Acts clarifying the legal status of Trade Unions and controlling the behaviour of strikers	1871
Trades Union Congress formed a Parliamentary Committee	1871
Introduction of voting by secret ballot in parliamentary and municipal elections	1872
Office of Petty Constable abolished	1872
Judicature Act created the Supreme Court	1873
Conspiracy and Protection of Property Act removed organized strikes from law of criminal conspiracy ..	1875
Public Health Act introduced new requirements for the maintenance of health	1875
Food and Drugs Act. The first serious attempt to exercise control over the standards of purity of food and drugs	1875
Registration of Trade Marks commenced	1875
Appellate jurisdiction restored to the House of Lords	1876
Church of England Temperance Society appointed their first Police Court Missionary	1876
Education became compulsory for children between the ages of five and fourteen	1877
Control of all prisons was vested in the Prison Commissioners	1877
All highways placed in the control of the Local Government Board	1878
Creation of the office of Director of Public Prosecutions	1879

The three courts of common law became separate divisions of the High Court	1881
Death of Disraeli	1881
Married Women's Property Act emancipated a wife's property from her husband's control	1882
Institution of the Patents Office	1883
Franchise Act introduced household suffrage for county seats	1884
Opening of the new Royal Courts of Justice	1884
Abolition of Sheriff's Tourns	1887
'Bloody Sunday' riot in Trafalgar Square	1887
Local Government Act created County Councils ..	1888
Sales of Goods Act gave purchasers protection against sellers for false descriptions of articles	1893
Report by the Gladstone Committee on prison conditions	1895
Introduction of Workmen's Compensation	1897
Death of Gladstone	1898
Trade Unions set up a Labour Representative Committee	1899
Death of Victoria	1901

Part X *THE MODERN PERIOD*

Accession of Edward VII	1901
First Borstal institution opened	1902
Poor Prisoner's Defence Act introduced free legal aid for certain poor defendants	1903
Campbell-Bannerman's minority Liberal Government formed	1905
Liberals swept into power at general Election	1906
Start of suffragist campaign of violence	1905
Trades Disputes Act removed organized strikes from the law of civil conspiracy	1906
House of Lords repeatedly obstructed Government programme of legislation	1906–1907

Professional Probation Service commenced	1907
Creation of Court of Criminal Appeal	1907
Asquith's Liberal Cabinet	1908–1915
'Borstal Training' became a recognized sentence of the courts	1908
House of Lords rejected the Government's Finance Bill	1909
Death of Edward VII. Accession of George V.	1910
Parliament Act curtailed the legislative powers of the House of Lords. Full term of a Parliament reduced from seven to five years	1911
Copyright of literary, artistic, dramatic and musical works extended to fifty years after the death of the creator	1911
Members of Parliament started to receive salaries	1911
Trade Unions empowered to collect political levies from their members if there was a right to 'opt out'	1913
First World War	1914–1918
Asquith's coalition Government	1915–1916
Lloyd George's Coalition Government	1916–1922
Representation of the People Act gave women of thirty the right to vote	1918
The Labour Party became the second largest party in the House of Commons	1922
Baldwin's Conservative Governments	1923–1924 & 1924–1925
Macdonald formed the first Labour Government with Liberal support	1924
Appointment of Probation Officers made compulsory in every Petty Sessional Division	1925
The General Strike	1926
Trades Disputes Act made certain sympathetic strikes illegal	1927
Women given identical franchise with men	1928
Macdonald's second labour minority Government with Liberal support	1929–1931

Poor Prisoners Defence scheme extended	1930
Macdonald's first and second National Governments	1931
Sir Oswald Mosley formed British Union of Fascists	1932
Grand Juries abolished	1933
Public Order Act banned wearing the political uniforms	1936
Baldwin's National Government	1935–1937
Death of George V. Accession of Edward VIII	1936
Abdication of Edward VIII. Accession of George VI	1936
Leader of the Opposition granted a salary	1937
A. P. Herbert's Matrimonial Causes Act extended grounds for divorce	1937
Chamberlain's National Government	1937
Cadogan Committee recommended abolition of corporal punishment	1938
Britain introduced peace-time conscription for the first time	1939
Second World War	1939–1945
Chamberlain's Wartime Government	1939–1940
Churchill's Coalition Government	1940–1945
Churchill's Caretaker Government	1945
Attlee's Labour Governments	1945–1950 1950–1951
Trades Disputes Act of 1927 repealed	1946
Representation of the People Act abolished the business and university votes	1948
Corporal punishment abolished	1948
Courts given power to discharge defendants conditionally or absolutely	1948
Peers lost their ancient privilege of being tried for treason or felony by their fellow-peers	1948
Legal Aid and Advice Act introduced legal aid for civil actions	1949
Homicide Act made certain forms of murder non-capital	1957

Contracts of Employment Act gave new rights to employees 1963

Harold Wilson's Labour Governments .. 1964–1966, 1966–1970, 1974, 1974 – 1976

Rendundancy Payments Act ensured employee's compensation on becoming redundant 1965

Sidney Silverman's Act abolished capital punishment for murder 1965

Courts empowered to suspend sentences of imprisonment 1967

Majority verdicts introduced for juries in criminal trials 1967

First Trades Descriptions Act 1968

Report of Donovan Commission on labour relations 1968

Race Relations Act forbade discrimination 1968

Labour Government published *In Place of Strife* .. 1969

Age of Majority lowered from twenty-one to eighteen 1969

Beeching Commission advocated the reorganization of the higher courts 1969

Edward Heath's Conservative Government .. 1970–1974

Divorce Reform Act made the sole ground for divorce the 'irretrievable breakdown' of a marriage 1970

Divorce Division of the High Court became the Family Division 1970

Equal Pay Act (effective in 1975) forbade any distinction in conditions of employment between men and women 1970

Industrial Relations Act 1971

Courts Act implemented a number of the proposals made by the Beeching Commission 1971

Courts given power to defer passing sentence and to make 'Community Service Orders' 1972

Fair Trading Act 1973

Provided for the appointment of a Director General of Fair Trading and of a Consumer Protection Advisory Committee

Harold Wilson's Labour Government 1974

Industrial Relations Act repealed	1974
Sex Discrimination Act .. .. Certain kinds of sex discrimination made unlawful	1975
James Callaghan replaced Harold Wilson as Prime Minister	1976
Bail Act .. .. Gave a general right to bail except on specified grounds	1976
Race Relations Act .. .. Made provision for preventing discrimination on racial grounds.	1976
Margaret Thatcher's Conservative Government	1979–1990
Brixton Riot	1981
I.R.A. bomb Grand Hotel, Brighton while Mrs. Thatcher and other Ministers were staying there ..	1984
Riot at Handsworth.	1985
Riot at Tottenham	1985
Public Order Act	1986
I.R.A. bomb at Royal Marines School of Music, Deal, 10 musicians killed.	1989
John Major replaces Margaret Thatcher as Prime Minister	1990
I.R.A. Mortar attack on 10 Downing Street	1991
Conservatives win General Election, John Major remains Prime Minister	1992

Part I

THE ROMAN OCCUPATION

(AD 41 – AD 410)

CHAPTER 1

A PROVINCE OF ROME

Britain was given her first experience of a Rule of Law during the four centuries of the Roman occupation.

When Julius Caesar invaded the south-east regions of the island with two legions in the summer of 55 BC, he intended nothing more than a punitive expedition as a reprisal for the assistance which the British had sent to one of the Gaulish tribes in their revolt against the Romans during the previous year. He returned to Britain in 54 BC with a larger force of infantry and cavalry and advanced twelve miles inland from the coast of Kent, but after some fierce and sporadic fighting he allowed the natives to sue for peace and, having collected both hostages and tribute, he once more retired from their shores.

At that time Britain was populated by a number of warlike Celtic tribes, together with the various communities of settlers which had come to the country at an even earlier period than the Celts from the continent of Europe. Julius Caesar wrote, 'the interior of Britain is inhabited by a race said to be aboriginal, the coast invaders from Belgium who having come over for the sake of spoil have settled in the country'. They lived on milk and flesh, he went on, and clothed themselves with skins. In battle they stained themselves a blue colour which gave them 'a more formidable appearance'. The Druids, the established priesthood of the Celts, were, according to Caesar, the 'arbiters in almost all disputes public and private', whose customary powers included the pronouncement of rewards and punishments.

One of the principal results of Julius Caesar's two landings in Britain was to unite the majority of the tribes in the south-eastern portion of the country under a single, common leadership.

On becoming Emperor of Rome, Tiberius Claudius

resolved to carry out a much more thorough invasion of Britain than his resolute predecessor had attempted during the previous century. In AD 43 Aulus Plautius landed with a force of four legions just north of the Thames estuary. After a short while he was joined by Claudius who then led his army on a victorious march to the interior, driving the tribal warriors right back across the borders of Wales and Scotland. While the Romans consolidated their hold on the south-east of the country, the struggle against the native chief Caratacus continued for almost nine years in and around the Welsh hills, until in AD 51 he was vanquished, captured and led in triumph through the streets of Rome. Even then the hill tribes of Wales continued their stubborn resistance and it was the absence of main Roman fighting units in Anglesey which gave Boadicea, Queen of the Iceni, the opportunity to stage her uprising in AD 61. The tide of rebellion swept rapidly through East Anglia. St Albans fell, Colchester fell, and soon the Roman garrison was forced to withdraw from London. But the insurrection ended almost inevitably in the defeat of the British when the regrouped Roman legions met and annihilated Boadicea's ill-trained and ill-equipped hordes in a merciless engagement which took place somewhere between London and Chester. In the ensuing massacre about 80,000 Britons were killed and Queen Boadicea committed suicide by poisoning herself.

After crushing Boadicea's revolt the Romans continued their harsh, repressive measures for a few more years before gradually ameliorating their policies and starting to spread their customs, their enterprise and their culture throughout the newly acquired province. The mild process of colonization was fostered in its early stages by the humane and benevolent influence of Agricola who became governor of Britain in AD 78.

The Romans administered Britain through a single prefect until AD 292 when Diocletian decided to divide the Roman empire into four parts. Thenceforth Britain was incorporated in the prefecture of Gaul and was ruled by a vice-prefect who resided at York. By that time the fortified Roman settlements throughout the country had developed into progressive cities and towns, steeped in the Roman conceptions of civilized urban existence and linked by an enduring network of straight and well-constructed military roads. The Roman-style city was built around a central square called a forum and in that square was a public hall – the basilica – which was used primarily as a court of law, for the Romans shared Aristotle's view that without law, man lived on the level of the lowliest of animals.

The legal system which the Roman soldiers, officials and immigrants brought with them to Britain was the established law of Rome which had been codified several centuries earlier in the Twelve Tables. Sir Henry Maine, in his classic study *Ancient Law*, has written,

> Among the chief advantages which the Twelve Tables and similar codes conferred on the societies which obtained them, was the protection against the frauds of the privileged oligarchy and also against the spontaneous deprivation and debasement of national institutions. The Roman code was merely an enunciation in words of the existing customs of the Roman people.

Originally Roman law had only extended its rights and its privileges to Roman citizens, but in the course of time its ambit was enlarged to include the Peregrini, the free non-citizens residing under the dominion of Rome.

The authority of the magistrates was all-important in shaping the development of Roman law, as its substantive principles were seldom prescribed by legislation. It was customary for a magistrate before his assumption of office to issue an edict in which he would proclaim the legal and procedural axioms he was proposing to follow. In due course these would be adopted by his successors with any modifications they thought fit to impose. Hence it is true to say that to a large extent the Roman magistrates devised their own law.

Under the Roman system of government each city had its own magistrates whose jurisdiction also embraced the surrounding territory outside the city's limits. Public order was maintained by a semi-military policing organization called the *stationarii milites*, any member of which could arrest a person suspected of committing a criminal offence and bring him before a higher officer known as an *eirenarcha* for a preliminary examination. If the *eirenarcha* was satisfied with the evidence against the suspect, he committed him for trial by a magistrate and probably conducted the prosecution case against him at the hearing. It was also permissible under Roman legal procedure for a private individual to carry out a prosecution himself. First of all he had to appear with the accused before a magistrate and to swear to the truth of his accusation. If the accused denied his guilt, the matter proceeded to trial with witnesses being examined and cross-examined by professional advocates, though it is generally believed that the defence could only call witnesses as to character. Should the trial end with an acquittal, the prosecutor might be punished if the magistrate considered that he had made his allegations from an improper motive. On being convicted the defendant could be sentenced to imprisonment, banishment, slavery, a flogging, or to execution.

In common with most of the other ancient legal codes, the Roman system made very little distinction between criminal offences, to be prosecuted by the state, and civil wrongs, which were only triable at the suit of some private person. Indeed it was the old belief that most of the crimes which merely injured an individual, such as theft or assault, were personal matters to be settled by and at the instigation of the victim. For a crime to justify interference by the state under Roman law it must have constituted a danger to the administration, or a gross violation of religious propriety or social usage – such offences as counterfeiting money, extortion by officials, parricide of a very near relation, the practice of witchcraft, sacrilege in a temple, or the selling of a free man in a slave market.

Many of the most widespread offences against the person and against property were treated by Roman law as being *privata delicta* – personal wrongs – but were still placed on a quasi-criminal footing and were punished either by personal vengeance, a penal sentence, or the payment of compensation. *Privata delicta* included thefts, assaults, malicious damage, and defamation. Personal vengeance still played a large part in the Roman system at the time of the occupation of Britain, though it had receded from its importance in bygone centuries when the kinsmen of a murdered man had been under a solemn obligation to slay his killer; even after the Twelve Tables the kinsmen bound to set the law in motion if the identity of the murderer was known to them. The Twelve Tables also preserved the right of a householder to kill a thief whom he had apprehended by night, and the right of a husband or father to instantly slay a lover whom he had caught in the act of adultery with his wife or his daughter. In the interests of public order, however, the Roman code deliberately substituted legal process for private vengeance as the remedy for a personal insult. By the Twelve Tables the composition of scurrilous songs and the perpetration of public affronts were both punishable with death. In the later development of the Roman law, defamatory statements were divided into two classes: those which were made in a public manner were punishable for the humiliation they imposed on the victim, and the truth of the allegation was no defence to the charge; those which were made in private were merely punishable for the distress they caused, but here truth provided an absolute defence on the ground that no man was entitled to legal protection for a reputation which he did not possess.

Roman law had a different procedure for purely civil matters in which there was no suggestion of criminality on the part of the defendant and where the plaintiff was merely attempting to enforce a legal right or to compel the payment of financial compensation. The parties first stated their contentions before a magistrate and if he thought that the issue was a proper one to go for trial he remitted the case to a deputy, usually an ordinary citizen without legal training, at the same time stating how the law should be applied to the facts in dispute. The deputy then heard the evidence, decided the facts and pronounced his verdict according to the legal directions of the magistrate. This process was used particularly to settle claims arising out of alleged negligence or disputed agreements. The basis of the enforceability of contracts under Roman law was the formality with which the agreement had been made, coupled with the solemnity of the words which had been spoken by the parties concerned.

For the Roman citizen, order and discipline began in his own household where the paterfamilias reigned supreme. In the older, imperial days, Maine has written, the father of the household has the power of life and death and an uncontrolled right of corporal chastisement over his children – 'he can modify their personal condition at pleasure; he can give a wife to his son; he can give his daughter in marriage; he can divorce his children of either sex; he can transfer them to another family by adoption; and he can sell them'. But by the time of the Roman empire this authority had been considerably diminished. 'The unqualified right of domestic chastisement has become a right of bringing domestic offences under the cognizance of a civil magistrate; the privilege of dictating marriage has declined into a conditional veto; the liberty of selling has been virtually abolished and adoption itself is destined to lose almost all its ancient importance. . .'

In the household of the Roman citizen a single woman, even after the death of her father, continued to be subjected to the guardianship of her closest male relations. Marriage only presented her with the substitution of one form of domination for another, owing to the ancient Roman doctrine of *manus*, by which a wife came under her husband's control on a similar basis to his sons and daughters and his slaves. There were at one time three forms of marriage which passed the wife into the *manus* of her husband. The first, *confarreatio*, was a religious ceremony conducted by a priest; the second, *coemptio*, a higher form of civil marriage, comprised the fictitious sale of a wife to her husband; and the third, *usus*, the lower form of civil marriage, was the acquirement of a wife by prescriptive right when she had lived in the husband's home for a period of one year without leaving it for three or more consecutive nights. Naturally enough, *manus* was viewed with increasing disfavour by a number of Roman women who found it both irksome and degrading. As an institution it fell into gradual disuse and it is doubtful if many of the Roman wives who came to Britain during the occupation had ever passed into the *manus* of their husbands. By then a new form of marriage was becoming prevalent in Rome, which was virtually an unwritten civil contract based on the binding force of mutual consent and requiring neither formalities nor ceremony for its initiation; there were, however, certain personal disabilities – for instance, if either of the parties was already married, or of unsound mind, or below the age of puberty – which could prevent it from taking place.

Since the Romans regarded marriage as a private arrangement, it came very little under the scrutiny of the courts. Divorce was brought about by informal agreement without the need for legal sanction, although if a wife was not within the *manus* of her husband her father could terminate her marriage whenever he chose to do so, even though divorce was contrary to her own and her husband's wishes. Constantine, the first Christian emperor of Rome, who ruled towards the latter part of the Roman occupation of Britain, endeavoured to institute a legal basis for divorce by allowing a wife to divorce her husband on such grounds as his wrongfully accusing her of adultery, attempting to induce her to commit adultery, or his taking a mistress into their marital home.

Unless he chose to release the children of his family, the paterfamilias in a Roman citizen's household retained his absolute domination over their lives for as long as he lived. They remained infants until they reached the age of puberty – fourteen in the case of a boy and twelve in the case of a girl. Thereafter they became minors until the age of twenty-five, and a son might have a tutor to take charge of his education and upbringing and a curator to supervise his possessions. If the son married, then his wife and his children would automatically pass into the power of his own paterfamilias.

Apart from an additional measure of security, the principal benefit accruing to a wife in *manus* or to a child in power was the conferment of a specific right of inheritance on the death of the husband or the paterfamilias. The fundamental purpose of a Roman will was to ensure the perpetuation of the family, with the fulfilment of its obligations and the preservation of its dignity. A testator would seek not only to make provision for those who had lived under his dominance, but also to appoint an heir who could be trusted with the continuance of his family tradition. In the time of the Roman empire a will could be made either formally, by the testator publicly declaring its terms before a court of law, or informally in a written document signed by the testator or acknowledged by him in the presence of seven witnesses.

A testator could bequeath both his movable and his immovable possessions. It has been suggested that it was the Roman officials and settlers who, by confiscating the areas they needed for building their villas and establishing their estates, first brought into Britain the notion that land could be privately owned. It is clear that before the Roman invasion the land in Britain was possessed by tribes rather than by individuals, and it is natural to suppose that during the occupation the families of the tribal chieftains soon assimilated the habits and the ideas of their new masters. Roman property law was sufficiently developed to recognize a simple form of leasehold, equally applicable to buildings and to land, in which provided the tenant continued to pay the agreed rent to his landlord he was legally entitled to remain in possession until the end of the period stated in the lease. There was too a rudimentary type of Roman mortgage whereby a person could use his house or his land to secure a money debt. The borrower did not have to part with his property but merely created a charge over it in favour of the creditor, giving him a right of sale if the debt was not repaid.

Although Roman law prohibited usury it dealt very harshly with defaulting debtors, treating them as persons who had deliberately avoided the fulfilment of their legal obligations. At one time the unsatisfied creditors were given the right either of killing their debtor and dividing up his carcase between them, or of selling him and his family into slavery. The *lex poetelia* in 326 BC mitigated this severity by providing that if the debtor surrendered everything he possessed he might retain his life and his liberty. Under the Roman empire an unpaid debt was no longer regarded as a capital offence but the penalty of slavery remained unless the debtor availed himself of the *lex poetelia* or some other equivalent enactment.

It would have been quite alien to the Roman way of life for their legal system to have imposed a general liability on an employer, or to have interfered in any way regarding the ordinary relationship between a master and servant. The patrician household was a self-contained unit catering almost exclusively for its own needs, and within its confines the rule of the paterfamilias was absolute. If one of his slaves committed an offence or caused any damage outside his own domain, the paterfamilias had a choice between surrendering the offender to the person he had wronged or paying an adequate sum by way of compensation. It is a significant indication of the legal status of the Roman slave that the Twelve Tables laid down that the owner of a beast which causes damage to another man's property should have a similar alternative of surrender or compensation.

Nevertheless, the Romans were a nation of traders and in their dealings with one another and with the subject peoples of their empire they placed considerable reliance upon the surveillance and the protection of their courts. As a matter of commercial practice Roman law accepted the validity of trading partnerships; these were initiated by the consent of the parties concerned and no legal formalities were necessary. There was no limit to the number of partners in a concern but each one could only make binding arrangements for the partnership with the consent of all the others and could not act as an agent on their behalf. On the death of a partner his share in the partnership came to an end, so he was not able to bequeath his interest by his will. The conception of the legal corporation – an association of individuals treated in law as though it were a single person – has its origins in the Roman *collegium*. A *collegium* comprised a minimum of three people; it was governed by its own rules and the members could sue or be sued through their agent. Even after the founder-members had died off or had been replaced, the *collegium* continued to have its separate legal existence. The *collegia* in Rome consisted not only of trading societies but also of religious bodies and exclusive, private organizations.

Both in Rome and in her provinces the majority of the smaller commercial transactions were still elemental and crude with the farmers, the artisans and the small traders depending principally on the integrity of those with whom they were dealing. Before money came into general use the ordinary method of purchase was by barter; once articles had been inspected and exchanged the deal was concluded and could not be reopened. Certain transactions, however, involved a promise or an undertaking for the future and necessitated an imposition of trust by one or both of the parties to the arrangement. In such circumstances it was quite customary for a person to pledge his honesty by swearing a solemn oath of good faith or by handing over to the other participant some article as an earnest of his sincerity. As the Roman law of contract was entirely undeveloped, if the recipient of the earnest refused to return it the only remedy open to the owner was to institute a prosecution for theft.

The Romans had always encouraged the right of association for the working man and for the humbler classes in general, not with the objects of creating solidarity or dissension but for the sake of companionship and pleasure and to inculcate a spirit of diligence and endeavour amongst them. The craft guilds of Rome enjoyed an ancient and privileged tradition and continued to flourish under the empire, together with the lesser guilds of artisans, manual workers, freed men and slaves. They met at regular intervals to take part in feasts and celebrations and to appoint their officers and to formulate their rules, under the benevolent eye of the authorities.

The system of law which the Romans brought to Britain was an admixture of the sophisticated and the primitive. It aimed at substituting the decision of a court for the assumption of a personal right; the curtailment and control of the custom of private vengeance; the introduction of the notion of equitable arbitration in place of the precept of individual power. It bestowed on Britain four centuries of civilizing influence and of the Pax Romana.

Throughout the period of the occupation the Romans had never succeeded in conquering the tribes in the north of Britain. The legions waged repeated campaigns against the tribesmen; they built ramparts to stem the aggressive incursions; they launched incessant sorties into the barbarian territory beyond. But it was all to no avail. The Scots from Western Caledonia, and the Picts, a Celtic tribe of uncertain origin from the north-east, continued their independence and their insubordination. In AD 367, at a time when the Saxons were stepping up their raids from the continent of Europe, the Picts and Scots invaded the British province and overran the whole country as far south as London. They were driven back again by Theodosius, the father of the emperor of the same name, but it proved to be only a temporary respite.

In AD 383 the Roman garrison in Britain was seriously weakened when the emperor Maximus transferred the bulk of the occupation army to campaign in Gaul. These forces never returned, but in AD 396 a single legion consisting for the most part of Germanic and native troops was sent to Britain for the purpose of resisting the northern raiders. Once again, in AD 407, the emperor Constantine withdrew the majority of the occupation forces to fight in Gaul, leaving the defensive line against the Picts and Scots almost unmanned.

The Roman occupation of Britain was ended in AD 410 when the Emperor Honorius sent a letter to all the cities in the province telling them that from then on they must be prepared to defend themselves. Unfortunately for the British, their long period of reliance on the power of Rome had left them with neither the will nor the ability to resist the incursions upon their coasts and across their frontiers. Having appealed to Honorius in vain for assistance in repelling a new attack by the Picts and Scots, they were driven eventually to the enlistment of bands of Germanic mercenaries to help them drive back the invaders. These mercenaries were rewarded with grants of land in the east of the country where they settled as troublesome and unwelcome guests, shortly to be joined by other warriors from their homelands. Inevitably they soon began to move westwards and in less than fifty years the Anglo-Saxons were in firm control of the greater part of Britain.

Part II

THE ANGLO-SAXON PERIOD

(AD 410 – AD 1066)

CHAPTER 2

THE TEUTONIC AND VIKING INVASIONS

The manifestations of Roman civilization, together with Roman ideas and institutions, were quickly dissipated after the withdrawal of the Roman legions. For some reason the Celtic tribes in Britain had never been Romanized to as great an extent as the subject peoples in most of the other parts of the Roman empire.

The Teutonic invaders who poured into Britain during the fifth Century – the Jutes from the northern and the Angles from the southern ends of the Danish peninsular, and the Saxons from northern Germany and Holland – came not so much to plunder as to settle. They were heathen tribes which had not experienced the dominance or the influence of Rome and they brought with them their own primitive religions, laws and customs. The Britons put up a bitter resistance but they were without a supreme leader or a unified control, and those who were not killed or enslaved were driven from their territories and forced to retreat gradually towards the western parts of the island. The conquering tribes then divided Britain into a mass of small states with seven or eight petty Teutonic kingdoms; by the end of the sixth century these minor entities had become merged into four principal independent kingdoms, Northumbria, Mercia, Wessex and Kent.

There can be little doubt that one of the most important events which occurred soon after the Anglo-Saxon invasion was the conversion of Britain to Christianity. Even when Christianity had become the religion of the Roman empire the new faith had made very little impact on Britain. However, in 597 Pope Gregory sent St Augustine at the head of a small band of missionaries to England for the purpose of converting the Anglo-Saxon invaders. St Augustine was phenomenally successful from the start; in 601 he baptized the King of Kent and thereafter the Christian faith spread rapidly throughout the country. By 660 it could be said that the whole of Britain had become Christian. Not only did Christianity bring to the people a new mode of thinking, but it introduced them to fresh sources of learning, philosophy and culture.

The Anglo-Saxon leaders first came to Britain not as kings and princes but as ealdormen. The institution of kingship did not take place until the settlements of the various kingdoms had been completed. The kings were chosen by election from the members of noble families who had shown particular prowess on the field of battle and had won particular respect fot their abilities in tribal administration. One of the effects of the conversion to Christianity was to surround the kings with a religious reverence, indeed their very appointment to office was often formalized in a Christian ceremony and it became accepted that the king was both a temporal ruler and an ecclesiastical dignitary. It was the priests who started to propagate the doctrine that the king was the fountain of law and order. But the ecclesiastical heirarchy in Britain – the Church was organized and established before the beginning of the eighth century – always abstained from propounding a tenet which even remotely suggested the existence of a divine right of kings, and they felt themselves at liberty to chide and admonish their kings for any moral or spiritual failings. Soon after the introduction of Christianity into Britain a new development took place which led towards the eventual unification of the whole country, in that it became customary for the king of one of the major kingdoms to be generally acknowledged as being the bretwalda, the supreme overlord of all the Anglo-Saxon settlements in the island. No particular kingdom had a prerogative right of supplying the bretwaldas: for almost a century they happened to be the successive kings of Northumbria; then for most of the eighth and for the early part of the ninth centuries it became the turn of Mercia; and finally from 825 to 1013, when the power of Wessex had reached its zenith, the Wessex kings enjoyed a virtual monopoly of the honour.

The administrative and social systems which the Anglo-Saxons adopted in Britain were based on the ancient form of Teutonic democracy. The whole country was divided into shires, the boundary lines of which were arbitrarily arranged for the purpose of convenience. The shire was a self-contained political unit and possessed its separate assembly which exercised legislative, judicial and administrative authority. The ealdorman was the principal official in every shire. The shire was subdivided into smaller components called hundreds which had their own assemblies with administrative and judicial powers. Every hundred comprised a number of townships, the smallest political units in Anglo-Saxon society, and each township again had its own assembly and its own administrative organization. The other two principal figures in the shire were the sheriff and the bishop. The sheriff was at that time an executive officer and the king's agent whose chief task was the collection of profits and taxes on behalf of the king. Although the sheriff might have presided at the shire court in the absence of the ealdorman, his legal and judicial functions did not become significant until a later age. After Britain was converted to Christianity the bishop achieved a growing influence in the shire and came to be regarded as the highest dignitary in the shire assembly after the ealdorman himself.

Under the Anglo-Saxon social structure in Britain the people were separated into two distinct sectors, the free and the unfree. There were several grades of freemen of differing status and importance but they were all essentially both citizens and soldiers. They were usually landowners but they might well be mere tenants. The unfree might be slaves, enfranchised slaves, or foreign settlers. It seems that British slavery, unlike the Roman equivalent, only obliged the slave to perform specific duties for his master; perhaps it was more like the later concept of serfdom. A person could become a slave through capture in war or by being demoted from his original ranking as a freeman in punishment for a criminal offence. The Christian Church in Britain took a benevolent interest in the welfare of slaves and under ecclesiastical influence the British slave was gradually merged into the nominally free, but subservient, category of the villani or peasants.

The highest assembly of all in Anglo-Saxon Britain was the assembly of the king, known as the witan, where the kings and the ealdormen held discussions on public policy.

Every freeman had the right to appear at the witan, not to take part in the deliberations but only to vote for or against the decisions when these had been reached.

The Viking invasions from Denmark and Norway on the east and the southern coasts of Britain commenced about 800. At first the Vikings came to ravage and to plunder, but as the years passed their landings increased in scale and intensity and their objective was not so much to despoil and return to their homelands as to establish permanent settlements. By the middle of the ninth century they had overrun most of East Anglia, Mercia and Northumbria and had occupied London. They were also mounting an increasingly successful attack against the sprawling kingdom of Wessex and it seemed altogether likely that they would be able to conquer the whole of Britain. Indeed, if it had not been for the fact that at the vital moment the Anglo-Saxons had found a leader who was capable of marshalling their resources, restoring their morale and unifying their efforts, Britain would probably have ended up as a Danish colony.

Alfred, son of the king of Wessex, was born about 848. At a very early age he had become the symbol of Anglo-Saxon resistance to the Danes and the only leader who seemed capable of defeating them in battle. He won his first big victory in 870, a year before he became king of Wessex. Other victories followed during the continuous fighting which lasted for the rest of his lifetime, in which he managed to recapture much of the territory the Danes had previously subjugated. At the time of his death in 899, King Alfred had succeeded in confining the Danes to an area in the north and east of Britain which henceforth became known as Danelaw. Moreover he had also ensured that Anglo-Saxon Britain would retain its independent identity, and indeed that the Anglo-Saxon settlements in the country would achieve a measure of political unity under the leadership of the successive kings of Wessex. It was during the tenth century that the name 'England' came into use as a collective territorial description of all the Anglo-Saxon kingdoms in Britain.

During the period of the supremacy of the kings of Wessex a radical alteration took place in the class structure of the new rulers of Britain. Prestige and political power began to depend less and less on a person's status in the old

Anglo-Saxon ranking, and more and more on his personal wealth and the amount of land in his possession. The powerful proprietors gathered about them bands of followers known as thanes whose allegiance was measured in terms of military service rather than on a loyalty based upon kinship, tribal connection, or territorial proximity. In due course the thane was rewarded with a grant of land from his master's holding, so that he himself became a member of the recently emergent landed nobility. By such a process the social distinctions of the past were gradually replaced by the more feudal gradations into greater lords, lesser lords, ordinary freeholders, and the servile mass of unpriviledged villani.

In the changing order of society the position of the king grew ever more remote and ever more sacrosanct. A transformation also took place in the status and function of the witan, which ceased to be a popular democratic assembly and became instead an exclusive oligarchical council principally attended by bishops and ealdormen and by a select circle of royally-favoured thanes.

This metamorphosis did not proceed unhindered by external interference. In the year 980 the Danes resumed their plundering raids along the British coast after a period of about a quarter of a century during which they had turned their attentions elsewhere. However, in the course of the next few decades it became abundantly clear that the latest Viking attacks were on a different level from those of the former century, for they did not consist of mere uncoordinated landings and settlements but were part of an integrated scheme for incorporating the whole of Britain into the expansionist Scandinavian empire.

In 1013 King Swein of Denmark landed on the east coast at the head of a powerful invading army. The British, wearied from the years of incessant Viking onslaughts, capitulated after a short struggle and King Aethelred of Wessex, then the Anglo-Saxon bretwalda, was promptly deposed and sought refuge at the court of his father-in-law, Richard the Fearless, Duke of Normandy. Swein was then acknowledged as king of all England, but it appears that he still continued to recognize the constitutional authority of the witan and when he died in 1014, although the Danish army of occupation chose his younger son Canute as his successor, the witan voted for the restoration of the exiled Aethelred. Two years later, after the death of Aethelred, Canute was crowned king of England. He later assumed the thrones of Denmark and Norway as well, and so the Scandinavian dream of a kingdom bridging the vast expanses of the North Sea was eventually fulfilled.

Canute regarded himself, not as a foreign conqueror but as an English king; apart from the limited areas incorporated in the territory known as Danelaw he accepted and governed according to both the customs and the laws of the Anglo-Saxon peoples. England under Canute was never treated as a subject colony; in fact he replaced the Danish officials and administrators with native Britons as quickly as men with adequate qualifications became available, and as soon as security permitted he sent home his Danish army. For simplicity of management he divided the country into four units, Wessex, Mercia, East Anglia and Northumberland, each of which he placed under a local chieftain. Canute died in 1035. Reared as they were to the notion of an elective monarchy, it must have seemed to most Anglo-Saxons like the closing of the long, benign reign of one of their own kings rather than the termination of the imperious rule of an alien intruder.

CHAPTER 3

ANGLO-SAXON LAW AND ORDER

The system of law which prevailed in Anglo-Saxon Britain was mainly Teutonic in origin and had been influenced very little from Celtic or from Roman sources. At their inception the legal precepts of the Anglo-Saxon invaders were based upon the traditions and customs of the Teuton tribes, though these were later modified and supplemented in the conditions brought about by the advent of feudalism and by the conversion of the country to Christianity.

Anglo-Saxon Britain was never fully feudal in the true sense of the word as no implicit obligation of military service was placed by the lords upon their tenents and villani. Nevertheless, Britain gradually developed her own brand of feudalism inasmuch as the landed proprietors began to exercise an increasing power and authority over their dependents, and offered them in return a measure of security and protection which could be supplied neither by the shire nor by the state.

After Britain became Christian there were very few alterations in her substantive laws but the Church thereafter exercised a certain formative effect on the future development of legal principles. Initially ecclesiastical law did not evolve as a distinct and separate growth; the harmony existing between the heads of the Church and the political leadership rendered such a divergence unnecessary. For the Anglo-Saxons had not suffered a forcible conversion but rather they had undergone a tranquil and voluntary transformation in the course of which they had abandoned most of their old religious beliefs and accepted entirely new ones in their stead. The members of the Christian priesthood were absorbed easily and naturally into the framework of Anglo-Saxon society. The bitter animosity which was to exist between the Church and the State only arose in a subsequent era.

Written laws were unknown in Anglo-Saxon Britain until after the introduction of Christianity; however, a series of codes were drawn up during the years in which the kings of Wessex were supreme, and these were consolidated by Canute during the early years of the eleventh century. Anglo-Saxon law made no clear distinction between criminal acts and private wrongs. Personal vengeance and the family blood-feud were interwoven into the authorized system and, certainly in the early part of this period, very little use was made of the courts either for restraining violence or for the settlement of disputes between individuals. The later Anglo-Saxon codes sought to define and to limit the circumstances in which it was permissible to kill and to maim as a matter of legal right. For example, a man was allowed to slay a person in defence of his lord or one of his relations; a thief could be put to death, but only if he was actually escaping with stolen property or if he was resisting apprehension; an adulterer could be killed, but solely by the husband or the father of the woman with whom he had committed the act. In such a way, whereas the ancient right of private vindication was still maintained, a strenuous effort was being made to reinforce the growth of authority and the establishment of a more stable polity by bringing as many disputants as possible under the control of the courts of law.

The barbarism of personal vengeance and the blood-feud were further ameliorated by the introduction of a scheme whereby someone with a legal right to kill a wrongdoer could give him an opportunity of paying a sum of money by way of compensation instead of forfeiting his life. At first the victims of offences – or the kin of the victims in the case of murders – were granted an unfettered choice of either demanding financial recompense or exacting the full penalty sanctioned by tradition. Later it was made obligatory for the wrongdoer to be offered the chance to make compensation, but if he was unable to do so, or he refused, he lost the protection of the law and could be hunted down and slain like a wild animal. Everyone in the Anglo-Saxon community had a financial value attached to his person, regulated according to his status in society, and this prescribed the amount which was payable in recompense for his injury or his death. The sum paid to an individual was called the bot; the sum paid to the relatives of a deceased was called the wer. Naturally the bot and the wer payable in the case of a thane were considerably higher than those payable in the case of one of the villani. In common with Roman law the older Anglo-Saxon system authorized the practice of noxal surrender, whereby an owner or a master could evade liability for the wrong committed by his animal or his slave by handing over the offender to be punished by the person who had suffered an injury from them.

Although the Anglo-Saxon law, especially in its earlier stages, was more concerned with the compensation of the victims of what are now known as criminal offences rather than with the punishment of the offenders, there were even then some forms of behaviour which were considered too heinous for private recompense and which were in consequence only punishable by the State. The first offences to be placed in this category were really elementary forms of treason – plotting to kill the king, and conspiring against a lord or master. Certain crimes against morality and religion were included at the instigation of the Church – heathenism in the worship of idols, pagan gods, the sun, the moon, fire and rivers; adultery, incest and fornication; witchcraft and treating with devils. In the course of time other offences became the concern of the State too, because of their detrimental effect on the safety and well-being of the community in general: amongst them were arson, rape, robbery, coining, and secret homicide. A further step towards the differentiation between public wrongs, or crimes, and private wrongs, or torts, came about through the system of reparation called wite. Apart from the payment of bot and wer to the persons who had suffered direct or indirect harm from a breach of the law, a payment of wite was sometimes taken by the king or the lord in whose territory the offence had been committed. By implication the king and the lord seemed to accept that they owed a duty of protection to the people living in or travelling through their domains.

In the early stages of the Anglo-Saxon occupation of Britain the enforcement of law and order was mainly dependent on self-help. If something was stolen it was up to the loser to find the thief and to try to recover his possessions, if necessary by force; if a murder was committed it was left to the kinsmen of the dead person to track down the murderer and to take their own vengeance. Even when the courts became better organized and self-help was discouraged, it remained the responsibility of the victim of an offence to apprehend the culprit and bring him to trial. During the tenth century the tithing system was started in an effort to ensure the speedier arrest and surer punishment of criminals. The basis of this new scheme was that the hundreds and townships became accountable for the preservation of law and order within their own boundaries. A tithing was simply an association of ten men from the same locality in the charge of one of their number known as a tithing-man or chief-pledge. If a member of the tithing committed an offence the other nine were under a duty to arrest and to bring him before a court; if they failed to do so they were liable to pay compensation for any damage he had caused, and they had in addition to meet any fine he might have incurred. Every man was obliged to enrol in a tithing unless he was exempted because of his status or the extent of his property. When a theft or a robbery occurred, the victim immediately notified the hundred-man, the official responsible for the policing duties in the hundred, who then marshalled the tithing-men in the relevant district and organized a pursuit of the criminal. Another method by which the rulers of Anglo-Saxon Britain sought to discourage crime was by compelling every man in the realm to find himself a borh or surety to guarantee his appearance at court if he should be called on to answer a charge. When a person was charged and failed to appear, it seems that the borh had to forfeit the full amount of the sum he had pledged as a recognizance. A man who could not produce a borh was liable to be arrested and detained in custody.

The Anglo-Saxon courts became established during the tenth century. Strictly speaking, they were assemblies rather than law courts and were based upon the regional demarcations of the shire and the hundred, though there were a host of petty private courts as well; indeed, with the growth of feudalism it was accepted that every lord had legal jurisdiction over all the tenants and villani on his estate. It is difficult to distinguish between powers and the scope of the early shire and hundred courts, both of which seem to have dealt with most forms of offence and of civil disputes which had arisen within their areas. There were no higher central courts exercising a superior jurisdiction to theirs and as they probably kept few, if any, records, their decisions were virtually absolute. Sessions were usually held in the same place, often in the open, and took place at regular intervals. There were no professional judges but cases were tried by a panel selected from the leaders of the community; later on the right and duty to sit as a judge were attached to various holdings of land.

The procedure at the shire courts and the hundred courts were identical. The plaintiff in a civil dispute, or the victim of a criminal offence, stated his grievance and made an oath that he was acting in good faith. The defendant then denied the allegation, again on oath, and undertook to abide by the judgement of the court. Having reached this stage, the judges decided which party must establish his case and what was to be the method of proof. The forms of proof which were used during the Anglo-Saxon period were generally either ordeal or compurgation of witnesses; initially trial by battle might have been used as well, but it certainly fell into abeyance until it was readopted after the Norman Conquest. The basis of proof by ordeal was that it was left to the deity to determine the truth of the matter, and hence this system was firmly supported by the priesthood of the Christian Church. The most common ordeals in Britain were by boiling water, by heat, and by blessed bread. In the ordeal by boiling water a person was made to plunge his arm into a vessel filled with boiling water – sometimes boiling oil was used instead. Afterwards his hand was bandaged up and if the scalding had healed within three days it was a sign that he had been telling the truth: if the sores were unhealed it indicated that he had lied. Similarly in the ordeal by heat the contestant had to suffer burning either by carrying a red-hot iron or by walking between two proximate fires, and the speed at which he recovered from his injuries was taken to be the test of his veracity. The ordeal by blessed bread was founded on the belief that someone who lied on oath would experience difficulty in swallowing consecrated food immediately afterwards. A variant of these forms of ordeal was occasionally employed in which the person was tied up and thrown in a pond or a river. If he sank it implied that the water had been willing to receive him as a truthful or an innocent man: if he floated it meant that that water had refused him and that he was a liar. When a court ordered proof by compurgation, or law-wager as it was also called, the party had to find a number of witnesses, how many depended on the discretion of the judges, who would swear to the genuineness of his contentions. These witnesses did not speak of the facts in issue from their personal knowledge, but they merely affirmed their belief that the party was speaking the truth. If the necessary number of witnesses was produced the case was won: if they were not forthcoming it was lost.

At the beginning of the eleventh century King Aethelred issued an ordinance in which he decreed that twelve of the principal thanes in each district should act as an accusatorial committee to prefer charges against any known lawbreakers in their localities. This was an interesting development in two respects. Firstly, it suggested that the initiation of criminal proceedings should be transferred from the victim of an offence to an independent representative body of the community; and secondly, it was a direct precursor of the grand jury system.

There were no regular prisons in Anglo-Saxon Britain. Criminals were punished mainly by fines, flogging, death and mutilation. There were various methods of penal execution: probably hanging and beheading were used at various times, and a law passed by Aethelred speaks of the offender being 'smitten so that neck break'. Mutilation too took differing forms, cutting off the hands or the feet, putting out the eyes, the excision of the nose, ears or upper lip, and even scalping. Outlawry was also used as a punishment in this period.

As regards family law, the Anglo-Saxons at first regarded marriage as a civil contract in which the prospective husband bargained with a woman's parents or guardians, and if a price was agreed he bought her from them. After the conversion to Christianity the whole concept of marriage was changed as the Church regarded it as being not a secular agreement but a holy sacrament. The husband no longer paid for his bride; instead he gave an undertaking to her parents or guardians to treat her properly 'according to God's law' and made a financial settlement upon the wife herself. The Church ordained that a religious ceremony was necessary in order to validate the marital union, and imposed regulations forbidding marriages between couples who fell within certain prohibited degrees of consanguinity. Before Christianity was established in Britain the Anglo-Saxons had recognized divorce by mutual consent without any formalities being required. A husband had also been able to divorce his wife on the grounds of her adultery or desertion. However, with the advent of the Christian faith a marriage tie came to be regarded as indissoluble. The Anglo-Saxons had no custom analogous to the Roman *patria potestas*, but a father had a right to administer corporal punishment to his children in moderation, and in circumstances of exigency he was permitted to sell a son or a daughter who was below the age of seven. He could forbid the marriage of a daughter under seventeen but could not compel her to marry against her will.

Unlike the Romans, a nation of citizens, the Anglo-Saxon tribes which invaded Britain were a pastoral people. With them it was cattle rather than land that had a real value, and the notion of private ownership of the soil was to some extent alien both to their outlook and to their way of life. The fields in every village were unenclosed, and were held, cultivated, and grazed in common by all the inhabitants; the forests on the outskirts which provided wood for their fires and timber for their homes were regarded as joint property. With the growth of feudalism, however, a fundamental change took place. Not only was the populace divided into owners and dependants, but land had become more valuable and was subjected to taxation in order to finance the defence of the nation. Further, the recognition of the lord as the autonomous possessor of his estate made more credible the subsequent Norman theory that the sovereign was the paramount proprietor of all the territory in the realm. In the Anglo-Saxon law at its later stages, land was freely disposable either by sale or by gift.

The Anglo-Saxon law of inheritance was considerably affected by the law of Rome, since the Christian Church regarded the legal principles of testation as falling closely within their particular province. It is true that there were several important differences between the two systems: for instance, the Romans debarred heretics and slaves from making wills, whilst equivalent disabilities did not exist in Britain; on the other hand, in Britain a youth under twenty-one could not make a valid will whereas in Rome he would have had full testamentary capacity. On the whole it was the policy of the Church to carry out the expressed intentions of the testator with regard to the division of his possessions, both chattels and realty, though probably a man's wife and children could claim a certain proportion of his estate if he had not made adequate provision for them. Sometimes testators would appoint guardians to supervise the implementation of their bequests and sometimes they would leave legacies to the local lord or to the king to increase the liklihood of their testamentary wishes being fulfilled. There was no set law of intestate succession in Anglo-Saxon Britain, each district applying its own customs.

On the eve of the Norman Conquest the Britain of the Anglo-Saxons was essentially a primitive, undeveloped and predominantly agrarian country in which a small number of the inhabitants lived in comfortable prosperity and the vast majority existed in conditions of the utmost poverty. Certainly lawlessness had diminished, communal responsibility had increased, and farming methods and commodity distribution were growing more efficient. Nevertheless, this was an age when the unrelenting hazards of nature, political turbulence, economic uncertainty, impotence in the face of epidemic and blight, and the still persisting menace of banditry were coercing many of the smaller freeholders to exchange their independence for a protected subservience on the estates of the more powerful proprietors. The consolidation of strength in the monarch over the lords, and in the lords over the people, marked a centralization of authority but a diminution of personal freedom at a time when the old rules and practices of law were coexisting with the new tenets based on developing feudal conditions.

In their commercial transactions, such as they were, the Anglo-Saxons could place small reliance on the surveillance of the courts. The law of contract was practically unknown in their form of jurisprudence and the actual form of an agreement of barter, loan or sale counted for very little; the essence of the deal was that if one person parted with his possessions to another it established a debt which in some way should be repaid. It was the Church which introduced a new concept to the legal principles of a contract by scrutinizing the intentions of the parties as evidenced by their words and actions and by penalizing unconscionable behaviour. The Church also encouraged the use of written documents as providing the clearest proof of intent.

When Canute died in 1035 he had already nominated his son Harthacnut as his heir to the English throne. Harthacnut was supported by the powerful adventurer Godwine, Earl of the West Saxons and the people of Wessex in general. However, another of Canute's three surviving sons, Harold, was chosen to succeed him by Mercia and Northumberland, so in order to resolve the matter without bloodshed the witan decreed that both these claimants should inherit the kingdom jointly. This arrangement did not last very long as Harthacnut incurred universal displeasure by remaining in Denmark, and two years later Harold I was crowned sole king of England. Harold died in 1040 at a time when Harthacnut was just preparing to invade the country and to depose him. In the event Harthacnut was able to land peacefully and to assume the English throne without further dissension. After a short, oppressive reign he died unmourned in 1042.

After Harthacnut's death it was the wish of the English nation to discontinue their association with the Scandinavian monarchy and to restore an Anglo-Saxon dynasty from the royal house of Wessex. Accordingly the witan, influenced by the indomitable Earl Godwine, decided to offer the throne to Edward, one of the sons of King Aethelred, who was destined to pass into history for his lineage as 'the last English King', and for his monastic temperament as 'Edward the Confessor'. Edward had spent almost thirty years at the Norman Court at Rouen before returning for his coronation. Although he married Godwine's daughter, in speech, character and outlook he was more Norman than English and his court was filled with his Norman favourites and advisors; so much so that Godwine staged an unsuccessful revolt in an effort to overthrow him in 1052. As a result, Godwine and his sons were exiled and Edward formally appointed William the Bastard, Duke of Normandy, as his heir to the English throne.

Edward died childless – according to popular belief his marriage was never even consummated – in January 1066. One of his last acts had been to rescind the nomination of the Duke of Normandy as his heir and to appoint Harold, second son of the then deceased Earl Godwine, in his stead.

Part III

THE NORMAN PERIOD

(1066–1154)

CHAPTER 4

THE NORMAN CONQUEST

A constitutional lawyer who was asked at the present time to decide whether Harold or William had the better claim to the English throne in 1066 would be faced with a difficult problem. As has been said, according to the customs of the Anglo-Saxon tribes the crown did not descend by primogeniture, but the king was selected by the assembly of notables from candidates of royal or princely stock.

William of Normandy, who was granted the permanent epithet of 'the bastard' and 'the great' at various phases of his life and was only called 'the Conqueror' by posterity, was the illegitimate son of Duke Robert of Normandy and a turner's daughter; his sole connection with a royal English lineage – and it was a rather slender one at that – had been through his aunt Emma, the wife in the first place of King Aethelred and later of King Canute. For his part, Harold possessed no royal or princely blood, but he placed his claim upon the fact that he had been designated heir to the crown as a death-wish of Edward the Confessor.

In the event, Harold attained the support of the witan for his seizure of the throne and, wasting no time, he arranged for his coronation on the day of Edward's funeral. Perhaps the leading figures in the realm were biased against William because of their bitter memories of Norman privilege and influence during the reign which had just ended; it is doubtful whether the ordinary English people cared one way or the other who was to become their next king, provided they were to be permitted a period of settled rule.

In September 1066 another contender for the English throne, King Hardraada of Norway, invaded the coast of Yorkshire and captured York city. Harold gathered together an army, marched north and inflicted a crushing defeat on the Norwegians at Stamford Bridge. Meanwhile William, with the blessing of the Pope and an army of about 7,000 knights drawn from Normandy, France and Italy, was awaiting a favourable wind to sail his fleet across the channel. On the morning of 28 September, only three days after the battle of Stamford Bridge, William landed his force at Pevensey in Sussex. If Harold had acted less precipitately the subsequent history of Britain might have been very different; as it was he hurried back to London leaving many of his best-trained archers behind him, and after a forced march to Sussex he assembled his tired and inexperienced army on the downs just outside Hastings, where they were attacked and massacred by William's numerically inferior force, Harold himself being struck in the eye by an arrow and mortally wounded.

After the battle of Hastings the witan was still disinclined to recognize the validity of William's claim to the English throne. Instead they nominated Edgar, a nephew of Edward the Confessor, who was unendowed with the attributes either of leadership or of resolution, but who was possessed of the necessary constitutional qualification in regard to the royal blood in his veins. William continued to press inland with his victorious army, and towards the close of 1066 he was in firm occupation of the whole of the south-eastern portion of England including London. Moreover, he had received obeisance from Edgar, the monarch-elect, and a number of other leading Anglo-Saxons. On Christmas Day he was sufficiently established to be crowned king of England in Westminister Abbey and to offer himself to the assembled congregation for their approval. In fact it was not until 1070 that the Norman conquest of the whole country was completed and William was able to parade his army for the last time at Salisbury and formally to disband it.

William I, as the Norman duke now became, did not consider that he was appropriating the English throne by right of conquest; he regarded himself as the lawful successor to Edward the Confessor. Furthermore, he intended to govern the English people according to their own laws, for there was much in their system which he greatly admired in the fields of administration, peace-keeping, law-enforcement and taxation of land, and which he desired to preserve, with suitable adaptation, as the basis of his own form of government. Whatever might have been the constitutional impropriety of William's accession, there can be little doubt that he was, in his day, one of the best military commanders and one of the most politically adroit rulers in Europe, and that during his reign England enjoyed a period of the most efficient and progressive administration which she had experienced since the days of the Roman occupation.

Since William wished to rule as an English king and not as a repressor of the English people, there was little vengeance and scant reprisal after he came to power. The knights who had served with him at Hastings were granted estates which were confiscated from the English nobles who had fought against him – that was natural justice perhaps; the senior officials throughout the land were gradually replaced by Norman administrators because of their competence and dependability; Lanfranc and Anselm, successive holders of the archbishopric of Canterbury, were brought in to thoroughly reorganize the English Church. But on the whole the infusion of Normans and of other peoples from the European continent, which continued throughout William's reign, was peacefully accomplished. In the social pattern which became established in the course of the next few decades most of the nobles were of Norman stock and the humbler classes were almost exclusively Anglo-Saxon; with regard to intermediate gradations, the artisans in the towns and the smallholders in the country districts, the integration was so complete that the families soon forgot about their racial origin. Within fifty years of William's invasion the generic description of 'Englishmen' was probably applied to every free resident in the realm quite irrespective of his ancestry.

The Normans introduced to England the type of feudalism which was then prevalent in France and in Normandy. At the lower level, in the relationship between the lord and his vassals, it did not bring about many radical alterations from the system which had existed in Anglo-Saxon times; but on the more gracious plain, besides a new form of tenure, which will be discussed in the next chapter, it embodied a concept of loyalty, mutual trust and chivalrous responsibility. In any event, the feudal principle bridged the divide between an era of tribal autonomy and custom on the one hand, and the advent of a centralized style of government together with a universally applicable system of law and order on the other.

Although William I only demanded the dignity and privileges which had been accorded to the Anglo-Saxon kings in the past, his dominant personality, his unique control and the circumstances of the Conquest gave him a power and an influence which surpassed those of any of his predecessors. Moreover, in the feudal scheme he had originated in England he established himself in a twofold position of authority: he was both the monarchical chief of state and also the personal lord of every inhabitant in the realm. In the first capacity he conducted national policy, levied taxes and dispensed justice, and in the second he exacted levies and military duties from his tenants. He succeeded in extending his rule to nearly every corner of the British Isles, subduing the Irish and the Welsh by force of arms, occupying the southern part of Scotland, and even receiving homage from the Scottish king.

While William I did not seek to bring about any basic changes in the English constitution, he manipulated certain developments which radically altered the scheme of executive government and judicial administration. The witan remained in being, but it was convened comparatively seldom and it became essentially Norman in character owing to the fact that most of the notables in the country happened to be Normans. It had ceased by then to be a popular assembly; attendance at its meetings was by invitation only, or rather by summons, and was no longer regarded as the entitlement of every free man. Furthermore, there seem to have been two distinctive types of witan – the first a select council of the eminent, and the second a general convocation of a large group of landowners; indeed, in 1086 William summoned a meeting of all the landowners in the kingdom. It has been suggested that this duality of the witan was the origin of the separate assemblies of the House of Lords and the House of Commons which, together with the monarch, were eventually to comprise the sole source of authority of the British legislature.

Another important innovation brought about by William I was the setting up of the Curia Regis, the King's Court, as the permanent executive committee of the witan with administrative, judicial and legislative functions. The Curia Regis was the power-centre of the nation, the hub of a unified government; it had no fixed location but always followed the person of the king, both in his travels around Britain and on his journeys further afield to the continent of Europe. The principal officials of the Curia were the justiciar, the chancellor, the treasurer, the chamberlain, the constables, and the king's justices. The justiciar commenced as a kind of regent who was only appointed on a temporary basis whenever the king was overseas; later on he became the full-time minister in charge of the financial and judicial control of the nation. Initially the chancellor's duties were mostly of a secretarial nature, although he was also concerned with legal business and he had a formal responsibility as keeper of the royal seal. The chancellor presided over the chancery, a body of trained clerks who formed what was virtually the first government department to come into existence. All matters relating to the national revenue came under the control of the Exchequer; this was staffed by the king's justices who were neither trained lawyers nor professional judges, but were sent out from time to time to various parts of the country to preside over local courts in the capacity of itinerant commissioners.

William I adopted the territorial divisions of Anglo-Saxon Britain. The boundaries of some of the old shires, for instance Sumorseatas and Dorseatas, remained unchanged; other new shires – or counties as they presently became – were artificially created to a pattern of convenience rather than of geographical or ethnic significance. The hundred, consisting of a combination of several townships, remained as the largest unit within the shire. The township, which resembled in size the medieval village, was ceasing to be a family group and developing into a community of tenants living in proximity to one another and all holding their land from a single lord. Every township was subdivided into tithings, the smallest segment of all, each of which had its own representative official called a tithingman.

Under Norman rule the independent or semi-independent status of the shires was eradicated and the ealdormen were divested of their former responsibilities and power. In fact William I only appointed new ealdormen where their location entailed a prescribed military duty such as the defence of a portion of the coastline. Ten years after the Norman invasion the last English ealdorman had been removed and in subsequent years the title 'earl' became a distinction of rank rather than a definition of office.

Whilst the ealdormen were rapidly losing their importance, the authority of the sheriffs was being greatly increased. The Norman kings regarded their sheriffs as instruments for implementing the royal will and the new centralization of control throughout every shire in England; they took their places as personal delegates of the sovereign and as such were in charge of the enforcement of law and order and the management of the courts and the prisons. In addition they directed the military forces and gathered in revenue for the national exchequer. It was the sheriff who always convened the County Court, which was still a public assembly and comprised the governing body of the shire.

During the reign of William I the English Church established a closer contact with the See of Rome and with the other Churches in Western Europe. The Anglo-Saxon prelates who were holding office at the time of the Conquest were allowed to retain their positions, but as vacancies occurred their successors were usually ecclesiastics of Norman or of continental extraction. At the time of William's death only one bishop and a small proportion of abbots were Englishmen by birth. This transformation brought with it both benefits and disadvantages: one of the benefits was that the new prelacy was composed of men of higher intellect and wider learning than the old; one of the disadvantages was that the foreign clerics seldom integrated with the local populace, and many of the bishops were more occupied with the indulgence of temporal grandeur than with the abstinence of spiritual devotion.

The social classes of Norman England were divided into three general groups. At the top end of the scale came the feudal lords and knights, below them were the ordinary free citizens, and at the lower end of the scale came the villani or serfs. In 1086 when the Domesday survey was carried out there were about 170 lords, only two of whom were Anglo-Saxons, holding their estates as tenants-in-chief directly from the king; there were, in that same year, about 5,000 knights. At the highest level Norman lords became known as 'barons'. In rural areas it is probable that labourers acting as foremen and those in more skilled occupations, such as carpenters, smiths and stonemasons, were mostly free citizens, whereas in towns the distinctions between free citizenship and serfdom was less easy to distinguish. William I, supported by the Christian Church, condemded the institution of slavery and under Norman rule the last vestiges of the old form of slavery were effaced from the English scene. The conditions of serfdom, however, in which approximately two-thirds of the rural population of England existed, were far removed from the status of full emancipation. A serf was tied to the land of his lord without the right to leave it. He usually paid rent for his holding in terms of service rather than in money – he might work on the lord's estate for so many days a week, or he might undertake to supply his lord with the loan of a certain number of horses, or to cut and to cart the wood for the lord's domestic use. Serfs could be punished by their lord for idleness, disobedience or faulty workmanship, and they were obliged to obtain his consent before they allowed their children to marry. For his part, the lord had certain responsibilities for the welfare of his serfs: he had to provide for them if they fell into destitution; he had to supply them with new homes if their houses were destroyed by fire; and he had to care for any of the infants on his estate who became orphans.

Throughout this period the English towns continued to expand. Sometimes new towns grew up around the impregnable stone castles with which the Normans studded the countryside, to fulfil the dual capacity of fortresses and homes. Although the bulk of the population still resided in rural areas the towns were playing an increasingly important role as the centres of commerce, distribution and supply, and in catering for the steadily developing trade links with Normandy, France, and Scandinavia.

William I seems to have assumed that he had a constitutional right to choose his successor to the throne. In 1087 he received a mortal injury whilst campaigning in France, and during the eight painful weeks which elapsed before his death he bequeathed the Duchy of Normandy to his elder son Robert, and the kingdom of England to his second son, William. These two brothers reached an agreement of doubtful validity, whereby if either of them should die childless his survivor would inherit his entire domains. William II ruled England until 1100 as a tyrannical despot, feared and detested by his Norman and his Anglo-Saxon subjects alike. Although he succeeded in maintaining public order and frequently consulted the national assembly on matters of policy, he developed a system of taxation of such severity as to amount to extortion. At the time of William II's death Robert was in the Holy Land waging a crusade, and the national assembly elected Henry, the youngest son of William I, to become the new English king. Robert carried out an ineffectual invasion but returned to Normandy after he had arranged a mutual inheritance pact with Henry on similar lines to the one which he had previously concluded with William II. Henry I was a competent administrator under whom the central government was considerably strengthened; he gave to the English nation what it principally desired – a period of internal stability, justice and protection from feudal oppression. In order to offset the growing power of the barons he sought to retrieve the activity and prestige of the old local courts of the shire and the hundred. Following the precedent set by his father and his brother, Henry I assumed the right of nominating his successor, and on the death of his only son he announced that his daughter, Matilda, would become heir to the throne. However, when Henry died in 1135 his directive was completely ignored by the national council and the crown was conferred on his nephew Stephen, the son of William the Conqueror's daughter, Adela. Stephen proved to be an inept and pusillanimous monarch who had no idea how to govern the country or how to control the host of turbulent barons; during his nineteen-year reign England was to disintegrate into a state of anarchy, insurrection and civil war.

After the Norman Conquest the emanation of authority in England underwent a significant shift. William I brought with him the autocratic conceptions of the continental rulers; the witan was superseded by a national council comprising the king's immediate associates – the principal officers of state and of the royal household – whose functions were both consultative and legislative but whose dominance was always subordinated to the personal absolutism of the king. The notion of monarchical despotism might have boded ill for the cherished customs and liberties of the Anglo-Saxon heritage had it not been for the jealousies and dissension which prevailed amongst the most powerful elements in the community. The Crown itself was debilitated by the distractions of rival claimants and foreign warfare; the Norman barons, haughty and insubordinate, were preoccupied by their lust for aggrandisement and their perpetual aggression against each other; the revitalized Church was striving with obsessive self-interest to establish a position of secular privilege and material proprietorship. In the outcome, the will of the ordinary people gained an added recognition and a new importance. When William II was threatened by a baron's insurrection, he immediately appeased the Church and offered good laws and justice to the populace; directly on his accession Henry I issued a charter restoring to the people the rights they had enjoyed by the laws of Edward the Confessor, and Stephen made a similar well-intentioned declaration at the very outset of his disordered reign.

The Norman kings did not issue many ordinances; they had neither a ready-made code of law nor a complex political philosophy to bestow upon the nation which they governed. Even the *Laws of Henry*, the first comprehensive English law book, which was compiled around 1115, was only an attempted codification of the existing Anglo-Saxon system. In a way the Norman kings adopted a method of rule which was both personalized and local, and they exercised a direct control over the various shires through the medium of the sheriffs. Their usual mode of determining facts or of gathering information for administrative purposes was to hold an inquest, which meant the summoning of a body of people in the neighbourhood concerned to answer on oath certain questions put to them by the sheriff or by some other royal representative. A classic example of an inquest on a national scale was the census of the entire population, the livestock and the land, carried out in 1086, the findings of which were recorded in the Domesday Book.

For the enforcement of law and order the Normans continued to rely on the Anglo-Saxon systems of tithings and borh which they amalgamated into a unified scheme known as frankpledge. Under frankpledge the tithings still consisted of ten persons presided over by a tithingman or chief-pledge, and each member was a borh or surety for the good behaviour of the others; again, membership of a tithing was compulsory for every freeman unless he was exempted by reason of his status or by the extent of his property. The duties imposed by frankpledge appear to have been less onerous than those prescribed under the Anglo-Saxon tithing scheme; there was no obligation to report the offences of one's fellow-pledges but only to arrest them if they were wanted by the authorities. If the arrested person absconded, the other pledges in his tithing had to establish that they had not abetted in his escape, and if he was not recaptured they became liable for any fine or compensatory payment he might have incurred. Frankpledge was supervised by the sheriff in every county at special sessions of Hundred Courts, called tourns, which were held either once or twice a year. Apart from ensuring that each man who was liable was properly enrolled in a tithing, the sheriff on these occasions received general reports from local officials about the state of crime in the hundred.

It is said that William I introduced the curfew procedure in England, ostensibly as a protection against the risks of fire but in reality to prevent the Anglo-Saxons from meeting together during the hours of darkness with subversive designs. The curfew bell had been used for some years in various towns on the continent of Europe. At that time rooms were usually heated by an open fire in the middle of the floor directly below a hole in the roof; the hazards from so many exposed flames was very real and when the bell was tolled the inhabitants were supposed to extinguish their fires and their lights and to retire for the night. William I ordered that the curfew bell was to sound in towns at eight o'clock every evening and that anyone who kept in a fire or who showed a light after that hour was to be severely punished. Such a measure must have had a considerable effect in the reduction of night crime. The strictness of William's rule was relaxed by Henry I who allowed the burning of lights after the curfew bell had been rung.

Police duties under the Norman system were performed by various unpaid officials, the sheriff in the shires, the bailiff in the hundreds, and the reeve and his four assistants in the townships. It was their responsibility to investigate serious offences, to arrest criminals, and to recover stolen property; in doing so they could call upon the assistance of the frankpledges. The rights of injured parties to self-help and private vengeance were being steadily diminished; whereas previously the victims of crimes, their kinsmen, friends, and neighbours had had to pursue and to apprehend the culprits, this task was now being increasingly undertaken by the local policing officials. Eventually the hundreds were placed under an obligation to raise hue and cry whenever a robbery had been committed within their boundaries; if the robber was not captured the hundred became liable to compensate the person who had suffered loss at his hands. The hundred had also to pay a collective fine if any Norman was murdered inside its area; this fine was recoverable unless the local officials could establish that the dead man was in fact an Englishman. The murder-fine, as it was called, was finally abolished during the fourteenth century.

CHAPTER 5

BIRTH OF THE COMMON LAW

At the time of the Norman Conquest there was no single system of law which was applied universally throughout the courts of England. The sessions held by the various Shire and Hundred Courts were still more akin to public meetings than to judicial tribunals, and the legal principles governing their decisions were dependent upon the customs of their own particular districts, which might be drawn from the laws of the Mercians, the Danes, or the West Saxons. The Norman kings both centralized the administration of justice and laid the foundations of the common law of England. They achieved this in two ways: firstly they established a King's Court, and secondly they sent out royal judges to supervise the work of the old local courts.

The King's Court originated as a special committee of the national assembly, with combined judicial and administrative functions. However, the two sides of its responsibility were gradually separated and the judicial component became infixed as the supreme legal tribunal, administering a species of law superior to any of those which were applied elsewhere in the country. The King's Court used the same methods of trial and the same methods of proof which had appertained before; it dealt only with the most eminent litigants and the most important causes, but in spite of this restriction it had soon commenced to formulate a body of juridical precepts which were at the same time of a logical consistency and of a transcendent authority. It is difficult to say whether any judges of the King's Court in the Norman era were professional judges in the true sense of the word. Certainly they were mostly ecclesiastics with a profound knowledge of canon law, which enabled them to sift a rational and coherent pattern out of the jumble of tribal dictates that had previously formed the fabric of the English law. The theory of jurisprudence was now being recognized as a subject of academic study. In 1139 Vacarious, a Lombardian scholar of Roman law, formed a group of students in Canterbury and by the end Stephen's reign both canon and Roman law were being taught at Oxford. It would seem probable that the royal judges, towards the end of the period, were by no means professionally unqualified before they assumed their judicial duties.

It was William I who originated the proposition that keeping the peace of the realm was a prerogative of the monarch and who first enunciated the axiom, of 'the king's peace'. This had an important effect on the administration of criminal law, for if the king was responsible for the maintenance of law and order it followed that the King's Courts had a duty to suppress crime – at any rate, crime of a serious nature. The tendency which had been developing even during the Anglo-Saxon era of regarding certain crimes as offences against the State was thus accelerated.

Even after the setting up of a King's Court the old local courts remained in being and retained much of their former significance. Soon after the Norman Conquest the practice commenced of royal commissioners being sent out to travel through the country on the king's business. At first the distinction between their fiscal and judicial work was not clearly drawn, but Stephen occasionally despatched these delegates specifically to try cases, both civil and criminal, on a roving commission. Henry I instituted resident justiciars in certain localities, with a status superior to that of the sheriff, to supervise the dispensation of royal justice; this new office grew in its scope and importance under Stephen. Apart altogether from their royal emissaries the Norman kings also traversed the country personally, taking with them their own court and conducting administrative and judicial matters as they went. Henry I in particular regarded these formal tours as an essential part of his monarchical duties; owing to the diligence with which he carried out these excursions, he became known to his subjects as 'the lion of justice'.

As the King's Court began to draw off so many of the more important cases, the County Court became recognized as the small man's tribunal dealing with everyday disputes amongst the ordinary people of the shire. Nevertheless the jurisdiction of the County Court was still wide and varied;

indeed it had power to hear almost every type of case which had emanated from its area, including petty criminal offences, infringements of personal rights, actions for unpaid debts and broken agreements, and simple causes relating to the possession of land. The judges in these courts continued to be selected from the leading people in the community, but in the course of time they were to be entirely superseded by members of the new royal judiciary. A defendant who declined to appear before the County Court when required to do so could be declared an outlaw. Apart from its judicial functions the powers of the court as the governing body of the county were enhanced during the Norman era, and under the direction of the sheriff it became responsible for the administrative, military, and financial management of the whole of the shire.

The Hundred Court met twelve times a year; it had a similar jurisdiction to that of a County Court but on a much smaller scale, and its judges were minor landowners who generally served in rotation. The civil side of its work diminished to such an extent that it is doubtful if the Hundred Court would have survived at all had it not been for the growing importance attaching to the sheriff's tourn. As was mentioned in the previous chapter, the sheriff used to preside over the Hundred Court on one or two occasions every year to ensure that the frankpledge system was operating properly within the area and also to carry out an investigation with regard to the maintenance of law and order. At the sheriff's tourn, which was also known as the court leet, each township was represented by its five leading citizens, the reeve and his four assistants, and each tithing by its chief-pledge. These officials were required to make presentments laying accusations against any persons in their districts who were suspected of having committed offences against the public peace. The presentments were considered by a jury of twelve free men from the hundred who could either accept or reject them; those which were accepted were passed to the sheriff who then ordered the arrest of the suspect, if he was not already in custody, and directed his trial either by the Hundred Court, the County Court or, if the accusation was sufficiently serious, by the King's Court.

There were several other kinds of local court under the Normans. Many large landowners obtained permission from the sovereign to hold their own courts leet on their estates, with a similar function and equivalent jurisdiction to the sheriff's tourn. Many lords also continued the feudal and the manorial courts for their tenants which they had inherited from their Anglo-Saxon predecessors. Certain boroughs were permitted under royal charters to hold borough courts, and the royal franchise was frequently granted for the holding of special forest courts and courts of law merchant. Henry I is said to have originated the custom of setting up *ad hoc* courts of enquiry known as 'eyres'. Although the eyre had a limited criminal jurisdiction, its chief purpose was to investigate some privilege of the Crown or the misconduct of a sheriff or some other royal official.

One of the principal changes in judicial administration which took place during this period was the establishment of separate ecclesiastical courts with their own exclusive jurisdiction, their own procedure, and applying their own independent tenets of law. It was perhaps ironical that such an autocratic monarch as William I should have initiated a division between the spiritual and the temporal spheres of judicial authority, which was to result in the creation of a new type of English court regarding the pope as the supreme legislator as well as the ultimate arbitor, and treating the canon law as being superior in every respect to the national law of England. After William's ordinance setting up ecclesiastical courts the bishops no longer sat with their lay colleagues in the County Courts, and the civil courts in general were debarred from trying any of those types of cases which were decreed by the prelacy as falling within their particular sphere. The jurisdiction which ecclesiastical courts assumed was by no means confined to clerical and theological matters, but included all matrimonial and testamentary causes, offences against morality such as adultery and incest, and certain other offences the Church viewed with especial disfavour, including usury, perjury, and defamation.

The ecclesiastical courts also claimed to have exclusive criminal jurisdiction over all clerks in Holy orders, and in consequence any cleric could refuse to be tried by a temporal court no matter how grave a charge had been laid against him. Since the harshest sentences an ecclesiastical court could pass on a defendant were to excomunicate him, to degrade him in his clerical status, or to order him to fulfil certain penances, it meant that a clerk who had committed a serious crime was immune from any of the prevalent methods of punishment.

The Normans did not make any fundamental changes in the procedure of the temporal courts; however, this period was marked by developments of outlook and variations in belief which inevitably altered the form and the emphasis of a legal trial. A higher regard seems to have been paid to the sanctity of the formal oath, and a more rational consideration was given to evidence, especially by the judges in the King's Courts who sometimes carried out their own enquiries into the facts in issue. The methods of proof ordered by the courts were still ordeal and compurgation of witnesses, and as in Anglo-Saxon times when compurgation was ordered the witnesses had to swear to the genuineness of a person's cause, not from their actual knowledge of the events but from a belief in his truthfulness; from the twelfth century onwards these compurgators were not liable to be charged with perjury.

The Normans also introduced, or it may be that they reintroduced, the system of trial by battle, which like trial by ordeal was based on the theory that divine providence would intercede in favour of the innocent. Originally only women, infants, and men over sixty years of age were exempted from this form of trial and were allowed to employ their chosen champions to fight on their behalf; later on a similar privilege was extended to all and sundry. The battle-trial was conducted with great formality according to a set ritual. It always started at dawn in presence of the judges, both contestants being clad in armour and each carrying a stave, shaped like a pickaxe, together with a four-cornered leather shield. As a preliminary in criminal cases the accused person had to plead 'not guilty', throw down his glove, and declare that he would defend it with his body; the accuser would then pick up the glove and reply that he was willing to make good his charge 'body for body'. In civil actions the parties merely swore oaths stating their belief in the truth of their cases. Whether the matter was criminal or civil, they also had to take an oath that they would forgo the employment of sorcery or enchantment in the forthcoming duel. If the case was a civil one and the defendant was still fighting when the stars first appeared in the evening, he was adjudged to have won his action; if it was a criminal case and the accused had maintained the fight until the appearance of the first stars he was acquitted and could recover damages from his accuser, but if he was vanquished or he had given up the fight at an earlier stage, then heaven had made it abundantly clear that he was guilty.

It is generally accepted by authoritative writers on the subject that the Normans were responsible for the introduction in England of the basic origins of the jury system. A clear distinction must be drawn, however, between the two different types of jury which were to play such an important role in the English criminal procedure at a later stage. The first was the jury of accusation – the grand jury – which only decided whether or not a suspect should be put on trial; the second was trial or petty jury which heard the evidence and decided whether he was quilty or innocent of the charge against him. The Normans certainly brought with them the jury of accusation, a derivation of their custom of ascertaining facts on administrative or fiscal matters by holding an inquest in the district concerned, when the jurors were, as the historian F. W. Maitland has stated, 'a body of neighbours summoned by some public officer to give, upon oath, a true answer to some question'. It has already been noted how a jury of this sort had to consider the presentments made by the policing officials at the sheriff's tourn, and it was also used by the King's Court and the other local courts to supply information about criminal offences or the improper conduct of officials in the area from which the jury was drawn. The inception of the petty jury came about in a subsequent period, but even under the Normans sworn inquests were sometimes held during the course of a trial when the jurors were required to supply an answer on some specific point which was in dispute.

The punishments inflicted on convicted criminals in the Norman period remained much the same as before, except that William I abolished the death penalty and substituted mutilation in its stead. The lords and the barons continued to run their private prisons in the dungeons and strongrooms of their castles, manors and gatehouses; and the official prison system was taking shape as well, since the sheriffs became liable during the eleventh century for the safe custody of all the prisoners in their counties whilst they were awaiting trial on criminal charges. No provision was made for proper prison buildings, so the sheriffs were obliged to make the best use of any local facilities that happened to be available.

In its emergent phases the common law was not the hallowed code of legal precepts it became in after-years nor was it clothed with the same inviolability. The king's judges were deliberately fashioning a system of law to be applied universally throughout the realm; they arranged and methodized the mass of tribal customs, regulations and conventions which had existed in England at the time of the Conquest and they added a blending from the principles of canon law and Roman jurisprudence. As yet there were no formal reports of decided cases and no collected records of judicial pronouncements; the only way the judges could infuse their revised and unified system was by propagating a new generic reasoning, and a unanimity of approach to forensic issues; and this they began to do with marked effect.

In respect of the law regarding the ownership and occupation of land, the impact of Norman conceptions was immediate, far-reaching and absolute. The invading army, after the Conquest, had transferred to England the type of land tenure to which they were accustomed in France and Normandy, as well as the continental notions and class structure of a feudal society. William I did not purloin the territories of his defeated enemies; as king of England he assumed the right of possession of all the land in the country, though he had an alternative claim inasmuch as the entire nation, by their failure to support him, had been guilty of treason and had thereby forfeited their entitlement to hold any property whatsoever. William proceeded to bestow grants of land, either on its former possessors or more often on his own followers. By the end of his reign most of the great estates in England had passed into Norman hands and even if an Englishman was still in partial possession he was generally there merely as the grantee of a Norman overlord. From that time forward it became a maxim of the English law that the real and ultimate owner of all the land in the kingdom was the Crown, and that the highest interest of the individual possessor was a strictly subordinate one amounting to little more than a virtual tenancy.

The Normans considered personal advancement in terms

of property rather than of office and they were apt to measure a person's ascendency less by the grandeur of his title than by the size of his estate. The Anglo-Saxon kings had only had a prerogative right to the ownership of a comparatively small amount of territory known as the folkland; the Norman kings, by virtue of their paramount position, were the supreme lords of every acre of land throughout the length and breadth of England. This possessory concept of monarchy had an important consequence with regard to succession. While the Crown had represented no more than the elusive embodiment of a spiritual authority combined with a terrestrial leadership, the elective system of the Anglo-Saxons had been fully acceptable; but when a proprietary overlordship was involved as well, inheritance on a hereditary basis began to seem more appropriate, and gradually the doctrine of primogeniture became applicable to the English throne.

The customary method of holding land in Norman England was by the feudal practice of military tenure. This meant that the lord held from his king, and the ordinary tenant from his lord, on a commitment to supply certain armed services when required to do so. A military tenancy passed from father to son but it had to be re-granted to the incoming tenant who was charged a fee, called a relief, before he was allowed to take up his estate. There were numerous other dues connected with military tenure whereby the king enriched himself at the expense of his lords, and the lords recompensed themselves at the expense of their tenants; for example, an heir who was a minor had to pay to inherit his estate, and an heiress in possession in her own right had to buy her lord's consent before she married. William II in particular made use of these feudal perquisites to develop an arbitrary means of extortion for refurbishing the royal revenue. Apart altogether from financial considerations of military tenure, the tenant undertook to supply a set quota of knights, horsemen or foot soldiers, according to the requirement placed upon the land which he occupied.

The land law of Norman England was rigid and precise and it is likely that the majority of the actions coming before the courts concerned the interpretation of agreements rather than complex matters of definition and title. Occupational tenancies and tenancies for a fixed duration of time were unknown with one exception, a legal subterfuge known as a 'moneylender's lease' whereby an impecunious landowner could raise a loan by leasing his property to a creditor for a sufficient period to justify the amount of the loan. Moneylender tenants were regarded with disdain by their neighbours, which was due partly to the falsity of their title and partly to the wholehearted condemnation of usury by the Church, carried to the extent of a doctrinal belief that it was unconscionable for a loan to be charged with any interest at all. During the Norman period the peasant population was expanding rapidly and townships were becoming absorbed into their surrounding manors. As a result competition for land amongst the serfs was growing intense and the lords of the manor and their bailiffs were able to impose increasingly rigorous terms upon their serf-tenants.

The law of inheritence was closely affected by Norman feudal principles. A person holding his land by military tenure, and a free man who occupied it in exchange for services, were allowed to devise their property by will, but according to Coke's *Institutes* they were unable, after the Conquest, to dispose of an estate greater than a term of years, except in localities where special provisions applied; further, land could only be passed by will to the issue of the original tenant. These stipulations were designed to provide a proximate connection between the king or the lord on the one hand and the tenant in occupation on the other, so that the feudal relationship would be indefinitely preserved. The free inheritence of land was a matter of perpetual dissention between the prelacy and the temporal authorities. The clergy had always encouraged the making of death-bed gifts, known as gifts in mortmain, where the penitent had donated his land and his other possessions to the Church, in the hope of redemption in the life hereafter; but from the point of view of a tenant-in-chief the Church, or any other corporation, was neither able to fulfil the terms of feudal service nor could it incur any of the feudal dues and penalties which usually provided him with such a lucrative source of income. When gifts in mortmain were prohibited, the clergy, who were well acquainted with Roman law, responded by the employment of uses or trusts. The method was simple: the landowner, unable to bequeath his property to the Church, conveyed it to a nominal purchaser subject to a trust entitling the Church to enjoy the full rights of occupation and ownership. With regard to a testator's personal estate, that is all his private possessions other than land or the buildings upon it, he was allowed to dispose of it as he thought fit, subject to certain rights which were granted to his wife and children.

The law of marriage, like the law of testamentary succession, was wholly within the jurisdiction of the ecclesiastical courts. Although the bond of wedlock was regarded as indissoluble, the Church had power to annul a marriage if either of the parties suffered from one of the defined canonical disabilities, which included an inability to procreate children, or if they were connected by certain degress of relationship either by blood or by matrimony. The exclusive right of annulment, together with the fact that the ecclesiastical courts had a discretion whether to abrogate a wedding or not, gave the Church an authority which helped considerably to heighten its influence in society. The legal consequence of a wedding was that the husband and wife became one person, with the wife merging her identity into that of her husband. This fictional unification gave rise to the long-standing rule at common law that one of the parties to a marriage could not give evidence against the other. Marriage for a wife implied a status of bondage; the ownership on her personal property and the management of her real estate were vested in her husband. Indeed her independence counted for so little that if she committed some criminal offence in his presence she was deemed to have acted under his coercion. It is a little surprising, perhaps, that the great eighteenth-century jurist Sir William Blackstone could have written in his commentaries that the female sex was 'so great a favourite' with the English common law.

Stephen's calamitous reign, the 'nineteen long winters'; ended on his death in 1154 with the country in a state of turmoil and the power of the barons rampant and unrestrained. A year earlier, by the Treaty of Wallingford, it had been agreed that he should occupy the throne for his lifetime and that he would be succeeded by Henry of Anjou, son of William I's sister Matilda, who had already been passed over for the crown of England.

Part IV

THE PLANTAGENET PERIOD

(1154 – 1399)

CHAPTER 6

THE STRUGGLE FOR POWER

Henry of Anjou, crowned as Henry II in 1154, became the first of a dynasty of kings under whose governance the structure of constitutional authority in England was finally to take shape. Correctly speaking they should have been known as the Angevin house; the name 'Plantagenet' appears to have derived from the habit adopted by Henry's father of wearing in his cap a sprig of broom-flower – the *plante genet*. Henry II was only twenty-one at the time of his accession to the English throne but he was already an experienced warrior and the ruler of most of France. Without undue difficulty he speedily crushed the rebellious barons by isolating them and subduing them individually with a well-trained army of continental mercenaries.

By then the term 'baron' was applied to all the noblemen who held their land directly from the king as tenants-in-chief without having any intermediate lord. The right of the barons to attend the King's Council was founded in the feudal principle that every tenant was entitled to attend at the court of his immediate superior. During the Plantagenet period the name 'parliament', from the French word *parlement*, became the accepted designation of the royal council, the exclusive assembly in which the king was given the opportunity to speak to his subordinates. As has been seen, the privilege of being present was no longer extended to all the barons, but was then restricted to the favoured few who had been personally summoned by the king. A clause in the Magna Carta endeavoured to restore the original entitlement by decreeing that each baron should receive a summons to every meeting of parliament that took place, although, no doubt, it must have been anticipated that the majority would probably have been unable to attend. Sir Edward Coke has stated in his *Institutes* that the summons to attend

Parliament 'ennobles the blood of the person summoned' and that therefore the nobility becomes hereditary descending through female as well as through male progeny. Naturally this concept of barony was a departure from the feudal notion which involved a form of land tenure. From the middle of the thirteenth century barons were called upon to attend Parliament by virtue of writs served on them in their personal capacities rather than by summonses which they received through being royal tenants. In 1388 Richard II began creating barons by letters patent, limiting the right of inheritance, usually to male heirs. With this, the last vestiges of the feudal origins of the barony were swept away.

Knighthood also lost its connection with land tenure during the Plantagenet era. At the commencement of Henry II's reign the tenant by knight-service was still obliged to render military service to the king, fully equipped and mounted at his own expense, for a set period every year, which generally amounted to forty days, if he was called upon to do so. In addition the knight owed certain civil duties to his lord and he was subject to various feudal fines and forfeitures. It soon became apparent that the stipulations of knight-service were ill adapted to campaigning on the continent of Europe where professional and mercenary armies were both more flexible and more efficient. It then became customary for the knight-tenant to commute his military liabilities for an annual money payment, known as scutage. Knighthood still persisted as an honorary and chivalrous distinction, created by a formal ceremony of investiture.

Having crushed the barons, Henry II might have seemed to be in a position of absolute supremacy, but in such a formative and empirical age the shifts and slants of the power struggle created a perpetual fluctuation and a constant instability. The next challenge to the king's authority was to come from the See of Rome. In the year after his accession Henry had appointed a London merchant's son, Thomas à Becket, to be his Chancellor; in 1162 Becket added to his dignities the archbishopric of Canterbury. Whereas Henry had resolved to undermine the special and privileged position which the clergy were establishing for themselves in England, Becket soon became a zealous advocate for the most inordinate ecclesiastical pretensions. By the Constitutions of Clarendon, drawn up in 1164, clerics lost their immunity from the criminal jurisdiction of the ordinary courts, and their right of appeal direct to the pope was forbidden without the king's specific consent. Further, the extensive land-holdings of the prelates were brought into line with the normal principles of feudal tenure, and the king was granted a right of veto in the appointment of English bishops. Becket at first agreed to the Constitutions, but presently withdrew his assent, fled the country, and sought refuge and support in France and Rome. In 1170 a reconciliation was patched up and Becket returned to England where he again assumed the archbishopric of Canterbury, an office in which the pope had reinstated him during his years of self-imposed exile. Further quarrels between Henry and Becket, culminating with the murder of the archbishop in his own cathedral, failed to resolve the fundamental issue regarding the degree to which the English prelacy and clergy should or should not be subjected to secular control.

For the last nineteen years of Henry II's reign he was harassed by treachery at home, and across the borders of the kingdom by his military struggles with the French and the bellicosity of the natives in Scotland and Ireland. In spite of this, his rule gave England a long period of comparative peace and order during which the machinery of government both at the central and the local levels was considerably strengthened and some sort of rudimentary civil service was established. On the death of Henry II in 1189, he was succeeded by his son Richard I who has taken his place as one of the popular heroes of the English historical tradition but who made little effective contribution to either the social or the constitutional development of his country. Shortly after coming to the throne he led the third crusade in an attempt to recapture Jerusalem from the Moslems, and he subsequently spent a considerable portion of his ten-year reign campaigning in France; it was there in 1199 that he was mortally wounded, after appointing his brother John as his successor.

The historian G. M. Trevelyan has described John as having 'a false and cruel nature, made to be hated'. The youngest son of Henry II, his treachery and his ruthless ambition became apparent at an early stage in his life when he plotted against his father, and again when he endeavoured to usurp the throne while his brother Richard was away crusading in the Holy Land. By the rules of primogeniture the crown should not have passed from Richard to John but should have been inherited by their twelve-year-old nephew Arthur, whose father had been Henry II's eldest son. It is generally believed that one of the first acts of John's reign was to dispose of this lawful claimant by having him brutally murdered. It was an apt beginning for a monarch whose name is principally associated with the national revolution which led to the procurement of the Magna Carta – the great charter of English liberties.

An important, though indirect, result of John's incompetent administration was that England severed her connection with the continent of Europe. Under Henry II and Richard I the English kingdom had merely ranked as the most important possession amongst the sovereign's widespread domains but by 1204 practically all John's continental dependencies had been lost; in particular, the traditional link with Normandy and the more recent association with Anjou had been destroyed. From then on Britain was to fashion her laws, her social structure, and her destiny as a completely separate entity from the remainder of Europe.

In 1208 the question of papal control – or papal interference – in English ecclesiastical affairs once more came to the fore. A dispute had arisen regarding the election of a new archbishop of Canterbury, and the bishops of that province had appealed to Pope Innocent III for a ruling. The pope had replied by appointing Stephen Langton, a nominee of his own, to fill the vacant see. King John, who was already supporting one of the existing claimants, refused to acknowledge Langton. In the ensuing four-year contention the pope placed England under an interdict, excommunicated her king, and offered the English throne to the king of France. John obtained scant support from his own subjects, who were seething with discontent owing to his oppressive methods of government and his onerous system of taxation. Eventually he felt obliged to capitulate to the pope, not only accepting Stephen Langton as Archbishop of Canterbury, but promising with abject humiliation to rule England from then on as a papal dependency.

All this formed part of the backcloth for the ultimate drama in 1215 when King John made his public constitutional surrender to his barons, his prelates, and his people at Runnymede. The national tumult which gave rise to Magna Carta was prompted partly by an almost legendary conception of idyllic freedom which had existed in England during the reign of Edward the Confessor, and partly by a sense of smouldering exasperation with the financial exactions involved in the scheme of feudal land tenure which had been introduced by the Normans. It also symbolized the first tremulous utterance of a people aspiring vaguely and distantly towards some form of representative government. In simple and practical terms the Magna Carta laid down that only three of the ancient feudal dues should normally be demanded by a lord. These were: firstly, the provision of his ransom money if he was captured by an enemy; secondly, a donation made at the knighting of his eldest son; and thirdly, a similar levy at the marriage of his eldest daughter. No other aids, as they were called, were to be imposed and the king could raise no additional revenue, except by order of the national council of the realm. For the future all the archbishops, bishops, abbots, earls, and the greater barons were to be personally summoned by the king to every meeting of the Council, and the remainder of the king's tenants-in-chief were to be summoned collectively; they would all have to receive forty days' notice informing them of the place and the purpose of the meeting.

The most quoted clause of the Magna Carta is the one in which the king made the solemn pledge that 'no freeman shall be taken or imprisoned, or be disseised of his freehold or liabilities, or free customs, or be outlawed or exiled, or any otherwise damaged, nor will we pass upon him, nor send upon him, but by lawful judgement of his peers, or by the law of the land'. This, Blackstone wrote, 'protected every individual of the nation in the free enjoyment of his life, his liberty and his property, unless declared to be forfeited by the judgement of his peers or the law of the land'.

Other clauses of the Magna Carta dealt with the practice and procedure in the courts and repaired many deficiencies in the law regarding matters which were becoming increasingly important with the expansion of trade and commerce. There can be little doubt that the barons, the prelates, and the people dispersed from Runnymede believing that the old Anglo-Saxon freedom had been largely restored and that they had succeeded in establishing the basic foundations of a constitutional form of government.

Like so many ancient British institutions the English Parliament was not fashioned by a single act of policy: it came into being through a long and gradual process of rectification and development. The witan – the popular assembly of the Anglo-Saxons – had been superceded by the Norman national council, a select committee of the king's advisers; and now the Magna Carta was dictating the creation of a vastly expanded legislature comprising an upper and a lower strata of delegates. There was nothing in the relevant clause which specified that there should be two separate consultative chambers, but the suggestion must have been inherent in the duality of the methods of summons. The notion of the three estates as the three distinct orders of the body politic – the nobles, the clergy, and the commoners – came later. There was no real reason why these should have been selected to form the composite organs of governmental administration, although Edward I, at a subsequent stage, had some idea of establishing a deliberate assembly on such a three-fold basis. By the end of 1215 the nucleus of the House of Lords was already in existence, due to the fact that all the greater barons had a theoretical right to be summoned to every meeting of the national council and that their nobility was recognized as carrying on from father to son. The representative nature of what was to become the House of Commons had not yet fully emerged but was in the process of formulating, as it was apparent that the vast majority of the lesser tenants-in-chief could not possibly attend the meetings of the Council and it was tacitly understood that the acts of those who were present would be fully binding upon those who stayed away. Thus the future constitution of the British Parliament was settled; the nobles would attend in their own hereditary right and the commoners in a representative capacity. The clergy, apart from the prelates who ranked as greater barons, being unwilling to compromise themselves politically, preferred to hold aloof from the assembly altogether.

It is doubtful if John had ever intended to adhere to the civil undertakings he had given in the Magna Carta. With the support of the pope he renounced them almost immediately, and a year later when he died he was on the eve of a military confrontation with his barons. Henry III, John's son, reigned for fifty-six years, during which time a relentless struggle was waged between the king and his Council with regard to a definition of parliamentary authority. On a number of occasions the barons compelled the king to ratify the Magna Carta, but he always did so, significantly, with the omission of the clause restricting the royal right to raise revenue without an affirmative vote of the national council; this was particularly relevant for, like the pope, he was constantly endeavouring to grind money out of the nation.

During Henry III's reign meetings of the national council took place fairly regularly and the representative nature of the lower strata of delegates, the future House of Commons, was becoming more evident. In 1224 every county was invited to send four knights to one of its meetings, though whether they were nominated or elected is not certain; in 1254 two knights from each county were summoned personally by royal writ; and a few years later every county was represented by four elected knights. At this stage it seems to have become accepted that all the meetings of the assembly – the term 'Parliament' was first used about 1246 – would be attended by elected knights as representatives of their countries. Apart from incessant haggling over the constitutional procurement of revenue, an increasing demand was now being heard that Parliament should have some say in the appointment of the chief officers of state, and that it should be granted wider administrative powers generally; but as yet there was no suggestion that its principal function should be the creation of new laws.

In 1258 the barons under the leadership of Simon de Montfort, the king's brother-in-law, compiled a series of declarations known as the Provisions of Oxford, reaffirming the terms of the Magna Carta and directing that not only the king's counsellors should attend at Parliament but also certain other great lords, 'on behalf of the whole community of the land', in order to 'consider the affairs of the king and the kingdom'. Henry III swore that he would comply with these principles. However, he obtained a bill of absolution from the pope releasing him from his oath, and in the civil war which followed the king was defeated and captured at the battle of Lewes. The victorious Simon then proclaimed a new English constitution and summoned a national Parliament in 1265 to which each county sent two knights, and each city and borough two citizens or burgesses. A second civil war broke out soon afterwards, when Simon was killed and his forces were vanquished. For the rest of his reign Henry III continued to summon meetings of Parliament attended by his own selected delegates; it was purely a matter for his personal discretion which particular nobles were summoned and which particular counties and towns were invited to send representatives.

Edward I, who came to the throne on his father's death in 1272, was a firm believer in the constitutional significance of Parliament and also in its potential function as the national body of legislation. During his reign the kingdom was at one stage extended to the whole of the British island; but the Scottish later recovered their independence, whereas the principality of Wales remained lastingly under the English Crown.

It would appear that Edward I adopted Simon de Montfort's precedent of summoning commoners to meetings of his Parliaments immediately he became king, though the composition of his assemblies was irregular and indistinct until it assumed a more definite shape with the Great Parliament of 1295 when knights, citizens, and burgesses began to be summoned as a matter of course to attend in a representative capacity. Edward I also initiated the practice of holding parliamentary sittings permanently at Westminster instead of arranging them at various towns in different parts of the country. Even then the actual delegates to Parliament had little real authority either individually or collectively; they came as petitioners before the king and he had the free choice whether to accept or to reject their petitions. In 1297 Edward I acknowledged a constitutional axiom that the king could not impose any taxes without the prior sanction of Parliament; but neither he nor some of his successors on the throne ever felt themselves completely bound by this restriction.

The advancement of the parliamentary principle was not assisted by the behaviour of either the clergy or the commoners. The clerics persistently maintained their indifference to the developing legislative assembly and preferred to exercise their influence in their own convocations.

The knights, the burgesses, and the citizens were reluctant to make the often hazardous and inconvenient journeys to Westminster for the sake of voting taxes which would eventually have to be found out of their own pockets. Nevertheless, a vast amount of legislation emanated from Edward I's Parliaments, affecting almost every branch of the English law.

Edward II, who succeeded his father in 1307, was a weak and indolent man, constantly swayed by his favourites of the moment. As a monarch he was no match for his prelates and his barons. In 1310, as a result of his inefficient administration, he was divested of all his powers and the country was ruled for one year by a 'Committee of Ordinances'. This was followed by a new baron's war, at the conclusion of which the king's Gascon favourite was captured and executed. The strife between Edward and his nobles continued intermittently and in 1318 his entire authority was once again removed from him and transferred to a council of ministers. In 1326 the king's wife Isabella raised the standard of national revolt against his rule, and the following year Parliament, exerting a new-found supremacy, deposed him from the throne and elected his eldest son in his place. The unfortunate Edward II was murdered with the utmost cruelty a short while later.

Edward III had been fourteen years old when the English crown was thrust upon him and during his minority a council of guardians was appointed to fulfill the royal function. As was to be expected, this situation gave rise to rivalries and schemings and eventually effective control was seized by his mother Queen Isabella, in conjunction with her favourite, Roger Mortimer. Edward's reign did not really commence until, as a result of a small revolution, Isabella was imprisoned and Mortimer was executed at Tyburn. The external policies of Edward III's reign were dominated in the first part by a struggle against the Scottish, and from 1337 onwards by the initial phases of the Hundred Years War with the French.

Up to this, Parliament had been held as a single assembly, though it is likely that at its meetings the various classes and orders had deliberated and voted separately. Edward III was responsible for the division of the delegates into two distinct bodies, the prelates and hereditary nobles being called the House of Lords, and the knights, citizens, and burgesses being named the House of Commons. To begin with both these bodies carried on their discussions in the same chamber, but about the year 1344 it was decided that it would be more convenient for the Commons to have their own separate meeting-place so they moved to the chapter-house of the Abbot of Westminster. The constitutional position of the two houses was very different: the Lords exercised their responsibilities as the direct successors of the witan and the national assembly; the Commons were a newly created element whose exact powers had yet to be defined. It was generally accepted that the nominal role of the commoners was still a subservient one. They were petitioners rather than legislators, and even if their petitions were accepted by the king, on the advice of the Lords, the House of Commons took no part in the framing of the subsequent enactments. In spite of this the House of Commons wielded considerable influence by its financial control over the governmental revenue; and the king, who was almost continuously in need of money, learnt to bargain for his subsidies by inviting the commoners to advise him on his policies and by showing a greater readiness to redress the grievances to which they respectfully drew his attention. The audacity of the Commons reached its zenith in 1376 when they complained about the burdens of taxation, purported to suspend several ministers, and pressed for a more vigorous conduct of the war against the French. The king, in exasperation, imprisoned the Speaker and dismissed Parliament forthwith.

A year later Edward III died. On the accession of his grandson Richard II, a new Parliament was summoned, the Speaker was released from goal, and the old complaints and demands were again renewed. Eventually the king and his ministers were forced to concede the principles that the House of Commons possessed the right to enquire into public abuses and, if necessary, to impeach any erring ministers of the Crown; that not only could they vote the necessary subsidies, but they might also supervise the expediture of the money which had been raised; and that Parliament ought to be convened annually rather than at the whim of the sovereign. The procedure of impeachment was that the Commons acted as the accusers and the inherent judicial jurisdiction of Parliament was exercised by the Lords. By such a means the Earl of Suffolk, the Lord Chancellor, was impeached in 1386 for his alleged misconduct in office.

Richard II, the last of the Plantagenet kings, is historically an enigmatic and a somewhat tragic character. It was his misfortune to come to the throne when he was only eleven at a moment when Parliament was beginning to realize the full measure of its power, and to spend almost his entire reign in the disturbing shadow of his two domineering uncles, John of Gaunt and the Duke of Gloucester. The weak and unpopular government during his minority provoked a popular rising in the south-east of England known as the Peasant's Revolt which, however, had no important political consequences. For eight years, from 1389 until 1397, Richard was permitted to reign quietly, peacefully and constitutionally; apart from this period he never really had a chance. Afterwards he tried for a brief spell to rule as an absolute monarch but ultimately, in 1399, John of Gaunt's son Henry raised a revolt against him and, abandoned by his people, Richard was forced by Parliament to sign a deed of abdication. Parliament then conferred the crown upon Henry. Richard was sentenced to perpetual imprisonment and a year later he died in captivity under somewhat mysterious circumstances at the age of thirty-three.

Henry IV ascended the throne of England partly as the grandson of Edward III, but what is more significant, at the instigation of the English Parliament and by virtue of their formal sanction.

CHAPTER 7

A REFORMATION OF JUSTICE

The social development and the increasing sophistication of the English State made it inevitable that the sources and structure of central authority should be expanded and diversified. It has been seen how legislative power, together with a growing executive control over national affairs, had been removed from the Council and appropriated by the composite assembly of the Houses of Parliament. Likewise, during the Plantagenet period, the council as such was destined to lose its historic function as the supreme judicial tribunal in the realm.

When Henry of Anjou came to the throne in 1154 the King's Court still notionally followed the person of the monarch and still constituted a special committee of the Council. During Henry's reign its two branches, the financial and the judicial, remained interwoven – so much so that certain barons of the exchequer were sometimes employed to try ordinary civil and criminal cases. However, in the prevailing conditions a travelling royal court was becoming more and more of an anachronism. An increasing confidence in the common law and in the methods, procedure, and remedies applied by the curia regis were resulting in a steady growth in the number of prospective litigants; the augmentation of the laws was constantly enlarging the royal jurisdiction; and the lengthy absences abroad of Henry II, and subsequently of Richard I, were nullifying the fiction of the king's personal judgement. To surmount these difficulties Henry II in 1178 appointed five officials from his household to sit permanently in the curia regis, adjudicating in all the causes which came before them except those of unusual difficulty which were to be reserved for the king himself.

Henry II also initiated the practice of sending out representatives of the curia regis to tour certain specified counties on royal business. At first these excursions were spasmodic and haphazard, but from 1176 onwards at least one part of the country was visited every year, and at the beginning of the fourteenth century the organization of various recognized circuits became more methodical and more precise. As well as hearing civil and criminal cases the itinerant justices took part in general administrative duties, especially the assessment of taxes in the areas under their surveillance.

The cleavage between the Council and the courts of common law really emanated from a clause in Magna Carta which provided that common pleas should no longer follow the royal court but should always be held at some definite place. This gave rise to the division of the curia regis into the Court of Common Pleas, stationed permanently at Westminster, and the Court of King's Bench which continued to travel around in the wake of the monarch. Initially these two common law courts remained closely associated with each other, but during the fourteenth century they began to keep their own separate records and to be manned by their own separate judges. The type of work which was handled by the Court of Common Pleas consisted for the most part of private actions between ordinary litigants; it also possessed a jurisdiction to supervise the old local courts and to correct any substantial errors made by them, and it could grant motions for new trials in civil cases. Until the final years of the Plantagenet period the Court of King's Bench continued to preserve its personal connection with the king, who theoretically presided at its hearings, and with the Council; it heard pleas of the Crown, that is, all those types of case which were considered to lie within the exclusive province of the curia regis, and it developed a wide and important jurisdiction in remedying the mistakes and overriding the proceedings of all the inferior courts.

A third common law court to emerge in the thirteenth century was the Court of Exchequer, which was only concerned with actions relating to the royal revenue. During its early history the judges, known as barons, were nominated from the exchequer clerks and their duties were partly judicial and partly fiscal; later on the Exchequer became solely a court of law and the barons were chosen from practising lawyers – though even then they had a lesser status than the judges of the King's Bench or Common Pleas.

Whereas the common law judges derived their immediate jurisdiction from the courts in which they sat, the itinerant justices acquired an *ad hoc* authority from the commissions under which they had been appointed. The customary commissions, one or more of which would be addressed to each itinerant justice, were: Gaol Delivery, ordering him to deliver the gaols in a stated locality and to try the prisoners confined in them; Oyer and Terminer, directing him to enquire into specified crimes committed in certain designated counties; and General Eyre, a very ancient commission enabling him to perform various local administrative duties connected with taxation and the enforcement of law and order.

The English professional judiciary dates from the time of Henry III. At the start of his reign the king's justices were still royal clerks but they were for the most part men in Holy orders with a detailed knowledge of the intricacies of canon law. At the close of the reign the royal bench was being steadily infiltrated by full-time lawyers drawn from a small but developing group who were earning their livelihood as pleaders before the King's Courts. By the end of the thirteenth century very few of the old-style, canon law clerical judges remained. The remodelled judiciary received inadequate and irregular salaries which were supplemented by a set scale of fees charged to litigants at each stage of the proceedings. The king's judges enjoyed no security of tenure; they held their office at the pleasure of the monarch and lost it at the moment of his death.

The creation of a permanent qualified judiciary was soon followed by the emergence of an organized and competent legal profession. In the course of the thirteenth century two types of advocate made their appearance in the courts: the first was the pleader, a specialist who assisted a client in the presentation of his case; the second was the attorney who could literally represent a client even though he himself was absent. In this distinction lies the historical basis of the two-fold British legal system. During the reign of Edward I professional pleaders were employed in a great many important cases and the art of pleading was increasingly respected for the skill and erudition it entailed. Two commissions, the first of which was set up in 1290 and the other in 1292, both made recommendations for the training of law students, and in 1292 Edward I directed his judges to nominate a certain number of attorneys and legal apprentices who would be granted the exclusive right to practise in the King's Courts.

After the Court of Common Pleas had become stationary at Westminster, as a result of the Magna Carta, the lawyers formed themselves into guilds and acquired an area of land just north of the Thames between the cities of London and Westminster. This led to the creation of the four great Inns of Court, Lincoln's Inn, Gray's Inn and the Middle and Inner Temples, together with ten lesser inns known collectively as the Inns of Chancery. At each inn the members and students had a hall where they dined in common, a library in which to study the common law, and chambers where they could reside when they were not living with their wives and families in the country.

There were two classes of pleaders at the Inns of Court, apprentices who ranked as bachelors of law, and serjeants who were equivalent to doctors of law; in a later age both these grades became known collectively as barristers. Student-pleaders were usually young men of noble birth who had entered an Inn of Court instead of attending at a university. The students were taught the common law by a staff of professors and they learnt their advocacy by means of discussion and argument. Eventually they qualified as apprentices, and if they were successful they might in the course of time be selected to join the august guild of serjeants. A serjeant was created by royal summons and enjoyed equality of status with a knight. Serjeants had their own inns and their own mode of dress; they supplied all the judges for the courts of King's Bench and Common Pleas, and they took precedence over the judges of the Court of Exchequer.

It is difficult to supply a cogent reason why the British legal profession should have acquired a second and junior brand of advocate. It may be that attornies, who were later to be known as solicitors, derived their inferior grading from the lower quality of their legal education, or else from the fact that their membership was originally drawn from a humbler stratum of society. However, it is clear that they were appointed, indirectly perhaps, by royal grant and that from an early stage they were considered to be officers of the courts. In the Plantagenet period there seems to have been very little distinction between the inexperienced pleaders and the legally qualified attornies – many of the latter, indeed, were members of the Inns of Court – but there were still some attornies without any academic legal training whatsoever. In a subsequent generation the judges and the benchers, who were the administrators of the Inns of Court, combined to exclude attornies from the various inns and also denied the right to plead in the royal courts to anyone who had not previously been called to the bar, a distinction only available to a barrister.

Even after Parliament and the common law courts had divided off to become separate organs, the Council remained as the hub of executive authority in the English State; its membership included all the principal officers of the realm such as the lord chancellor, the treasurer, higher officials of the king's household, and an assortment of other notabilities like prominent barons, distinguished lawyers, and leading ecclesiastics. The Council also retained a judicial function, quite apart from the royal judges and the courts of common law, applying its own legal precepts and operating its own procedures. It claimed a jurisdiction so wide and so obsecure that it was viewed with suspicion by lawyers and by laymen alike, and although it could not impose the death penalty it had ample power to exact pecuniary penalties or to order the infliction of corporal punishment.

The House of Lords at this time considered that it possessed a jurisdiction superior both to the Council and the courts of common law – a jurisdiction, in fact, which was based upon the constitutional supremacy of Parliament. During the fourteenth century a system arose whereby a lower court could apply to the judges who sat in the Lords for a ruling on a difficult point of law; but the House of Lords regarded its appellate role as being of considerably less importance than its recently assumed right of controlling the conduct of royal officials, and even members of the Council, through the instrument of impeachment. When Lord Latimer was impeached in 1376 he protested that he could not be put on trial without an accuser appearing against him; he was informed that an impeachment by Parliament was a prosecution on behalf of the king. It is possible that Richard

II had this pronouncement in his mind eleven years later when he asked his judges for their opinion as to whether or not one of his officers could be impeached without his consent. It was the unanimous opinion of the royal bench that Parliament was not empowered to act on the king's behalf without first obtaining his authority.

Undoubtedly the chief rivals to the courts of common law at this time were the ecclesiastical courts which continued to administer the old canon law. All through the Plantagenet period the antagonism between the Church and the State was gradually building up to a climax – it was, in many ways, a conflict between an indigenous loyalty to national institutions and a subservience to the dominion of a foreign potentate. For a while an acrid struggle took place between the royal and ecclesiastical courts as each sought to broaden the limits of its jurisdiction. Eventually it was agreed, albeit somewhat grudgingly by both sides, that the royal courts would have an exclusive power to deal with all cases concerning law land, contract, and tort, and the trial of almost every type of crime; for their part, the ecclesiastical courts would retain their inherent right to try all offences against religion, such as heresy and blasphemy, offences against morality, including incest and adultery, and litigation concerning marriage, wills, and intestate succession. The jurisdictional lines of demarcation were sometimes difficult to define and the royal courts were continually issuing writs of prohibition to restrain the ecclesiastical courts from hearing cases considered to be outside the ambit of their control.

Early in Henry II's reign a clerk in Holy orders who had been charged before a temporal court was handed over to an ecclesiastical court for trial, and if convicted he was returned to the temporal court to be sentenced. Before the end of the reign the strange doctrine of Benefit of Clergy had arisen allowing the criminous clerks, as they were called, to evade the jurisdiction of the temporal courts altogether. The procedure which became established under Henry III was that the criminous clerk could be tried and convicted of felony by a temporal court, and had then to 'plead his clergy' in order to be transferred to an ecclesiastical court for sentence; the fact that he was genuinely in Holy orders was usually established by his clerical dress, a written certification, or by proof of his literacy. In 1350 the privilege of Benefit was extended to the holders of a number of ancillary ecclesiastical offices such as exorcists and doorkeepers. Before the end of the fourteenth century Benefit of Clergy had developed into one of the most incongruous fictions in British legal history for it had become available to any person who could read, even if he had never had the remotest connection with the Church. It was, in fact, an absolute charter for the literate, whereby they might totally evade any effective punishment if they were convicted of a felony.

With the growth of the new royal courts it was only to be expected that the old local courts would rapidly diminish in importance and this is, indeed, what actually happened. During the early part of the thirteenth century a full session of the County Court was still reminiscent of a meeting of one of the ancient popular assemblies, with the prelates, nobles, freeholders, and community representatives all taking part in deliberations regarding law enforcement, fiscal matters, and regional administration. Before the end of the fourteenth century it had lost practically the whole of its executive function and had receded into an inferior court of law. Since 1277 the civil jurisdiction of the County Court had been limited to disputes in which the amount at stake was two pounds or less; in practice most of its cases were simple actions for trespass and debt, as the more substantial litigation was either being dealt with by the itinerant judges or was being transferred to the royal courts. The criminal jurisdiction of the County Courts was also drastically curtailed; in 1166 they lost their competence to try accusations of murder, robbery, or theft, and ten years later treason, forgery, and arson were added to the list of offences which were only triable by the king's judges.

The Hundred Court survived as an organ of parochial government; it remained too the assembly at which the sheriff conducted his tourn on one or two occasions every year. As for its civil jurisdiction, this narrowed down to the hearing of petty disputes concerning boundaries and paltry claims arising out of debts and trespassess. The sheriff's tourn was still used for the supervision of the decaying frankpledge system and for receiving presentments from local jurors relating to crimes committed in their areas; the sheriff himself could only deal with comparatively trivial offences, like beatings, brawls, and minor breaches of the peace.

The feudal courts shared in the general decline which resulted from the movement towards centralized justice. Although Edward I was opposed to private jurisdictions, during the course of the fourteenth century many lords of the manor maintained their own courts leet in which they exercised judicial power and administrative control over their tenants. Certain boroughs were granted charters entitling them to hold courts leet in their localities; the jurisdictions were always closely defined and the judges usually consisted of a group of local aldermen.

The common law of England might well have evolved from its incipient stages with a flexibility, a vigour, and a rational cogency; instead it soon became confined in a legalistic strait-jacket. The only form of civil process in the royal courts was by way of one of the recognized forms of action, initiated by one of the prescribed original writs. Litigation was always complicated, expensive, and problematical; the writs were restrictive and precise; the procedural regulations of the courts were stringent and inflexible. If a would-be plaintiff applied for the wrong writ, or chose an inappropriate form of action, or if he commenced his case in one of the common law courts when it would have been apposite to another, then he would be faulted without the merits of his claim even being considered, and he would have to bear not only his own legal costs but the by no means immoderate court fees as well.

In spite of the formalism and constraint of the procedure in the royal courts, the growth of the common law was never completely stultified, as new types of original writ and new forms of action were being continually devised by the chancery with the approval of the king's judges. Although statutory law was increasing both in scope and in volume and the judiciary were accepting the authority of parliamentary legislation, the law was being developed mainly through the discussions and the legal arguments which were taking place from day to day in the superior courts. Thus the foundation was laid for one of the principal characteristics of the British juridical system, the reliance placed upon the sanctity of precedent. The first known law report was prepared in 1292 and thereafter a long series of Year Books, containing descriptions of legal proceedings, was produced annually until the fifteenth century. But lawyers in the royal courts had to depend for the most part on the scribbled notes of their colleagues regarding previous judicial decisions to add a weight and validity to their submissions. A student or a practitioner in this period also had available to him a handful of erudite and comprehensive law books: Glanvil, written in the reign of Henry II, Bracton in the reign of Henry III, and Fleta and Britton in the reign of Edward I.

Sir Henry Maine has remarked that positive law in progressive societies constantly tends to fall behind public opinion and that various expedients, such as legal fictions, statutory legislation, and equity, have been adopted for achieving a state of social harmony. Jurists and political philosophers have always envisaged a system of law superior to the man-made conceptions of the ordinary courts and untrammelled by the practical realities by which these are bound. For such a reason they have introduced the notion of a legally compulsive code of conduct, fashioned for the occasion and based upon the dictates of honesty and conscience. It was described by Aristotle as being 'a better sort of justice', and it was perceived by Roman jurists as the natural law appertaining to all mankind, in distinction from the fragmentary laws which were created by states for their own policy and well-being. In England it was known as equity.

The basis of English equity was the supreme jurisdiction of the monarch to hear and to adjudicate on petitions addressed to him by his subjects, quite apart from any litigation which took place in the ordinary courts. During the Plantagenet period this power, although nominally exercised by the king, was delegated in practice to the lord chancellor who had become recognized as the head of the judicial system and who was also in control of the issue of original writs. The early chancellors were all ecclesiastics and their decisions were based on different precepts from those which were applied in the courts of common law; further, as they were not tied by the governance of precedent, they were able to achieve an independence of thought and a fluidity of reasoning which were denied to the royal judges. During the fourteenth century when the common law courts were growing more and more inflexible, the need for such an equitable jurisdiction became increasingly apparent, and the lord chancellor could give his judgements on the facts presented in the petitions or else he could actually try the cases with the parties present before him. In time equity was to develop into a completely separate legal system with its own judges and its own courts, unlike the Roman concept of natural law which was administered coexistently with the ordinary civil law and always took precedence over it.

During the early part of Henry II's reign the ascendency of the sheriffs was still at its zenith, for in addition to their extensive judicial powers they were the principal officials responsible for the maintenance of law and order. Their decline commenced in 1170 when, owing to their corruption and the abuse of their authority, Henry II appointed the Inquest of Sheriffs to carry out a general enquiry into their conduct. One of the direct results from this is believed to have been the institution of the office of coroner; it also led to a gradual depletion of the jurisdiction of the sheriffs and eventually to their complete eclipse in the sphere of local government in Britain.

Throughout the thirteenth and fourteenth centuries there were usually four coroners in each county. They were unpaid officials elected by the County Courts and one of their most important functions was to restrain the venality of the sheriffs. Ostensibly they supervised the financial interests of the crown at a regional level, but in addition they sat beside the sheriffs whenever the latter were exercising their judicial functions, keeping a record of their decisions and recording the verdicts of the juries. Shortly after his accession to the throne Edward I laid down that every case of violent death should be reported to the nearest coroner so that he could investigate the matter, and if he suspected foul play he could arrest the culprit and hand him over to the sheriff; coroners also had to enquire into every case of housebreaking within their localities. In the course of time they accumulated many further responsibilities. They maintained the authorized register of private prosecutions and of sentences of outlawry, they received the confessions of escaping criminals who had taken sanctuary, they had certain duties in regard to the detention of suspects and in ensuring that such persons duly appeared for their trials, and they empanelled juries and held inquests, not only to enquire into unexplained deaths but also to examine discoveries of shipwrecks, royal fishes and treasure trove, as these were all possible sources of revenue to the Crown. In fact the powers of the coroners and the sheriffs became partly interdependent and partly overlapping. Both offices were to be surpassed at a later date by the rise of the justices of the peace.

CHAPTER 8

CHANGING PATTERNS

The preservation of law and order under the Plantagenet monarchs was left very largely to the community in general, and especially to the amateur, unpaid, civic policing officials in each locality. Indeed, the Assizes of Clarendon and Northampton during the latter part of the twelfth century had placed a specific duty on ordinary inhabitants to apprehend criminals and to deliver them to the proper authorities. The Assize of Arms in 1181 detailed the types of weapon which every free man, according to his status, should always have available for the pursuit of fugitive offenders.

Within the expanding urban areas the prevalence of nocturnal crime was increasing to an alarming extent. Henry III sought to control this lawlessness by ordering that watches be set by night in every city and borough town in the realm. Thirty years later, Edward I found it necessary to impose particular restrictions on the City of London: all gates were to be closed and all residents were to stay indoors during the hours of curfew, the streets were to be patrolled by all-night watches, and visitors to taverns and lodging houses were to be closely scrutinized. The Statute of Winchester in 1285 introduced the system of watch and ward for all cities and borough towns. According to Blackstone, this was supposed to afford the inhabitants a continuous protection, the ward being on duty by day and the watch by night. The 1285 statute also decreed that the gates of walled towns would be closed from sunset to sunrise and any strangers wandering abroad during that time were liable to be arrested and detained until morning.

The Statute of Winchester made further provision for law enforcement in country districts. The arms of all free citizens were to be inspected twice a year to ensure they were complying with the regulations. Sheriffs were reminded of their duty to raise Hue and Cry whenever a law-breaker had made his escape, and all free men aged between fifteen and sixty of their obligation to join in the pursuit. If a robbery was committed inside its boundaries, the hundred was made liable if the robber was not arrested within forty days.

In the days of decentralized administration and poor communications the Hue and Cry procedure was the only effective method of apprehending a fugitive offender. Directly Hue and Cry had been raised by a responsible official, every competent male citizen was supposed to leave his recreation or to lay aside his work and join in the chase, which continued from hundred to hundred and from county to county until the miscreant had either been hunted down or had surrendered. The fugitive himself had no rights: if he sought asylum in a private house he could be dragged out of it; if he resisted arrest he could be maimed or slain by his pursuers. He was only safe if he could reach the consecrated soil of a recognized sanctuary, in which case he was permitted to confess his guilt to a coroner and then to abjure the realm. Abjuration entailed perpetual banishment to any Christian land beyond the seas. The privilege of claiming sanctuary did not extend to a person who had committed sacrilege or treason.

From the fourteenth century onwards the cornerstone of internal law and order in England was the justice of the peace. The power and importance attained by these officials as judicial and executive officers, and also in the field of local government, were both unforseen and unintended and were derived principally from the class structure of rural life in the English counties, and from the complete absence, in a developing society, of any medium of administration at a regional level. The history of the justices of the peace began in 1195 when Richard I issued commissions to certain knights to become keepers of the peace in the more unruly areas of his kingdom. The knights who were so appointed appear to have done little more originally than to render general assistance to the sheriffs. Throughout the reign of Edward II various attempts were made to enlarge the authority of the keepers of the peace; in 1314 they were given the power of arrest, and in 1316 the jurisdiction to enquire into felonies and trespasses. On his accession in 1327 Edward III gave statutory recognition to the keepers in an enactment which provided that 'In every county good and lawful men . . . should be assigned to keep the peace'. In 1328 they were granted the right to inpose punishment, and in 1330 the power to receive presentments from juries and to send the people presented for trial by the royal judges.

Probably the Council still preferred the judicial function to remain essentially in the hands of judges appointed by the king, whereas the House of Commons were giving their full support to the notion of a local judicial officer elected by the County Court. Before 1344, although the keepers of the peace were often sent out on commission in company with other royal commissioners, they possessed no inherent judicial powers to form a court of their own. However, by a statute enacted in 1344 they were authorized to sit with lawyers and 'to hear and determine felonies and trespasses done against the peace . . . and to inflict punishment reasonably'. In 1361 a further Act created a new official, the justice of the peace, in substitution for the keeper of the peace. There were to be three or four justices of the peace in every county, to restrain rioters and other breakers of the law and to 'pursue, arrest, take and chastise them'. The justices were empowered to try offenders on lesser charges and to send those charged with more serious crimes for trial by the king's judges. Two years later, justices of the peace were ordered to hold their sessions four times a year; this was the origin of the County Quarter Sessions which in a future age were not only to exercise considerable judicial authority but were also to wield the power of local government in all the counties.

The justices of the peace in any rural area were drawn exclusively from the local gentry. At the outset no essential qualifications were prescribed, but in 1389 it was directed that they should be 'knights, esquires or gentlemen of the land'. Their numbers were increased to six per county in 1388, and to eight per county in 1390. With the system of criminal appeals falling into disuse, all prosecutions at common law had to be tried on indictment, following a presentment by a jury or a finding by a coroner's inquest. However, numerous statutes were passed making specific offences triable in a summary manner, sometimes by one justice of the peace and sometimes by two. With regard to this summary procedure, Blackstone has tersely commented, 'the common law is a stranger to it'.

The origin of the office of petty constable is somewhat obscure. It seems clear that by the middle of the fourteenth century, when the frankpledge system was disintegrating, he had inherited the role of the old Saxon and Norman communal policing officials. The petty constable was appointed by the local court; he had to take a formal oath to keep the peace and to arrest 'all those who shall make any contest, riot, debate or affray' and to bring the culprits before the sheriffs. The office was unpaid and the duties were performed by the constable in his spare time. After the institution of justices of the peace he came under their control to an ever-increasing extent.

Even towards the end of the fourteenth century the preservation of the peace remained very largely in the hands of the ordinary citizens. They were still liable to collective fines if certain offences had been committed or a detained criminal had been permitted to escape in their localities; men who were physically capable were bound to follow the Hue and Cry; and there was a general obligation to actively assist in the arrest and detention of all law-breakers.

It has been long accepted by legal and constitutional historians that the celebrated clause in the Magna Carta which provided that no freeman should be convicted except 'by the lawful judgment of his peers, or by the law of the land' was not the precursor of trial by jury. Indeed, the very concept of the trial jury would have been abhorrent to the barons, who only had in mind that they themselves should never be tried or sentenced by any judges they considered to be inferior to themselves. At that time the jury of presentment was coming into regular use in the royal courts, the jurors considering the allegations against the suspects both from their own personal knowledge and from the information supplied to them by others. They reached their verdicts by a simple majority, either rejecting the accusations or presenting the suspect for trial.

The trial jury as such made its initial appearance towards the end of the twelfth century, when a person accused by way of criminal appeal was sometimes allowed to purchase the right to be tried by a jury as an alternative to customary modes of trial by battle, compurgation, or ordeal. Both trial by battle and trial by ordeal were condemned by the Lateran Council at Rome in 1215, and as it then became imperative for a new form of trial to be adopted, there was probably little alternative to the petty jury. It was thus, at the indirect instigation of Pope Innocent III rather than as a matter of coherent policy, that trial by jury was incorporated as a fundamental precept of the British legal system. The original petty jurors were by no means impartial assessors. They were deliberately selected from those who might already have knowledge of the relevant facts, and although they were not expected to be eye-witnesses, they were encouraged to gain their information from their own private enquiries. The size of the trial jury was settled at twelve persons and it was determined in 1367 that their verdicts must always be unanimous. There was also an old-established rule that the jurors should not be allowed to separate during the course of their deliberations. It is uncertain why or when the custom arose of denying the jury food or drink until they had returned their verdict; it has been suggested that it was merely a device to hasten their agreement. In time the principle became so rigid that many judges considered that a verdict would be a nullity if it came to light that any jurors had either eaten or drunk during their retirement.

At first it was not unusual for the jury of presentment to form the trial jury as well, but later on special trial jurors were selected from the hundreds, and after 1351 it was forbidden for any juror to try a case which he had actually presented. The crown exercised a considerable influence over the outcome of a jury trial since the jurors were carefully chosen by the king's officers; in any event, the accused person was at a considerable disadvantage as he was neither allowed to have a lawyer to defend him nor could he call any witnesses to give evidence on his own behalf. Even when trial by jury became customary the defendant still had a right to choose trial by battle, ordeal, or compurgation as an alternative.

The trial jury came to play an equally important part in civil actions, where the jurors were more in the nature of witnesses to answer questions of fact addressed to them by the judge. During the thirteenth and fourteenth centuries the use of the trial jury was adopted in the local courts as well as in the courts of common law.

Through the passage of the centuries the Magna Carta has come to be enshrined as the fountainhead of English freedom, and the field at Runnymede has been accepted as symbolizing the great awakening to a sense of national justice. Such an adulatory image is somewhat misconceived; the Magna Carta was devised essentially for the upper classes and paid little heed to the serfs, who still formed the abject mass of the nation. The England of 1300, for all its sparsity of habitation and latent fertility, was an economically over-populated country with the bulk of its people living on a slender margin of subsistence. The serfs were the cultivators of the soil – the great unfree; their lords had an absolute power over them, for legally they ranked as the chattels of their masters. The lord could drive them, beat them, and imprison them at will and he could refuse to let them leave his domains. And yet the position of the serf during the Plantagenet period was growing more and more enigmatic; the common law and the royal judges were constantly proclaiming the virtues of liberty; as against every person except their own lords the serfs enjoyed their full legal rights; many of them possessed their authorized armament and took their part in the Hue and Cry; many of them served on juries of presentment and on juries of trial. Their subservience and bondage derived from ancient feudal custom, as did their poverty and their lack of possessory right.

Then came the Black Death, the devastating epidemic of bubonic plague which started in Central Asia and was carried by fleas and rats in the ships which were plying the trade routes to Europe. It reached England in 1348. The Black Death was usually fatal as the physicians knew of neither cure nor treatment for those who were infected with it. In the absence of proper statistics it is impossible to assess the English mortality rate, but estimates vary at between a quarter and a half of the entire population. The social aftermath of this huge reduction in the agricultural labour force was immense. A large proportion of the serfs no longer felt bound by the ancient feudal restrictions; some took up employment for wages, others moved into holdings of their own. The landlords responded to the fall in food prices by reducing the size of their farms, improving their methods of husbandry, and concentrating on the production of wool to meet the demands of the expanding textile industry. Indeed, the growth of the woolen and cloth trades induced a substantial number of serfs to forsake the servitude and dependence of manor for the latitude and sufficiency of the manufacturing crafts in the villages and towns.

The important economic results of the Black Death were the fall in the value of farms and the rise in the cost of labour. Understandably the peasantry were not slow to appreciate the transformation which had taken place in their position and they demanded and obtained an escalating scale of wages. At this stage, Parliament stepped in. The Statute of Labourers, which came into force in 1349, was a new departure in the governance of England – the substitution of state control of the national labour force for the surveillance formerly exercised by the feudal lords. The aims of the 1349 statute were simply to ensure that there would be an adequate supply of agricultural workers at the wage-rates which had been current before the plague. It was enacted that every man and woman under the age of sixty, unless they had land or money of their own, or were merchants or craftsmen, could be compelled to work on the land at the old rates of payment. The wages of artificers, urban labourers, and servants generally were subjected to a similar restriction. Further legislation followed with the primary objects of prohibiting idleness, curbing wage increases, and preventing the free movement of the menial classes from one neighbourhood to another. A labourer or artificer who left his master without permission could be arrested and returned to his former place of employment; in addition he might be punished by imprisonment, branding, or outlawry. An Act passed in 1388 forbade servants and labourers to leave the hundreds where they were living in order to obtain work elsewhere without first obtaining a letter patent under the king's seal. A short while later the justices of the peace, who were in charge of the implementation of all these regulations, were empowered to settle and proclaim the wages of the various categories of day labourers on two occasions every year.

In a society reared to a feudal tradition these stringent powers of direction and control did not seem unduly arbitrary. In any event the labouring classes were neither united nor organized. At common law any combination of masters or workmen for the purpose of imposing conditions or restrictions in connection with employment was considered to be an unlawful conspiracy. At the same time the merchant guilds, each managing its own particular trade, were growing in importance. Every merchant guild had obtained a royal charter which gave its members a virtual monopoly to carry on a particular type of trade. Later on, craftsmen formed their own fraternities, known as craft guilds. Both merchant guilds and craft guilds were in reality monopolistic societies established for the sole object of self-protection. The usual method of entry to a craft guild, certainly after the middle of the fourteenth century, was by way of apprenticeship. The apprentice would enter a contract with his master, normally for seven years, to be taught the essentials of his chosen craft. At the conclusion of his training he himself would become a full member of the guild. This method of selection enabled the craft guilds to exercise a close supervision over their standards and their membership.

One unfortunate result of the partial emancipation of the serfs was the casting upon the labour market of so many inadequates who were now no longer, in the last resort, the responsibility of the lord of their manor. This led to an increase in destitution. Only the impotent poor were permitted by law to solicit alms; those who were fit and who either could not obtain or could not hold employment were forbidden to wander or to beg, but were denied any form of national or local relief whatsoever.

During the Plantagenet period the legal principles of the occupation of land were being fashioned into a permanent shape. Broadly speaking there were two types of occupancy, free tenure and unfree tenure. With regard to free tenure, it has already been observed that the incidents of knight-service were giving place to the payment of a fixed money-rent, and a similar tendency was apparent in the other types of free tenancy as well. However, several of the old requirements of feudal procedure still lingered on. The tenant was supposed to take an oath of fealty to his lord; the heir had to pay a relief on succeeding to the property; if the tenant died without an heir the land reverted to the lord; and if he were convicted of high treason it was forfeited to the king in its entirety. Originally the unfree tenant gave labour-service in return for his holding and he too was subjected to the ancient obligations of feudal taxation, of which the three principal payments were made on the knighting of the lord's eldest son, the marrying of his eldest daughter, or as a contribution towards his ransom if he were captured in battle. Owing to the scarcity of labour after the Black Death and increased prosperity occasioned by the wool trade, the feudal elements of unfree tenure were gradually replaced by the fixed-rent system, the lord hiring out the land to a tenant for regular periodical payments of money.

During the fourteenth century the lawyers were starting to propound the conception that it was possible to define various estates in land, each of which incorporated certain specific rights and duties on the part of both the owner and the occupier. Even a free tenant was restricted in his power to alienate his property, but this was mainly for the protection of his heir. The closest the holder of a free tenure could come to making an absolute gift of his property was by donating it 'in tail', in other words, to the recipient and the heirs of his body. After 1285 if property had passed in this way it reverted to the donor or his heirs on the failure of the donee's issue. The use of trusts continued to be employed in order to allow property-owners to dispose of their land as they wished; in this respect the Mortmain Acts were strengthened to prevent the Church, already the owner of a considerable quantity of property both on a personal as well as a corporate basis, from the further enlargement of its holding.

Whereas a man was unable to bequeath his real estate he could devise the whole of his personalty either by a verbal will made before two honest witnesses, or by a written testament signed and sealed by himself. In common with Roman law, a youth attained testamentary capacity at the age of fourteen, and a girl at the age of twelve. The position of married women differed between ecclesiastical law, which allowed her full testamentary capacity, and common law, which considered that since all their possessions were vested in their husbands, any wills they purported to make were bound to be mere nullities. If a man died intestate leaving a widow but no children, his widow took half of his personal estate; if he left a widow and children, his widow took one third and his children one third of his personal estate between them. A statute in 1357 directed that when any person had died intestate, 'the next and most powerful friends' of the deceased should be appointed to administer the estate.

All matters appertaining to wills and intestacy were in

the province of the ecclesiastical courts, which also had jurisdiction over the formation and the dissolution of marriages. The legal effect of a valid marital union was that the husband and wife were joined together as one person with the wife falling completely under the dominion of her husband. During the subsistence of the marriage the wife could own no personal property and could make no valid contracts; her husband had the custody and control of all her real estate but she was entitled to bequeath it to her heir on her death. Whereas a wife retained full responsibility for her criminal acts, her husband was wholly liable for her torts. It is of interest to note that children under the age of eight were considered to be incapable of committing a felony; they could, however, be held responsible for their minor offences or for their torts if they were shown to have acted voluntarily.

Although industry was expanding throughout the fourteenth century the commercial company was still unknown. An association of merchants for trading purposes, unless it was incorporated by statute, charter, or prescription, possessed no privileges and was at best a partnership, in which all the members were equally liable for the collective business debts, and in any litigation they could only sue or be sued under all their individual names rather than under the name of the association. In private transactions the conception of a legally enforceable contract had become recognized by the courts. Unlike canon law which implemented agreements on the ground of the moral obligation involved, the English common law adopted the essential requirement of consideration, that is to say each of the parties to the contract must have passed to the other something of positive value, which could be a payment, a right, a profit, an interest, or a benefit.

At this time any legal protection of the nature of a patent was unknown; on the other hand, from the time of Edward III the Plantagenet kings made a practice of granting monopolies, usually to one person or a group of people, permitting them to exercise the sole trading rights in some particular commodity. For instance, contemporary reports make reference to royal monopoloies for exporting tin without paying the customary tax and for selling certain types of wine in the City of London. Edward III granted a number of monopolies to foreign merchants to manufacture cloth by special processes, in return for an undertaking by them to come to England and to teach the English clothmakers their arts and skills. The consumer, too, was granted little protection by the general law, except for the fact that the makers of gold and silver wares were subjected to strict regulations in respect of the marking of their articles, mainly to prevent fraud. The exact standards of purity for articles made of gold and of silver were stipulated by a statute passed in 1300.

It would seem that civil actions for defamation were not uncommon during this period, but they were heard in the ecclesiastical or the local courts and never in the courts of common law. Defamation was not regarded as a crime until the new offence of *scandalum magnatum* was created in 1275. This prohibited the dissemination of rumours affecting the reputations of the magnates of realm, and was introduced to facilitate the maintenance of internal order by curbing rumours, apprehension and mistrust. Nevertheless it was a dangerous weapon to place in the hands of the executive and, as will be seen, it was frequently abused by them in future years. In 1379 a further statute defined the classes of the eminent who were to be considered as magnates for the purposes of this offence.

Part V

THE PERIOD OF THE HOUSES OF LANCASTER AND YORK

(1399 – 1485)

CHAPTER 9

THE WARS OF THE ROSES

The English nation in 1399 was stirring restlessly. The old order and the old convention were being swept away by the progress of events and what was emerging in their place seemed both unenduring and imprecise. The balance of political authority between the king, the Council and Parliament was still unsettled; the social conformation which would supplant the confined autocracy of feudalism was as yet obscure; the orientation to the needs of a commercial community had scarcely commenced; new ideas and a muted enlightment were spreading; and even the teaching of the Church and the habits of the clergy were undergoing criticism, especially from John Wycliffe's adherents, the Lollards. In such an atmosphere the country turned to their new sovereign Henry of Lancaster to steer them through the uncertainties of the future and to finally rid them of the outworn relics of the past.

As so often happens when a people have acclaimed a new deliverer, the initial moments of exultation were short-lived and were soon followed by a despondent realization that the change of leadership had by no means signified a change of fortune. Henry IV was, in fact, a very ordinary king who produced no original policies. For almost the whole of his fourteen-year reign he was harassed by civil strife at home while he struggled to maintain the unremitting, inconclusive foreign wars against France and Scotland. Constitutionally he governed with his parliament, and Parliament in gratitude enacted in 1406 that, despite his lack of hereditary claim to the throne, the crown should eventually pass from him to his sons as a legitimate dynastic succession. Henry V succeeded his father without opposition in 1413; he devoted all his energies to the prosecution of the French war and won a series of tactical victories which had little effect on the overall strategical situation. He died in 1422 at a time when his heir and namesake was less than twelve months old.

Henry VI, the last of the Lancastrian kings, although pious and intellectual, was totally deficient in the qualities of leadership. He had the misfortune to be the occupant of the English throne during the final disastrous phase of the Hundred Years War when the French were recapturing the whole of their country except for a small area around the hinterland of Calais. A number of factors besides the blow to the national prestige contributed towards Henry's unpopularity: the disbanded and disconsolate soldiers from France swelling the ranks of the unemployed; the influence and machinations of the foreign-born queen; and the patent weakness of character of the king himself. In 1454 Henry succumbed to a bout of insanity and Richard, Duke of York was appointed Protector. In fact, Richard, a descendant of Edward III, was the Yorkist claimant to the throne. When Henry recovered his sanity in 1455 Richard took up arms against him and the Wars of the Roses commenced.

The civil war between the houses of York and Lancaster lasted to the end of this period with intermittent battles, truces, occupations, retreats and regroupings. Apart from the actual regions in which the fighting was taking place, life in England continued fairly normally. Most victories were followed by the slaughter of a proportion of the leaders of the vanquished armies; sometimes they were followed too by improvised allegiances, proclamations, and amended genealogical tables of succession before the battles moved on to different localities. Might was regarded as right and the victors for the moment were always accorded a retrospective constitutional validity.

Richard, Duke of York, was killed during the Lancastrian victory at the battle of Wakefield in 1460. His second son Edward immediately took up the Yorkist cause in his stead. Edward led his forces into London in the spring of 1461 where he was proclaimed as King Edward IV by the citizens, an accession which was legitimated by Parliament when they conveniently declared that Henry V had been a usurper. Henry VI, although deposed, remained at liberty until his capture and subsequent imprisonment in 1465. Apart from a brief interlude in 1470 when he was obliged to flee the country and when Henry VI was freed from prison and temporarily restored to the throne, Edward IV ruled England until his death in 1483. He was a sovereign of undoubted ability, but he dissipated his opportunities through his despotism, his cruelty, and his personal self-indulgence. He was succeeded by his twelve-year-old son Edward V.

During Edward V's minority his uncle Richard, a younger brother of the late king, was appointed regent. Richard, who desired the crown for himself, persuaded a compliant Parliament to declare that Edward IV's marriage had been invalid, thus opening the way for his own accession to the throne as King Richard III. Whilst Edward V and his brother were alive, Richard was aware that his position would always be fraught with danger, so he decided to eliminate this latent threat by arranging for the imprisonment in the Tower and the subsequent murder of the two young princes. Richard III's brief reign lasted a bare two years; he was defeated and slain at the battle of Bosworth in 1485 when his army succumbed to the forces of Henry Tudor, who was then the claimant to the throne for the House of Lancaster. Henry VII, the founder of the Tudor dynasty, was acclaimed King of England on the battlefield.

Throughout the three decades of the Wars of the Roses the constitutional development of England was dormant, although the theoretical rights and privileges of the House of Lords and the House of Commons were in no way diminished. It was, perhaps, because of Parliament's constant subservience to the conquerors and its instant condemnation of the vanquished that its residual powers were preserved. For their part the leaders of the rival factions invariably sought parliamentary sanction for the validity of their credentials, even if they showed small desire for parliamentary assistance in the general governance of the kingdom. Henry VI only once convened a parliament during the last eleven years of his reign; Edward IV had none at all for five consecutive years; and Richard III ruled with a single parliament for the whole of his brief spell on the throne.

Nevertheless, during the course of the fifteenth century the process of legislation was still continuing and it was becoming accepted that there was no authority superior to that of the king whilst acting in conjunction with his parliament. It had been tacitly suggested by certain monarchs that they had retained the prerogative right of legislating by royal ordinances – a function quite independent of parliamentary statutes – but this contention was never really put to the test. In the absence of any written constitution, wide and important areas of jurisdiction were naturally uncertain; for instance, the ability to declare or to conclude foreign wars, and the competence to settle the succession to the throne.

The character of the House of Lords had now undergone a total change. No longer was it a representative council of men who had acquired dominance and prestige by their own efforts; it had become in essence an assembly for those who were personally privileged to attend by virtue of an inherited rank and status. There were five dignities of peerage, each of which carried a seat in the upper house. They were, in order of precedence: dukes, a title first created by Edward III for the benefit of his sons; marquesses, an ancient office which became a social distinction under Richard II; earls, a survival of the long-abeyant Anglo-Saxon official; viscounts, originated as peers by Henry VI; and lastly, of course, the ordinary barons. The ecclesiastical dignitaries, the archbishops, bishops, priors and abbots, were probably numerically equal to, and might have outnumbered, their lay brethren.

The House of Commons fought hard to preserve and even to enlarge the powers they had achieved in the preceding era. They audited public accounts and scrutinized national expenditure. They curbed the activities of corrupt or over-arrogant counsellors and in the last resort attempted to bring about their dismissal and punishment, both by the force of their criticism and by a newly improvised device called an Act of Attainder which was, in fact, a parliamentary statute convicting a person without a trial. The Commons still contended that they possessed the sole and absolute right of levying taxes, but this was a claim which the monarchy never wholly accepted. As to membership of the lower house, at the beginning of this period all freeholders present at a County Court were eligible to vote for their representatives, but a statute of 1430 restricted the franchise to those freeholders who were resident in the county and who owned property to the annual value of forty shillings. A short while later many cities and boroughs deliberately abnegated their electoral rights and permitted them to fall into the hands of various rich landowners or small groups of self-appointed burgesses. There was no actual qualification for election to the Commons until 1445 when an Act provided that candidates must be selected thenceforth from 'notable knights, notable squires, gentlemen by birth'.

The judiciary and the senior members of the legal profession maintained a commendable impartiality during the Wars of the Roses, despite all attempts to commit them to one side or the other. Both the royal judges and the king's serjeants declined a request from the House of Lords that they should express an authoritative view of the legitimacy of the Duke of York's claims to the throne, on the ground that this was not a matter of law. Likewise in Henry VI's reign the judges refused a proposal that they should define the scope of parliamentary privilege. Throughout the fighting the courts managed to continue with their normal work, largely ignoring the unsettled background, and quite irrespective of whether the Yorkists or the Lancastrians happened for the moment to be uppermost.

A contemporary description of the training of barristers was given by Sir John Fortescue in his book *De Laudibus Legum Angliae*, written during the reign of Edward IV when Fortescue, who had been chief justice of the King's Bench under Henry VI, had been living in exile on the Continent. The ten Inns of Chancery, said Fortescue, each had at least two hundred students who, when they had become proficient in elements of the law, were absorbed into the four Inns of Court. 'Most of those who learn the law in the Inns', he went on, 'are the sons of nobles and there is scarcely a man learned in the laws who is not noble or sprung of noble lineage'. Fortescue tells us that during the vacations the students learnt the Holy Scriptures, and that many fathers sent their sons to the Inns, not with a view to their practising law, 'but for the sake of the acquisition of virtue and the discouragement of vice'. There is no doubt, too, that a number of youths studied law to equip them more fully for the eventual management of their family estates. 'Scarcely any turbulence, quarrels or disturbance' ever occurred in the Inns of Court, said Fortescue; and all offenders were expelled from their Inns, which punishment was more dreaded than 'imprisonment and fetters'.

The standard of the judges and that of the lawyers during

this period seems to have been fairly high and civil litigation was plentiful. The professionalism and strength of the courts of common law and the itinerant justices was gradually undermining the status and utility of the older local courts. By the beginning of the reign of Edward IV the County Court had become totally unimportant and the judicial work of the Hundred Court had receded into virtual extinction. A statute of 1461 deprived sheriffs of the power of arresting offenders or of levying fines, and directed that they should transmit all indictable offences to the justices of the peace; this was tantamount to abolishing the sheriff's tourn. Meanwhile the justices of the peace were going from strength to strength, especially with regard to their powers in Quarter Sessions where, apart from their expanding administrative control, they were permitted to try every type of crime except treason, and merely to send the more difficult cases for trial by the royal judges. In 1414 it was stipulated that justices of the peace must reside within the counties covered by their commissions, and in 1439 that they must own land there to the value of at least £20 a year. The ordinary justice's commissions authorized them to keep the peace, to punish offenders, to take sworn inquests, and to hear and determine certain offences.

The fifteenth century saw the birth of the Court of Chancery. Formerly, the lord chancellor had exercised his equitable jurisdiction in his capacity as a senior member of the Council; after 1474 he started to act on his own intrinsic authority, leaving the Council, for the moment, as a purely executive committee with an inert reserve of judicial power. There was a danger initially that lord chancellors might conceive the ambit of their equitable jurisdiction to be so extensive that they would usurp the functions of the common law courts, as well as nullifying the developing legal precepts and even jeopardizing the future of trial by jury. Fortunately for the English legal system, successive lord chancellors adopted the principle that equity would only assist when common law offered no redress; the demands for such intervention were numerous; juries were corruptible, the remedies of common law were circumscribed, the formalistic axioms and the intricate rules of procedure could be frustrated and debased. In theory equity was ever present to satisfy the requirements of good conscience, taking account particularly of cases which involved fraudulent dealing or breach of confidence.

The procedure of a chancery suit was speedier, simpler, and cheaper than that of an action at common law. It started with a petition from the plaintiff to the lord chancellor setting out a grievance and praying for relief. The defendant was granted an opportunity of answering the allegation, and there might then be further written pleadings and oral examinations of both parties before the lord chancellor gave his judgment. As he was not restrained by precedent, he could fashion his decisions to meet the circumstances, though lawyers soon began compiling his adjudications in an effort to create a body of equitable case-law. A plaintiff wishing to sue at common law still had to find an appropriate original writ; when he had done so he filed a statement of claim reciting the substance of his case. The defendant countered by filing a reply. Both the litigants were closely bound by these preliminary pleadings so it was essential that they should be skilfully drafted. An intense rivalry soon developed between equity and common law, matching the antagonism which already existed between the common law and the ecclesiastical courts, and, indeed, between the courts of King's Bench, Common Pleas and Exchequer.

By this time crimes were clearly distinguished from torts; and all the more serious offences, those which could only be tried in the royal courts, were classified as felonies. Included amongst the more common types of felony were homicide, wounding, rape, burglary, robbery, and theft. Treasons were treated as a separate class of offence and were divided into two groups: high treason which involved a breach of allegiance to the sovereign, and petit treason, a less heinous crime which entailed an act of treachery by a servant towards his master or by a wife towards her husband. The scope of actions for tort was constantly widening with the multiplication of original writs. In general these were designed to cover most non-criminal forms of behaviour which resulted in injury, damage, or harm to the person or the property of another, whether committed deliberately or accidentally.

Trial by jury had now become an essential feature of English common law. However, the jurors appear to have had a different function at civil and at criminal trials. In a civil case they were independent assessors of the facts, for Fortescue has said that each of the parties, either personally or through their counsel, first explained their contentions to the jury, after which they were at liberty to produce before the court 'all such witnesses as they please . . . who being charged upon their oaths shall give in evidence all that they know touching the truth of the fact concerning which the parties are at issue'. On the other hand criminal jurors, according to Fortescue, consisted of 'twelve men, persons of good character, neighbours where the fact was committed, and well acquainted with the lives and conversations of the witnesses'; in other words, they formulated their verdict partly upon the evidence and partly upon their own knowledge of the circumstances. The defendant at a criminal trial had to go through the formality of electing trial by jury. After he had pleaded 'not guilty', the clerk of the court used to say to him, 'Culprit, how will you be tried?' To which he was supposed to reply, 'By God and my country'. When he refused to plead, or refused to choose his form of trial, and the charge was one of treason or misdemeanour, a jury was empanelled to say whether he stood 'mute of malice' or 'mute through visitation of God'. If the jurors decided he stood 'mute of malice' a plea of guilty was recorded if their verdict was 'mute by visitation of God', the trial took place as it would have done on a plea of 'not guilty'. With a charge of felony it was different. The ordinary punishment for felony was death and it was considered morally improper to execute a defendant who had neither confessed his guilt nor agreed to a jury trial. Originally defendants were starved until they consented to plead, but in Henry IV's reign there started the barbaric process known as *peine forte et dure*, by which a prisoner charged with felony who would not plead was taken to an adjoining room where he was stretched on his back naked, and iron weights were placed on his body, 'as much as he could bear and more'. He continued like this, only being given bad bread and stagnant water for sustenance, until either he died or he was coerced into pleading.

The ecclesiastical courts had a procedure of their own which could best be described as 'inquisitorial'. The judge conducted the trial himself, acting as advocate, prosecutor, and juror. Each diocese had its own consistory court presided over by a chancellor, usually a specialist in canon law, who sat as a representative of the bishop. The ecclesiastical provinces of Canterbury and York each had its provincial court. Appeals lay from the consistory courts to the provincial courts and thence to the See of Rome. The most serious crime over which the ecclesiastical courts had jurisdiction was the offence of heresy, but this was being dealt with more and more on indictment by courts of assizes and Quarter Sessions. The penalty for heresy, first authorized during the reign of Henry IV, was burning at the stake. Ecclesiastical courts were also losing their exclusive jurisdiction over testamentary suits as these fell increasingly into the ambit of Chancery, but they were maintaining their absolute control over all matters relating to marriage and divorce. According to canon law only the pope could grant the complete dissolution of a valid marriage, a divorce *a vinculo matrimonii*, and he seldom if ever did so. The consistory court, however, was able to grant a divorce *a mensa et thora*, which was little more than a judicial separation and did not permit either of the parties to remarry. It was always possible to evade the principle of indissolubility and to obtain a decree of annulment, by proving that a blood-relationship of the remotest possible nature or a mythical spiritual affinity had existed between a husband and wife at the time of their marriage; or else by reliance on the doctrine of precontract, a fictitious assertion that prior to the wedding one of the parties had agreed to marry someone else. It was for an alleged precontract that Parliament, at the instigation of Richard III, had declared that the marriage of Edward IV was invalid.

During this century of insecure or irresolute monarchs many over-powerful landowners were striving constantly to enlarge their estates at the expense of their neighbours, availing themselves of fraudulent legal claims and devious marriage settlements, or even by forcible invasions of adjacent property. When an action came before the courts both sides often resorted to bribery and intimidation of the witnesses and jurors. There were then three principle classes of tenure in England: firstly freeholds, which were usually held directly from the Crown; secondly copyholds, which arose when a tenant had been in occupation a sufficient length of time to have his holding recorded in a copy of the rolls in the manorial court, for the common law recognized a legal permanence created by custom; and thirdly tenancies-at-will, the sort of tenure applicable to the majority of the residents on an estate who had not occupied long enough to acquire the status of copyholders.

Throughout the English countryside the process of switching over from tillage to pasture continued as the price of wool maintained its high level, particularly in the Low Countries. As a further measure to increase the economic deployment of their land the owners of large estates began to evict their tenants-at-will and to enclose large areas of wasteland, driving out the squatters who had settled there and who had been grazing their cattle without interference on the vast uncultivated valleys and plains.

In spite of the fact that the courts were becoming more inclined to assist maltreated tenants, the lawyers were continually devising new stratagems to frustrate their legal rights; for instance, the collusive action for 'recovery' between the vendor and the purchaser of property to enable the sitting tenant to be peremptorily evicted. By the close of the fifteenth century most of the land in the kingdom was held on trust. The advantages to the owner of such an arrangement were considerable. Apart from having greater freedom to sell or to bequeath his property, it was not subject to forfeiture if he was convicted of treason – an appreciable consideration during the ebb and flow of ascendancy in the Wars of the Roses. A trust was simply arranged by the owner conveying his property on trust to a reliable friend. Such transactions were not recognized by common law, but as the friend was under a moral obligation to fulfil the desires of the real owner the trust was upheld and its conditions were enforced by the Court of Chancery.

The draconian legislation for curbing the wages and restricting the freedom of the labouring classes continued. An Act in 1406 directed that artificers and labourers must take an oath to obey the statutes already in force or be placed in the stocks. It further required that children should be put to 'such labour as their mothers and fathers are of, or as their estates require' on pain of fine or imprisonment. It seems that the regulations were not properly implemented even then, as a statute in 1414 commenced by reciting that servants and labourers were still fleeing from county to county in defiance of the law, and it went on to urge sheriffs and justices of the peace to be more strict and more vigilant. In 1427 any two justices of the peace were authorized to settle and proclaim the scale of wages to be applied in their own districts. A statute passed in 1444 actually fixed the wages of various categories of labourers and artisans; it also decreed that persons refusing to work must be committed to jail, and that any farm labourer who wished to leave his employment must give his master six months' notice prior to his departure. Occasionally groups of workers endeavoured to form associations for improving their conditions, but these were all short-lived. The masons had the only permanent organization and in 1425 their annual conventions were banned on the ground that 'the good courses and effect of the Statutes of Labourers are publicly violated and broken, in subversion of the law, and grievous harm of all the commonalty', by their continuence.

In this empirical society with its rudimentary and ineffective policing arrangements the punishment of convicted criminals was directed solely to the purposes of deterrence and retribution. It was thought that the surest method of instilling a universal obeisance to the law was by publicly exhibiting the agony of the delinquent, and that such a vengeance exacted on their behalf would gratify the innate desire of the honest and upright members of the community. Punishments must therefore be brutal and dramatic: public hangings, the floggings of both men and women at the whipping-post or tied to the cart-tail; or else, a lesser penalty, a period of exposure and ridicule in the pillory or stocks. Every felony carried the sentence of death, with the proviso that if the defendant were literate he could claim Benefit of Clergy, irrespective of the magnitude of his crime. To offset this absurd procedure felonies were starting to be classified as 'clergyable', for which Benefit was allowed, and 'non-clergyable', for which it was not available. The pillory had probably been introduced in England by the Anglo-Saxons. In the thirteenth century a comprehensive list of pillory-offences was drawn up, which included the fraudulent use of weights and measures, perjury, and the composition of libellous or seditious writings. In the usual type of pillory the victims stood on a platform with their necks and wrists clamped in a wooden frame. Although men and women were liable to have their heads completely shaved as an additional humiliation, it was stipulated that they should 'suffer no peril to their bodies' whilst undergoing their sentences. The stocks, which fulfilled a similar function to the pillory, were employed in a far more arbitrary and informal manner, mainly by the justices of the peace. A statute in 1406 made it compulsory for every town and village to have a set of stocks. These were used for the punishment of trivial offenders such as drunkards, profaners, gamblers, and vagrants.

Sentences of imprisonment were sometimes, though rarely, imposed by the courts, the gaols being principally utilized for the detention of those awaiting trial and those who had been convicted and were still waiting for the execution of their punishments. Prisons were leased by private arrangement to unsalaried gaolers who engaged their own staffs. A gaoler ran his prison as a commercial undertaking. He hired out accommodation, beds and bedding at exorbitant charges to the prisoners who were able to pay for them; he appointed himself the sole retailer for all the food, drink, firewood, coals, and candles which were sold in his gaol; he collected admission fees from newly arrived prisoners, and release fees from those who had been acquitted, before they were allowed to leave his gaol. He received another payment known as 'easement of irons', by which a prisoner could purchase the right of being more lightly fettered or even of not being fettered at all. A prisoner in gaol had to maintain himself or to be maintained by his friends, otherwise he was forced to rely on the meagre rations donated by charitable well-wishers – or to starve.

The common law was supposed to protect prisoners from what was called 'hard usage', but in fact they were savagely treated by gaolers and turnkeys alike. They were herded together with little or no segregation, male and female, young and old, tried and untried, criminal and debtor, living in the most appalling squalour and degradation and subjected to continual whippings, torture and extortion. Perhaps the greatest dread in all their minds was an outbreak of the perennial and deadly disease called 'gaol fever' which could decimate the inmates of a prison in a matter of a few weeks. One of the earliest references to this endemic infection is to be found in Stow's *Survey of London*, where he mentions that a very bad epidemic occurred in the London prisons in the year 1414.

Part VI

THE TUDOR PERIOD

(1485–1603)

CHAPTER 10

THE SOURCES OF AUTHORITY

At the conclusion of the Wars of the Roses the embryonic English constitution had successfully survived thirty years of civil strife, irresolute rule, and factional instability. There can be little doubt that the mass of the nation were willing to acquiesce in an era of firm – even of despotic – leadership; but there were grave doubts whether a strong and purposeful governance could ever be attained within the existing framework, based as it was upon the surveillance of a censorious Parliament and the sanctity of the common law.

Henry VII was to lay the foundations for many of the later achievements of the Tudor dynasty. By establishing himself as an absolute monarch he suppressed the recalcitrant nobility whilst he effected a policy of internal order and commercial prosperity. He did not abolish the existing organs of administration, the Council, Parliament, the common law courts, and the justices of the peace; but rather he subordinated them to his will and redefined their roles in a unified system of control. At the same time he minimized the financial dependence of the Crown on the House of Commons by building up a large personal fortune.

In 1509 Henry VIII inherited both his father's throne and his father's wealth. Throughout his reign he wielded an arbitrary power which had been unprecedented in the reign of any previous national monarch. Yet in all his despotism, in all his acts of cruelty, his excesses, and his unscrupulousness, he was careful to seek the justification of the law; even his worst tyrannies were clothed with a propriety which prevented a regression in the social, legal, or political evolution of his country. Henry had little trouble in achieving his purpose. The Council did his bidding, Parliament grovelled to him, even judges and jurors would comply with his wishes in any case which involved his interests, his safety, or his schemings. Not only was he a very popular king but he was a monarch who interpreted, and to large measure fulfilled, the aspirations of his people.

Henry's attitude towards the constitution and his endeavour to respect the law were typified by his methods of handling his own matrimonial problems. When he decided to terminate his marriage with his first wife, Catherine of Aragon, he tried to obtain a formal annulment from the pope on the ground that his bride had been his brother's widow. It is thought that the pope might well have acceded to Henry's request had it not been for his fear of antagonizing Catherine's nephew, the emperor Charles V. Early in 1533, before the pope had given an official ruling, Henry married Anne Boleyn; next, the king obtained papal sanction for the appointment of Thomas Cranmer as archbishop of Canterbury and persuaded Parliament to abolish appeals to Rome on all ecclesiastical matters. The new archbishop dutifully declared the nullity of Henry's marriage with Catherine and the validity of his marriage with Anne; this view was subsequently confirmed by an ecclesiastical commission which had been set up by the primate. Three years later when Henry was displeased with Anne Boleyn, Cranmer annulled his marriage with her, and a special court of the House of Lords condemned her of adultery and sentenced her to death. Henry's fourth marriage with the plain and humourless German princess, Anne of Cleeves was formally dissolved by a convocation presided over by Cranmer on the scarcely credible ground that the union had never been consummated. And finally, Henry's fifth wife, Catherine Howard, was convicted of adultery before he arranged to have her beheaded.

The religious changes innovated by Henry VIII, which were supported by the mass of the nation, were brought about by parliamentary enactment rather than by royal decree. Henry had not wished to effect a religious reformation, but to leave matters of doctrine and ritual unaltered and simply to emancipate his country from the power of Rome by substituting the Crown for the pope as the highest ecclesiastical authority. At that time the standing of the Church was at an extremely low ebb, due principally to its corrupt and oppressive practices and the dissolute lives of the clergy. Any move which would subordinate the priesthood to the control of the law and would eliminate the last vestiges of foreign jurisdiction in Britain was bound to receive universal approbation. A series of statutes between 1531 and 1536 established a national Church with the king at its head and bestowed on the monarch a personal control in ecclesiastical affairs and in the making of appointments to the prelacy. The aftermath of this reorientation, and of the inevitable reprisals taken by Rome, was a divisive conflict of loyalty and belief which gave rise to the religious intolerance and persecution which were to persist throughout the remainder of the Tudor period.

The suppression of the monastries, which followed closely upon the institution of the national Church, had a twofold purpose. In the first place the monasteries would certainly have become the centres of dissident resistance to the change, and in the second, a judicious distribution of confiscated monastic wealth would be bound to create a group of influential persons with a vested interest in the preservation of the new order. Once again Henry accomplished his purpose under a cloak of legality. He sent out a team of official visitors to inspect a number of monasteries and to report upon the work and the habits of their monks. As a result of the revelations of the investigators, which were largely factual but probably exaggerated, the smaller monasteries were suppressed by Act of Parliament in 1536. The greater monasteries either yielded under duress and were surrendered to the king by their abbots and priors, or else, by a rather dubious interpretation of the law, they were held to have fallen into the king's hands by the attainder of their stubborn prelate. The monastic lands and a large part of the monastic wealth were distributed among the new nobility.

In 1544, three years before Henry VIII's death, Parliament passed a statute at the king's behest settling the succession to the throne on his three children in the order Edward, Mary, and Elizabeth, in spite of the fact that his two daughters had formerly been declared illegitimate owing to the alleged defects in his unions with their respective mothers. In addition, the Act decreed that in default of issue of the king's children the Crown would pass to such persons as Henry designated in his will.

The sickly Edward VI succeeded his father in 1547 whilst still a minor, and during his six-year reign Britain was ruled first by the Duke of Somerset and then by the Duke of

Northumberland. It was Northumberland who persuaded the ineffectual young king to disinherit his two sisters and to nominate Northumberland's own daughter-in-law Lady Jane Grey, a great-granddaughter of Henry VII, as the heir to the throne. Whilst both Somerset and Northumberland were in control of the nation's affairs the national Church drifted further and further from its Roman heritage. An English prayer-book was introduced, and a form of communion in the English language; an Act was passed allowing the clergy to marry; and in 1551 the Forty-two Articles were promulgated as the doctrinal exposition of a distinctive sect of the Christian faith. The appropriation of monastic resources continued, but by now it had lost a large part of its popular appeal and there were risings in favour both of the reinstatement of the old church services and of the partial restoration of the monasteries to their former uses.

When Edward died at the age of fifteen in 1553 the tragic and gentle Jane Grey was proclaimed queen by the Council. Her 'reign' only lasted nine days as the nation gave its solid support to the rightful claimant, Henry VIII's elder daughter Mary, whose entitlement was based both on her birthright and on a parliamentary enactment. Jane Grey was captured, imprisoned in the Tower, and beheaded seven months later for high treason, and Mary became the first crowned queen to occupy the English throne. True to the Tudor tradition Mary ensured the constitutional validity of her title to the throne when a short time after her accession Parliament declared that Catherine of Aragon had been the lawful wife of Henry VIII and that Mary was their legitimate daughter. Later, a parliamentary declaration confirmed that a queen of England possessed exactly the same privileges and powers as those of an English king.

Mary's reign is chiefly associated with its most deplorable and degrading features: the unrelenting religious persecution of the newly formed Church, in which at least 300 so-called heretics were burnt to death at the stake; the political abasement to the power of Rome when the Lords and the Commons knelt to the papal delegate to crave forgiveness for the nation's misdemeanours; the appointment of a hated foreign potentate, Philip of Spain as titular king of England after his marriage to the queen; and the disastrous war at the close of Mary's life in which the French recaptured Calais, the last remaining British foothold on the European continent. In spite of the queen's doctrinal bigotry, and she had been brought up in the faith of the Catholic Church so she was impelled by a natural determination to reverse the innovations of the two previous reigns, she probably tried, nonetheless, to be a conscientious and steadfast ruler; certainly she did not tamper unduly with the established principles of authority and government. Had she possessed the popularity, tact, and foresight of her sister Elizabeth, she might have been more successful in achieving her one abiding aim. As it was, she died in 1558 frustrated and desolate, abandoned by her husband, hated by her people, to be labelled by posterity with the permanent descriptive appellation of 'Bloody Mary'.

It was under the last Tudor monarch, Queen Elizabeth I that Britain attained the flowering of her greatness, independence and self-esteem. Elizabeth's guiding passions were her fervent patriotism and her burning beliefs in the royal prerogative and the supremacy of the law. During her reign the national Church was fully and lastingly established. Probably she would have preferred to revert to Henry VIII's dogma of Catholicism without the pope, but the recent bitter memories of Catholic-inspired persecution made any reconciliation with Rome impossible. Although Henry's anti-papal legislation was largely restored, the queen's despotism in religious matters was milder than that of her immediate forebears. She refused the title of Head of the Church which she was offered by Parliament; she declined to sanction the marriage of the clergy; the Forty-two Articles of Edward were curtailed to thirty-nine by way of a partial compromise; and she sought deliberately to make the prescribed ritual of the Church as little offensive to Catholic believers as possible, at the same time insisting that the new religion was established by law and therefore that it must be scrupulously observed.

During Elizabeth's long reign the British people took a growing pride in political constitution, and in their steadily maturing legal system which was beginning to arouse the interest, even the admiration, of foreigners. They were, of course, proud too of their martial glories, their expanding commerce, the exploration and discoveries of their seamen, the increasing enlightenment of their nation, and the extent of its contribution to the Arts. Britain was becoming a definite entity: Wales was now fully integrated under the Crown, and the kingdom of Ireland was being drawn closer and closer into the ambit of British rule.

The Tudor kings and queens controlled the country principally through the medium of the Council, a standing committee which handled all the routine business of government. It usually comprised about thirty members who were appointed and dismissed at the will of the sovereign. The majority of the leading officials in the country and at the court were members of the Council. For instance, the lord chancellor, one or both of the chief justices, and perhaps another judge represented the law; the two archbishops and a few ordinary bishops represented the Church; the lord treasurer represented the Exchequer; and for the rest it consisted of the keeper of the king's privy seal and such other persons of influence and power who might be selected. Early in the sixteenth century a distinction arose between the Privy Council, a smaller and more select body, and the ordinary Council; however, all councillors had to take the same oath of office.

During the reign of Henry VII the Council started to separate its administrative and its judicial functions, the latter being mainly performed by councillors sitting in the starred chamber of the Palace of Westminister, which gave rise to the court being known as the 'Star Chamber'. In spite of the tarnished reputation the Star Chamber has acquired both in legal and in general history, it fulfilled a vital and beneficial role in the Tudor period and was largely instrumental in the establishment, and later in the maintenance, of law and order throughout the country. The Star Chamber was put on a statutory basis by an Act of 1487, and other subsequent statutes gradually enlarged its jurisdiction.

The need was manifest at that time for a special central court which would be realistic, intrepid, and incorruptible in its application of the law, not only because of the deficiencies in existing legal remedies, but also because of the widespread bribery and intimidation of jurors and witnesses which were disrupting the course of justice. The Star Chamber accumulated an extensive jurisdiction; it embraced many forms of behaviour which were injurious to the public but were not punishable either by statute or at common law –

these included conspiracies, perjuries, attempts to commit offences, forgeries, and certain forms of fraud and of interference with the legal process. Moreover, it was powerful enough to deal with those whose wealth or status had bestowed on them a virtual immunity from criminal trial. The Star Chamber was particularly vigilant in regard to those forms of conduct which might endanger the safety of the State or impede the preservation of public order. It exercised a stringent control over the publication and dissemination of printed matter. The invention of printing had been seen immediately as a potential menace to the government and a proclamation during the reign of Henry VIII had forbidden the importation into England of books printed abroad in English, or of the printing of any books in England, unless they had been previously approved by the Council. The publishers, printers, and owners of any literature said to be treasonable or heretical could be severely punished. The Star Chamber was responsible too for disciplining corrupt and vexatious juries, and it had a special concern with seditious statements tending to provoke disorders, and even with ordinary libels directed at private individuals as these often resulted in breaches of the peace and duelling, a practice which the authorities were most anxious to suppress. In addition the court possessed a wide jurisdiction in civil matters, usually trying cases in which the Crown was a party, or forms of action in which the common law provided no adequate redress.

Initially the Star Chamber was by no means an unpopular court. It is true that it sometimes resorted to torture either to exact confessions or to elicit the names of accomplices, but its sittings were held in public and its punishments, usually fines or moderate floggings, were not considered to be severe. It was not empowered to impose the death penalty and therefore it could not try charges of treason or felony. Moreover, although the procedure was largely inquisitorial the standard of justice compared very favourably with that of the ordinary criminal courts. Holdsworth has remarked that 'the accused had every opportunity to collect his evidence and to state his case; and in all stages he had the assistance of counsel'. The civil procedure in the Star Chamber resembled that of the Court of Chancery. Both for civil and for criminal cases the court was accustomed to sit with a surprisingly large number of members – Stephen refers to occasions on which thirty or forty were present – some of whom nearly always were professional judges.

The Council, as such, still continued to sit in a judicial capacity, but only very infrequently. Unlike the Star Chamber its sessions were held in private and it seems likely that it functioned principally as a secret, extra-judicial tribunal rather than a court of law.

In spite of the despotic power of the Tudor monarchs a composite structure of governmental responsibility was gradually taking shape. At the apex, of course, was the sovereign. The feudal concept still persisted in the minds of lawyers that the king was a superior being to all the other lords in the realm. There was a wide area in which his prerogative was absolute – in foreign relations, declarations of peace and of war, and his edicts in times of civil turmoil and insurrection at home. The authority of a royal proclamation was as yet not clearly defined. It had been decided in the reign of Edward VI that its compulsive force was inferior to that of a parliamentary statute, but under Henry VIII its former authority was partially restored.

Parliament, although closely controlled by the Crown and the Council, was broadening its responsibilities into a new dimension. No longer was it merely a chamber which humbly petitioned to the king, but it was becoming an independent body which discussed, adapted, and legislated. What is more, the theory was being readily accepted that the laws of Parliament were inviolate and were equally binding upon the rich and the poor, on the powerful as well as on the impotent. Any legislation of importance was still being initiated from the top, by the king and the Council, but it was the Lords and the Commons which decided the eventual form and substance of a statute. From the time of Henry VIII Parliaments were no longer dissolved after each single session but were prorogued, that is to say they were kept in a state of passive suspension to be reconvened as often as the occasion demanded, for a number of years.

Even though the Tudor monarchs recognized and respected that Parliament enjoyed a specific function in the governance of Britain they neither admitted nor desired the concept of parliamentary independence. Under Henry VIII the voting of members was rigorously controlled, especially by

Thomas Cromwell, a master of political manipulation and intrigue. In addition, many peers at that time were heavily in debt to the Crown, which made them readily compliant with the king's commands. Edward VI and Elizabeth created many artificial constituencies – rotten boroughs – to secure the election of their own supporters, and during the latter part of the sixteenth century candidates who would be amenable to the royal will were often specially selected by the sheriffs. The Speaker of the House of Commons was a salaried nominee of the crown whose duties, for the most part, consisted of explaining the wishes and views of the Council to the House, and endeavouring to ensure their acceptance.

When Elizabeth I came to the throne a major social transformation was taking place in Britain. The feudal epoch was a thing of the past; the crumbling turrets of the castles no longer dominated the countryside, and the barons with their localized autonomy had become extinct. It was an age when the power of the State was dominant in the lives of the people and the supremacy of the law had become a constant reality. It was an age, too, which had been characterized by the advent of a great and durable middle class, a disparate sector of the community encompassing at one extreme the well-to-do professional gentlemen and the rich, land-owning merchants, and at the other the lesser traders and the yeoman-farmers. Villain status had disappeared completely by then and the lower classes were comprised of small shopkeepers, agricultural labourers, and artisans.

With this change in the social structure there came a change in the composition of the House of Commons. In the new Elizabethan Britain the majority of the members for the shires and a good few of the representatives of the cities and boroughs were drawn from the higher strata of the emergent middle class. They were men of a sturdy and independent disposition, conscious of their rights and their privileges, undaunted by the power of the Council and remote from the influence of the court. In their discussions they fearlessly digressed into such matters as the queen's intended marriage, the future succession to the throne, and the limits of the royal prerogative. They treated the Speaker as their servant and their spokesman and refused to be either coerced or intimidated by him.

By the close of the Tudor period a most significant alliance had developed between Parliament and the common lawyers. It was based on the belief that Parliament was the supreme law-making body and that the laws of Parliament were the only manmade laws which were totally binding on the courts. The ordinances of the Council and the proclamations, even the prerogatives, of the Crown were suddenly exposed to doubt and questioning. A constitutional problem of the gravest magnitude was imminent. Only the tact, the skill, and the popularity of a monarch like Queen Elizabeth could have deferred the impending confrontation – and the eventual day of reckoning.

CHAPTER 11

THE SYSTEM OF CONTROL

The rule of law which the Tudor monarchs envisaged for the British people was the combination of a disciplined respect for their superiors and a methodized justice in their dealings with each other.

The same brand of harsh and implacable discipline was applied throughout the realm; even those in the highest places, the Council, the court, the prelacy, and Parliament, were not in any way immune. Perverse and insubordinate statesmen and senior officials were disposed of by means of Bills of Attainder rather than by impeachment – in fact there was not a single impeachment during the whole of the Tudor period. Attainder was an expedient whereby a person could be condemned without trial by means of a simple parliamentary vote; it was the device employed by Henry VIII for the condemnation of his ministers Cardinal Wolsey and Thomas Cromwell, and his fifth wife Catherine Howard. Although Parliament was still referred to at times as the 'Court of Parliament' – a relic of the time of the ancient *curia regis* – it now possessed no significant judicial function. It is true that the House of Lords had jurisdiction to try peers on charges of treason and felony, a right which had been affirmed by statute in the reign of Edward III and which still persisted. For this purpose it sat under the presidency of the Lord High Steward, an *ex officio* appointment for every trial. The constitution of the House in this judicial capacity varied according to whether or not Parliament was in session. If a peer was charged with a misdemeanour he appeared before the regular criminal courts.

One important result of the Reformation was that the office of lord chancellor came to be regarded as more suitable for a lawyer than for an ecclesiastic. Wolsey was the last of the old-style chancellors, Sir Thomas More was the first of the new. Almost inevitably during the course of the sixteenth century the Court of Chancery was ceasing to be a forum for the personal views and predilections of an andividual chancellor and was assuming the qualities of an ordinary legal court. But even then the principles of equity continued to be based upon what was conceived as a precept of rational understanding or the divine-inspired canons of the universe. Under the lawyer–chancellors the processes of equity and the processes of common law drew closer together. Equity became more systematized; it began to supplement the common law courts and to adjust and harmonize their decisions. Moreover, the lines of demarcation between the two systems became clearer, and it was accepted that the Court of Chancery would only intervene in a case before a court of common law if the application of established legal axioms would lead to gross injustice, or if the circumstances were tainted by fraud, deceit, or unconscionable behaviour. The actual organization of the chancery gave it better facilities than those which existed in the common law courts for the examination of complicated accounts, thus heightening its suitability for the settlement of any disputes concerning the administration of estates, the dissolution of partnerships, or the misappropriation of funds held in trust. The Court of Requests, founded by Henry VII in 1493, was a special court for the attainment of equitable remedies by impecunious litigants.

The lord chancellor was assisted in his judicial functions by a staff of chancery masters, of whom there were originally twelve. According to the early legal treatise *Fleta* they were 'honest and prudent clerks who were sworn to be faithful to the king and who had a full knowledge of the laws of England'. The principal amongst them was known as the master of the rolls, and in the course of time he came to be regarded as the deputy of the lord-chancellor. The officials in the Court of Requests were called masters of requests.

The threefold division of common law courts into the King's Bench, the Common Pleas and the Exchequer remained unaltered during the Tudor period. The King's Bench and the Common Pleas continued to overlap one another, and even the Exchequer was beginning to encroach on their respective jurisdictions. In 1579 the barons of the

Exchequer were elevated in status and placed on a level with the judges of the other two courts; henceforth the Exchequer was recognized as a fully-fledged court of common law in every sense of the term.

Neither the judiciary nor the legal profession ever fell under the domination of the Council, which may be accounted for – partly at any rate – by the fact that the Council had always held the law in considerable esteem. In fact the interests of the judges and the interests of the privy councillors in preserving an orderly obedience to the dictates of the State were in every way identical. If the occasion demanded, the judiciary were not afraid to criticize an arbitrary or a tyrannical action on the part of the executive; the independence of the Bench from political interference was more than an empty catch-phrase even at that distant point of time. It would be absurd, of course, to claim that no judges were ever subservient to the royal will, that they were never corrupt or incompetent, or that they never behaved in a dishonourable manner. However, it may be stated with some degree of certainty that in an age when coercion was prevalent, when vengeance was unrestrained, and when the standards of morality in public affairs were barely minimal at their very highest, it was still appreciated by most members of the judiciary that the complete integrity of the Bench was one of the finest endowments which they could bestow upon the nation.

The theory and practice of the common law were still taught at the four Inns of Court, which also educated their students in the requisite standards of ethical behaviour within the profession. After 1596 no one was admitted as a member of an Inn unless he could show that he had residential chambers there. In those secluded sanctuaries of culture and tradition the students helped to formulate the British legal heritage. Writing with the perceptive detachment of a historian, Holdsworth has said,

> The strict technical training which was given by the Inns of Court, and the high ideals which they set before their students, ensured the professional competency of the Bench, and a high standard of professional honour in both Bench and Bar. All through the sixteenth century there was an abundance of good men at the Bar; and good judicial appointments were made. As a result the respect both of the king and of the people for the common law was in no way diminished.

The life and learning of the Inns was controlled jointly by the judges and the serjeants; the degree of serjeant had now to be accorded to every barrister before he received a judicial appointment.

During the Middle Ages it had always been accepted that the common law was not a universal system for every type of English court; for instance, civil law, based on the municipal law of the Roman empire, was applied by the Court of Admiralty, and canon law, founded largely upon regulations enacted by the general councils and provincial synods of the Church, was administered in the ecclesiastical courts. The universities of Oxford and Cambridge had acquired a complete monopoly in the teaching of civil and canon law and for the conferment of degrees in these two subjects, but after the Reformation, when the study of canon law had fallen into disfavour, both universities saw fit to remove it from their curricula. At the time of the Reformation the ecclesiastical courts abandoned the use of the orthodox canon law and substituted for it a form of clerical law which was homespun and national. Their subservience to papal authority was finally eliminated by the abolition of appeals to Rome from their decisions and the creation of an ecclesiastical appellate procedure within the sovereignty of Britain.

The Court of High Commission, a completely new tribunal, was created during the reign of Elizabeth I to exercise the queen's undefined powers as head of the established Church. The High Commission, which possessed jurisdiction over ecclesiastical offences including heresy, was a spiritual Star Chamber employed by the Council for the probing of people's minds and for unearthing their innermost religious beliefs; in a short time it became a dreaded instrument of persecution.

The various courts and the various systems of law maintained a constant rivalry with each other. The King's Bench and the Common Pleas found a powerful weapon in the writ of habeas corpus, which they used to compel litigants and prisoners to appear before them when their actions or their trials were taking place before some other court. In civil and in criminal trials the sworn proof of the witness was becoming all-important, and in the sixteenth century it was possible to compel a reluctant witness to come to court by issuing him with a subpoena. The conduct of civil actions was falling into two distinct phases: firstly, the preliminary pleadings, either verbal or written, setting out the facts and assertions on which the litigant was seeking to rely; and secondly, the presentation of the case in court, entailing the subtleties of advocacy, the examination and the cross-examination of witnesses, the formulation of arguments, and the application of legal principles. Gradually these two professional functions were growing more separate, an attorney settling the pleadings while a serjeant or an ordinary member of the Bar took over the case at the actual hearing in court. It was during the Tudor period that four Inns forbade attornies to be called to the Bar, thus consolidating what was to become the perpetual duality of the British legal profession.

The most striking feature of the criminal procedure in that age is the rank injustice it occasioned to the accused. If a person was arrested and kept in custody until his trial he was granted no facilities for the preparation of his defence; he was not told the names of the prosecution witnesses or the nature of the evidence against him; and if the charge was one of treason or felony he was not allowed the assistance of counsel to defend him. Before 1589 he was not able to call any witnesses on his own behalf, and even after that year defence witnesses were not permitted to give evidence on oath, probably on the basic assumption that they would have committed perjury. The trial commenced with the arraignment of the accused and the swearing in of the jury. There were often several counsel for the Crown who divided the prosecution case between them, each rising in turn to denounce the accused, to level accusations, to call witnesses, and to read out depositions and statements. The whole trial, Stephen has written,

> was a long argument between the prisoner and the counsel for the Crown, in which they questioned each other and grappled with each other's arguments with the utmost eagerness and closeness of reasoning. The judges occasionally took part in the discussion; but, in the main, the debate was between the parties.

There were no effective rules of evidence, and such as there were, it was supposed, had a biblical derivation. The trial concluded with the judge's summing-up and the verdict of the jury.

An attempt was made in the reign of Henry VII to decrease the absurdities of Benefit of Clergy. It was enacted that a defendant who succeeded in his claim for Benefit was to be branded on the brawn of the thumb, and if on a subsequent occasion he 'pleaded his clergy' again his claim would be disallowed unless he actually was a clerk in Holy orders. Also, it was decided that petty treason was an offence for which Benefit of Clergy would never be available. During the two hundred years which followed, the British criminal code continued to be unscientifically divided into 'clergyable' and 'non-clergyable' offences'. Until 1576 a defendant who had pleaded his clergy successfully was still handed over to ecclesiastical authorities for a fictitious punishment; after that year the lay courts dealt with the matter themselves and were empowered to impose a term of imprisonment not exceeding one year on the defendant.

During this period there was as yet no clear distinction, in the modern sense, between the function of a juror and the function of a witness; indeed it was considered essential that a set proportion of the jury, the figure was varied from time to time, resided in the district in which the case had originated so that they could employ their personal knowledge in reaching their verdict. A property qualification for jurors was introduced in 1487, but in spite of that the standards of integrity of the average jury remained low, principally because of their readiness, as has been noticed in the previous chapter, to succumb to bribery or intimidation. The Star Chamber was inclined to treat any acquittal which was manifestly against the weight of the evidence as being perverse, and the jurors who had returned it were punished accordingly, usually by fine or imprisonment. As stated earlier, they were also penalized if it came to light that they had eaten or drank before they had concluded their deliberations.

The office of sheriff had continued to decline in importance, partially because the old regional units, the hundred, the township, and the tithing, of which he had been the foremost local dignitary, had now been replaced by another territorial composition, and partially because new officials had now taken over the majority of his principal duties.

It has already been seen how the sheriff's former judicial responsibilities were gradually ceded to the coroner and the justice of the peace; in 1585 he also lost his ancient control of the shire's military forces to the recently-created royal representative, the lord lieutenant of the county. The coroners still combined their primary function of holding inquests with their subsidiary task of maintaining records of accusations, outlawries, and abjurations. Their position was no longer honorary as from Henry VII's reign they received a fee for every inquest of death they conducted. In 1554 their judicial work was placed on a more formal basis with a statute which required them to write down the evidence of all witnesses who appeared before them, and whenever they committed a case for trial to bind over the material witnesses to testify at the hearing.

During each Tudor reign the civic responsibilities of the county Quarter Sessions were being gradually enlarged until by the close of the sixteenth century the extent of its authority had reached into nearly every sphere of local government. Under Henry VIII the justices of the peace became liable for the supervision of the inns and the ale-houses, and they were placed in charge of the maintenance of public bridges and the enforcement of regulations with regard to weights and measures. Under Edward VI they were given control of a new system for licensing premises for the sale of ale and beer. Under Mary they were allocated the upkeep of the roads. And finally, under Elizabeth they were entrusted with the entire direction of poor law relief, they were empowered to control the wages of almost every type of manual worker, and they were deputed to establish and to manage a network of houses of correction where rogues and vagabonds could be set to compulsory labour.

It was at Quarter Sessions too that the justices of the peace discharged their principal judicial functions. A meeting of a county Quarter Sessions was not a mere session of a court of law; it was much more like a convocation of the delegates, spokesmen, and officials of the county, reminiscent of the shire assembly of a bygone era. Theoretically the justices sitting in their Quarter Sessions possessed the criminal jurisdiction of the royal judges, but in practice all cases of unusual importance or unusual difficulty were taken by a judge of assize. The judges also exercised a general surveillance over the justices, quashing their proceedings when necessary, correcting their errors, and compelling them to perform their duties. Even so, the power of the justices was immense and during the sixteenth century it was by no means uncommon for Quarter Sessions to sentence a prisoner to death.

Generally speaking, minor offences in the nature of nuisances or disturbances were disposed of summarily by the justices of the peace, and it was only the more serious cases which they committed for trial by a jury. A series of statutes had created a considerable body of summary jurisdiction but failed to prescribe any regular procedure for summary trials. As a result, says Bertram Osborne, 'the accused would be taken to a justice's house where the proceedings, if such a word can be used to describe the travesty of a trial conducted in secret in the justices' parlour, might end in the imposition of a heavy fine or a sentence of imprisonment'. Indeed on some occasions, for instance if the justice came upon a drunk or a brawler, he could order the culprit to be fined, whipped or set in the stocks without any further formality.

Before 1554 justices of the peace had no express authority to issue a warrant for the arrest of a suspect, as a person could only be lawfully arrested after he had been indicted for an offence. Further, justices, sheriffs and constables in general had no greater power of arrest than those possessed by the ordinary citizen. It seems, however, that an unofficial process was growing up whereby the justices were having suspects arrested on warrant, and then holding private investigations to assess the strength of the evidence against them before deciding whether of not to commit cases for trial. Two Acts passed in 1554 and 1555 legalized this procedure in respect of charges of felony, as it was provided that justices must hold down a preliminary enquiry into a non-summary offence, putting down the statements of the witnesses in writing; if the accused was committed for trial the witnesses were to be bound over to attend and give evidence. These statutes did not contemplate a formal judicial hearing so much as a collation and appraisal of the prosecution case. It did not help the accused person, who was not usually present when the witnesses' depositions were being taken and was not allowed to read them as they were intended merely for the information of the court of trial.

The justices of the peace had inherited from the sheriffs

the right of granting bail to a prisoner under arrest. The Statute of Westminster in 1275 had classified certain offences as 'bailable' and others as 'non-bailable', but apparently the justices were ignoring these provisions as an Act in 1487 recited that many non-bailable offenders had been allowed bail and had escaped 'to the great displeasure of the king and annoyance of his people'. It was ordered that thenceforth bail would only be granted by not less than two justices. An Act of 1554 re-emphasized that the provisions of the Statute of Westminster were still applicable.

With the increase in the powers of the justices there came a corresponding increase in the powers of the constables. There were two types of constable, the high constable, who was the executive officer of the hundred, and the petty constable, originally associated with the township but now becoming recognized as an official of the parish. After the Reformation, parishes lost their old ecclesiastical significance and became the smallest unit of secular administration. Service as a petty constable was a compulsory, unpaid parish duty, similar to a term of service as a churchwarden or a surveyor of the highways; it usually lasted for one year and was supposed to be filled by every adult male parishioner in rotation. However, it was possible for a man to avoid his turn by paying someone else to act for him, and in a number of parishes there were permanent 'professional' deputy constables. At best the office was time-consuming and burdensome and petty constables were notoriously people of humble status and low intellect. Both high constables and petty constables were appointed by Quarter Sessions, though the latter were often nominated by parish vestries. In addition to daytime security arrangements, the towns were patrolled at night by watchmen, an obligatory service imposed on all ablebodied males. Like constables, watchmen wore no uniform and carried no armament.

Describing the essential duties of a petty constable, the Elizabethan jurist William Lambarde said that these were threefold, 'first, in foreseeing that nothing be done that tendeth either directly or by means, to the breach of the peace; secondly, in the quieting and pacifying those that are occupied in the breach of the peace; and thirdly, in punishing such as have already broken the peace'. Constables could only use their powers in their own localities, where they were expected to act largely on their own initiative. The statutes of the sixteenth century tended to give them a special authority and thereby to increase their personal importance.

CHAPTER 12

THE PROGRESS OF THE LAW

The defects which had marred the common law in an earlier age – the slowness, the expense, the technicality, and the inadequacies in the methods of trial – were being largely rectified during the sixteenth century, leaving the system with considerable advantages over its rivals. As a scheme of jurisprudence it was becoming comprehensive as well as precise; it had derived its erudition from the legal training at the Inns of Court; it had been enriched by the scholarship and sagacity of the judges; and the integrity of both Bench and Bar had lent it substance.

In civil process the common law and equity were advancing side by side. The basis of a contract was now accepted by the common lawyers as being dependent on mutual agreement rather than on the formalities of initiation; but the common law courts could only remedy a breach of contract by awarding damages to the injured party, whereas the Court of Chancery could apply the equitable remedy of specific performance, by which the offender was compelled to discharge his obligations. The concept of tort was enlarging too, with common law actions founded upon negligence, and even on deceit, though matters of fraudulent behaviour mostly remained within the ambit of the Court of Chancery.

The growth of statutory offences added steadily to the criminal jurisdiction of the common law courts. In view of the personal authoritarian rule of the Tudor monarchs it was not altogether surprising that there should be an appeciable extension in the definitions of treason. During Henry VIII's reign it became treasonable behaviour, 'by writing, printing, or other external act to do or cause to be done anything to the peril of the king, or to the disturbance or interruption of his enjoyment of the crown, or of the succession'; and likewise, 'to wish, will or desire by words or writing, or by any craft to imagine, invent, practise or attempt any bodily harm to the king, the queen or their heirs'. Other statutes followed, becoming still more stringent until by an Act of 1571, in the reign of Elizabeth, it was declared to be treason for a person, 'by printing, writing or words to compass or imagine any bodily harm to the queen or to levy war against her within or without her realm', or to assist in the invasion of Britain by foreigners. The punishment for treason was barbaric in the extreme. The convicted male traitor was drawn to the gallows behind a cart, he was hanged by the neck and cut down whilst he was still alive, he was disembowelled and castrated and his intestines were burned before his eyes, and finally he was decapitated and his body was chopped into four quarters. Women were punished for treason in a different manner: 'as the decency due to their sex', Blackstone explained, 'forbids the exposing and public mangling of their bodies, the sentence is to be drawn to the gallows, and there to be burnt alive'.

During the Tudor period a number of new felonies were added to the statute book, mostly concerned with morality, religion, and the greater protection of property. Forgery became an offence for the first time; sodomy and the violation of young girls became statutory felonies, as did bigamy in the year of Queen Elizabeth's death. Religious offences were now being shifted from the ineffectual administration of the ecclesiastical courts to the more competent jurisdiction of the courts of common law, though there was still a certain amount of overlapping, especially after 1559, the year of the establishment of the Court of High Commission. In Henry VIII's reign came the first of a series of Acts directed at the practice of witchcraft. There had been ordinances against witches and other forms of magic since earliest times, but the Reformation had generated an upsurge of religious fervour and had indirectly stirred up an unhealthy obsession with the supernatural. In 1541 it was made a non-clergyable felony to practise various kinds of 'invocations or conjurations of spirits, witchcrafts, enchantments or sorceries'. It might have been thought that this list would prove sufficient for the desired purpose, but in 1562 it was augmented to include all communion with evil spirits for any reason whatsoever, and also the employment of witchcraft to cause a person's death. The punishment for a non-clergyable felony or for a clergyable felony where benefit had been refused was still death by hanging.

In the sixteenth century there was a growth too in the number of statutory misdemeanours. The term 'misdemeanour' was now being generally applied to all offences of a less serious nature than treasons or felonies. When the last relics of self-help and private vengeance were obliterated from the British legal system the distinction between harmful conduct amounting to a crime, and harmful conduct which merely gave rise to a civil action for damages, was drawn with far greater precision, although there were still some instances where the injured person could choose to proceed with either remedy. Misdemeanours, which were always tried in accordance with the ordinary criminal procedure, covered a wide range of unlawful behaviour, ranging from drunkenness and swearing at one end of the scale to assault and perjury at the other. There were even misdemeanours concerned with witchcraft – for instance the use of sorcery to procure unlawful love or to discover concealed treasure. The punishment for a common law misdemeanour, and also for a statutory misdemeanour when no specific penalty was prescribed, was a whipping. However, the statutes in question often provided that the offender should be fined, or imprisoned, or placed in the stocks or the pillory instead.

The Tudors continued the policy of statutory wage control. An Act of 1495 settled the rates of payment of artificers and labourers, and made it a misdemeanour for workmen in the building trade to take part in 'any assembly to assault, harm, or hurt any person consigned to control or oversee them in their working'. The statute was ineffective and was repealed after one year, but it was reintroduced by Henry VIII in 1514.

The Tudor labour laws were closely associated with the regulations for controlling vagrancy and destitution. Since the end of the feudal era there had been no organized relief for the homeless, the workless, and the starving, except the charitable assistance which had been provided by the monasteries. When the monasteries were suppressed, a swarm of vagrants was disgorged on the countryside. 'All through the Tudor reigns', G. M. Trevelyan has written, 'the "beggars coming to town" preyed on the fears of dwellers in the lonely farms and hamlets, and exercised the minds of magistrates, Privy Councillors and Parliaments'. In an attempt to offset this new scourge and to curb the alarming increase in the number of robberies and thefts, an Act was passed in 1530 to the effect that 'any person, being whole and mighty in body and able to labour, found begging or being vagrant and giving no satisfactory account how he lawfully obtained his living' might be arrested by a constable and taken before a justice of the peace. If satisfied that the prisoner had offended against the statute the justice would order him to be stripped naked, tied to a cart's tail, and whipped through the streets 'till his body should be bloody'; finally, the vagrant had to take an oath to return to his place of birth or the place where he had last lived for three years, and there to labour 'as a true man ought to do'. The same Act enabled the justices to issue licences to the genuine poor, aged and impotent, allowing them to beg in specified localities. If they begged outside the stated limits they were to be punished.

Subsequent Tudor legislation in the area of labour law was an odd mixture of savagery towards the idle vagrant and sympathy towards the authentic pauper. There were two further statutes in Henry VIII's reign. The first provided that a person who had been whipped under the 1530 Act and who still did not find work should have the upper part of his right ear cut off, and if he persisted in his refusal to work after that he was to be tried and executed as a felon. The second Act entrusted the care of 'the poor, impotent, lame, feeble, sick and diseased' to the parishes where they had been born or in which they had resided for three years, but little or no guidance was given as to what was to be done for their welfare.

The most draconian anti-vagrancy statute of the Tudor period was passed in the reign of Edward VI. An Act of 1547 commenced by reciting that many maimed, lamed, sore, and aged persons 'do fill the streets or highways of divers cities, towns, markets and fairs'. To curb this nuisance, genuine paupers and the very old should thenceforth be found lodging at the public expense by the parishes responsible for their welfare, and all other vagrants should be sent back to the place of their birth or the place of their last abode. The Act went on to direct that any serving man found wandering without a master should be branded with the letter 'V' and should be adjudged the slave for two years of anyone who could make him work 'by chaining, beating or otherwise'. If the vagrant escaped from his new master he was to be branded in the face and enslaved for life; for a subsequent escape he could be executed. The children of vagabonds could be removed from their parents and allocated as servants or apprentices to anyone who chose to take them. This barbarous statute was repealed after three years and Edward VI's subsequent legislation prescribed in detail how the aged, the poor, and the impotent should be conveyed from district to district at public cost in an effort to return them to their places of origin. A further Act provided that any person might take the child of a vagabond, aged between five and fourteen, 'to be brought up in any honest labour and occupation till such child, if a woman, attained the age of fifteen or was married, and if a man child until eighteen'.

Edward VI tampered very little with the established labour laws except for the passage of an Act which made it an offence for artificers, workmen or labourers to conspire together with a view to controlling their rates of pay or their hours of work. In 1562, soon after Elizabeth I had come to the throne, a new Statute of Labourers was passed which consolidated or amended all the previous legislation on this subject as well as introducing several original proposals. The justices in sessions were entrusted with the determination of wage-rates within their own localities and they were also given wide powers to press men, women, and children into compulsory service in the land, particularly during harvest-time. The regulations concerning the movement and control of labour were considerably tightened. No one employed in husbandry or trade was allowed to leave the county where he was working in order to seek a job in some other county unless he had first obtained an official permit; if he infringed this requirement both he and his new master would be committing criminal offences. Any unemployed craftsman who was offered work in the 'art or mystery wherein he had been exercised' was obliged to accept it. All these provisions were backed up with appropriate penalties of whipping and imprisonment and the statute also laid down some meticulous directions as to the rights and obligations of masters and servants during the course of an employment.

A statute of 1572, for the punishment of vagrants and the relief of the poor, stated in its preamble that 'all parts of this realm of England and Wales be presently with rogues, vagabonds, and sturdy beggars exceedingly pestered', and that in consequence there had been 'an abundance of horrible murders, thefts, and other great outrages'. Persons leading vagrant lives were to be 'grievously whipped' and branded, and if they returned again to vagabondage they were liable to be condemned as felons and executed. The Act also provided that the justices must compile a register of 'the poor, aged and impotent' who had been born in their areas or had lived there for three years, and they should then impose a tax on the local inhabitants for the maintenance of these people. The relevant parishes were given the responsibility of housing their own paupers. In 1576 another statute authorized the justices of the peace to purchase materials and to impose compulsory labour on the 'poor and needy'; further, the justices were required to establish houses of correction in which vagrants would be 'straitly kept, as well in diet as in work, and also punished from time to time'. An Act of 1597 appointed new, unpaid officials, some of whom would be churchwardens of parishes and some the nominees of the justices, to take charge of all the arrangements connected with the welfare of the poor. Five years later, in 1601, came the well-known statute which is usually regarded as the inauguration of the British Poor Law system, though it re-enacted verbatim the Act of 1597. However, it clarified the types of property which would be liable for poor rate, and specified the responsibilities of children for their pauper parents and of parents for their pauper children. Thus by the early years of the seventeenth century the care of the indigent, the elderly, and the disabled had been effectively removed from the ecclesiastical authorities and placed under the control of the justices of the peace.

At the opening of the Tudor period few of the large towns in Britain had not possessed their own craft guilds, but from the reign of Henry VIII onwards their importance had steadily diminished owing to increasing competition in trade and the changing social and industrial conditions in the country generally. Despite the decline of the craft guilds, however, the institution of apprenticeship had achieved a degree of permanence and an Act of 1563 provided that no one should exercise a 'trade or mystery' without being apprenticed in it for a period of seven years.

Whereas the merchants of an earlier period had traded individually, joint trading became popular when Britain began to develop extensive interests overseas, particularly during the reign of Elizabeth I. Before they operated abroad the merchants required a special charter from the Crown which granted them virtually a commercial monopoly in a specified region. All the partners who combined under each charter would form a company and would transact their business together using joint-stock, to which each of them had contributed his due share. Initially these companies would only function for a single venture – probably for one trading voyage of a chartered ship – but later it became customary for them to prolong their existence for several years. The joint-stock companies grew ever more powerful and prosperous, exercising most of the subsidiary powers of government in the areas covered by their charters.

An important development in the commercial field was the founding of the British law of bankruptcy by a statute of 1542 in Henry VIII's reign. The Act was directed against fraudulent debtors and empowered the lord chancellor to seize the property of the of bankrupt and to divide it amongst his lawful creditors. A subsequent statute restricted the principles of bankruptcy to traders, and enumerated certain actions on their part which would have the legal effect of making them bankrupt. The lord chancellor was empowered to appoint commissioners to take over their property and to supervise its distribution among their creditors under the overall direction of the Court of Chancery.

The law of patents in Britain owed its origin to the monarchs' ancient custom of granting monopolies to their favourites for the sale or manufacture of certain commodities. Sir Edward Coke expressed the view that the king was entitled at common law to award to an inventor, or to the importer of some invention, a temporary monopoly of his particular device. Henry VIII certainly conferred a number of monopolies for new inventions and Elizabeth I gave out so many that she encountered severe criticism from the House of Commons. Eventually in 1601 she was obliged to issue a proclamation withdrawing certain monopolies and declaring that all her subjects who suffered loss as a result of her future grants might have recourse to the ordinary courts of law, and not solely to the Star Chamber which had been assuming an exclusive jurisdiction over the issuing and the enforcement of monopolies when any legal issues were involved.

When Henry VII ascended the throne most of the land in Britain was held in trust, which had resulted in the avoidance of feudal dues and perquisites as well as affording an increased opportunity for a number of different types of fraudulent transaction. In an effort to remedy this situation the Statute of Uses of 1535 enacted that a trustee of land should hold it with the full burdens and benefits of an actual owner or, in other words, that the legal and the equitable estates would be amalgamated. Accordingly, it became virtually impossible for any land to be devised by will and this caused a great deal of inconvenience. In 1540 another statute made possible the devise of unencumbered freehold land, provided that the will was made in writing and that the recipient was a real person and not a corporation.

The prevalence of enclosures and the absorption of confiscated church lands into neighbouring properties tended to increase the size of both farms and private estates. Owing to the continuing prosperity of the wool trade the landed gentry were now enjoying an affluence quite unknown to their forbears; they were branching out, too, into large-scale agriculture, and during the reign of Elizabeth the cultivation of corn became almost as profitable as the rearing of sheep. The owners of the great estates were still seeking to limit them to a direct line of hereditary succession, usually by means of entails, but the ingenuity of the lawyers was constantly devising methods of breaking the entails and freeing the property from restriction.

A considerable amount of land was held by copyhold tenure. The substitution of money-rents for services had failed to simplify the obscure conditions of many of these tenancies, as each depended on the individual customs of the particular manor concerned. In his book *Early Law and Custom* Sir Henry

Maine has drawn attention to the strong resemblance between British copyhold tenure and French peasant tenure at this period, and he has gone on to assert that whereas the resulting grievances of the French cultivating peasantry, coupled with their hatred of the territorial nobility, were amongst the major causes of the French Revolution, the wisdom and firmness of the English courts in settling disputes between landlords and copyhold-tenants ensured a peaceful and satisfactory outcome to a difficult situation. At any rate, copyhold became another form of landownership, and Coke when writing in the seventeenth century stated that there was then almost no difference at all between copyhold and freehold tenure.

The Reformation in Britain affected the principles of marriage and divorce very little. The ecclesiastical courts still retained their matrimonial jurisdiction and continued to apply the canon law to the causes which came before them. There was a move towards greater freedom of divorce, and even a contention that an absolute divorce could be granted on legal grounds, but the matter was finally resolved by a specific ruling in 1602 that an ecclesiastical court had no power to dissolve a marriage completely. A formal wedding ceremony was becoming more customary, and although it was decreed by the Council of Trent in Elizabeth's reign that a religious consecration was essential this ruling had no binding force in Britain. Even so, the British theories on marriage and divorce had diverged in no way from the theories of the Church of Rome.

The status of married women was still a very inferior one and they remained totally incapable of owning any personal property or of dealing with their real property after marriage. Various legal stratagems were employed for defeating, or partially defeating, these restrictions, including the use of carefully constructed trusts, but only the comparatively wealthy could afford the benefit of such arrangements.

The 'golden days of good Queen Bess' ended with Elizabeth's death in 1603. She was succeeded by James I, son of her cousin, Mary, Queen of Scots, whom she had had beheaded in 1587.

Part VII

THE STUART PERIOD

(1603 – 1714)

CHAPTER 13

THE CONSTITUTIONAL TURMOIL

The latent conflict of authority between the monarchy, Parliament, and the common law was brought to a head by James I who formulated, if he did not originate, the obsessive and inflammatory doctrine of the divine right of kings.

There were at that time two distinct theories with regard to the undefined nature of the royal prerogative. On the one hand, James and his supporters believed that it was the paramount power in the State: in the mortal sphere the king could do no wrong; his will was superior to that of the legislature, and his whims could override the decisions of the courts. For their part, the parliamentarians and the common lawyers held that the royal prerogative was divisible: on a certain plain, such as the determination of foreign policy or the declaration of peace and war, it was absolute and unquestionable; but in many other respects it was subject to limitation and control. As a result of this dissension James I never led the British nation: he merely headed his own party against a steadily mounting opposition.

The new king crossed swords with his first Parliament within a year of his accession to the throne. The cause of the dispute was the parliamentary privileges which were claimed by the House of Commons as being their 'undoubted birthright and inheritence' but which were regarded by the monarch as being derived from his royal 'grace and permission'. The privileges in question were the right of the House to decide upon disputed elections, the immunity of members from arrest, freedom of speech in debates, and the entitlement to arrange their own order of business. James took issue with the Commons over the first two of these in 1604 and the whole matter of parliamentary privilege smouldered, flaring up intermittently, for the remainder of his reign.

The king was also at loggerheads with his judiciary. The common law judges had always been under the direct control of the monarch and they held office during the royal pleasure; indeed, when they toured on circuit their duties consisted partly of attending to the king's political and administrative business, for they had to ensure that the official governmental policies were being effected in the counties, and to report generally upon the drifts of local feeling and reaction. Hitherto there had been no perceptible disparity of interest between the Bench and the Crown, but now that the country was being split into two divergent factions a new situation was arising and the judges were tending to be drawn into one or other of the opposing camps. The Star Chamber, whose role had been in many ways complementary to that of the courts of common law, was changing its function and was becoming an oppressive instrument of royal power which tyrannized over the king's enemies and habitually employed the use of torture in its pre-trial procedure – although it managed still to win the praise of two of the ablest lawyers of the age, Edward Coke and Francis Bacon.

Coke's fervent belief in the supremacy of the common law had inevitably brought him into conflict with James I. In 1607 a barrister named Fuller was fined and imprisoned by the Court of High Commission for an attack he had made on the jurisdiction of that court whilst applying for a writ of prohibition against it. The judges of the King's Bench immediately declared that the High Commission could not punish a counsel for anything he had said in the course of his legal submissions, and further, they affirmed their power to decide the limits of any ecclesiastical court's jurisdiction. The matter was referred to James who consulted Coke, then chief justice of Common Pleas. Coke angered the king by asserting the superiority of the common law and the unfettered right of the judiciary to decide its meaning. A further clash occurred in 1610 when the judges ruled that the High Commission had no power to imprison for adultery, and Coke, once again defying the views of the king, expressed the opinion that the Church and its courts were subject not only to the sovereignty of the Crown but also the the predominance of the courts of common law.

In the prevailing circumstances Coke's convictions were

bound to impel him to the side of the parliamentary party. When James raised the duties on imports and exports by proclamation, following the practice of the last two Tudor monarchs, the House of Commons severely criticized this use of the royal prerogative, alleging 'that proclamations have been of late years much more frequent than heretofore and that they are extended not only to the liberty but also to the goods, inheritence and livelihood of man'. Coke adjudicated on the matter in a celebrated judgment wherein he declared that the king could not change any part of the common law, nor could he create new offences by proclamation without the approval of Parliament.

In an effort to decrease Coke's opportunities for interference James removed him from the Court of Common Pleas in 1613 and appointed him chief justice of the King's Bench, but even there Coke found opportunities to continue his opposition. Eventually, in 1616 the judges, under Coke's leadership, attempted to restrict the king's control of litigation in which his personal interest was involved. James took the unusual course of summoning his entire judiciary to a meeting of the Council in order to sternly rebuke them for their conduct. All the judges were willing to submit to the royal authority except Edward Coke, who was dismissed from office for his intransigence. Apart from his forthright views on constitutional issues Coke's judicial career is chiefly memorable on account of his quarrel with Lord Chancellor Ellesmere concerning the right of the Court of Chancery to intervene in cases before the courts of common law. The matter was referred to James I in 1616 and the king issued an order upholding the claims of the Court of Chancery, thereby confirming equity's favoured position with regard to the common law.

Throughout the reign of James I Parliament made use of two principle weapons against the king. The first was a revival of impeachments, brought against his leading ministers for alleged acts of tyranny and corruption; the second was the deliberate restriction of the king's finances, particularly when he was endeavouring to sustain a continental war. On the death of James I in 1625 the outstanding constitutional differences seemed to be no nearer to solution.

James's son Charles I inherited all his father's theories regarding the divine right of kings, and the new monarch's quarrels with his Parliament started almost immediately on his accession. For all its militancy the parliamentary opposition at that time in no way contemplated violence or civil strife. The members of the House of Commons were truly representative of a solid body of the nation which, although it gave its complete loyalty to the Crown, was yet unwilling to compromise in its determination to obtain redress for its prevailing grievances, and also to curb the more extravagant powers of the royal prerogative. In 1625 Charles's first Parliament refused to vote him adequate supplies unless he would appoint a group of counsellors who enjoyed its confidence to supervise his finances. The king would not agree to this condition and Parliament was dissolved. However, a year later his need for money became desperate and he was obliged to convene his second Parliament, which forthwith instituted impeachment proceedings against the king's favourite, the arrogant Duke of Buckingham, and in its turn was peremptorily dissolved.

Neither James I nor Charles I ever accepted the claim of the House of Commons that it was entitled to appropriate supplies for specific purposes, and subsequently to examine the details of the relevant expenditure. There were two principal sources of royal income: when a king ascended the throne he would be granted by Parliament an annual allowance sufficient to meet the ordinary, predictable costs of government; when he required additional revenue he would have to come back to the Commons and ask for it. It was the latter form of subsidization over which the Commons sought to exercise a strict control.

Charles now found himself without a parliament, with a war on his hands, and with no means of paying his soldiers and his sailors. To meet his financial requirements he resorted to the exaction of forced loans from his richer subjects and the imprisonment of those who declined to subscribe. He also billeted his troops, compulsorily and without payment, on private households, and allowed his army officers to enact a brand of martial law upon the civil community. In 1627 a knight named Darnel and four other men who had been imprisoned for refusing to contribute to a forced loan applied for a writ of habeas corpus to the King's Bench. Habeas corpus was a common law writ which seems to have stemmed from the clause in the Magna

Carta forbidding imprisonment 'otherwise than by lawful process'; in practice the writ issued as an order from one of the superior courts directing a person who was holding someone in captivity to produce his prisoner so that the matter could be investigated. After hearing careful argument in Darnel's case the judges ruled that if a man had been committed into custody at the king's command a writ of habeas corpus could not properly be granted.

Charles summoned another Parliament in 1628. The House of Commons took up the matter of habeas corpus right away and passed several resolutions opposing the decision in Darnel's case. Negotiations were entered between the Lords, the Commons and the king with a view to arranging a compromise under which Parliament would grant Charles his urgently needed supplies in return for his appeasing some of their principal grievances. The matter on which the king was most reluctant to yield was his purported right to imprison his subjects at his own discretion, which was, he contended, essential to the security of the State. Eventually some sort of a settlement was reached and Parliament passed a measure called the Petition of Right. This petition recited that the Magna Carta and other statutes had recently been disregarded; the king's subjects had been unlawfully imprisoned 'without cause shown', and they had been wrongfully refused writs of habeas corpus on the ground that their captivity was ordered by the sovereign. Further, the petition condemned martial law, declaring it to be 'wholly and directly contrary to the law of the realm'. The patched-up agreement between Charles and his legislature was only short-lived; before very long other disputes arose and the king dissolved Parliament in 1629.

For eleven years, from 1629 to 1640, Charles I endeavoured to govern without any parliament, and during this period he ranged himself ever more solidly against the mass of his people and against their elected representatives. It seemed that there was no one in a position to stand up to the king. The strength and the independence of the judiciary had been nullified by constant political pressure, the frequency of arbitrary dismissals from the Bench, and the appointment of a new style of judicial placeman who bowed to the will of the sovereign at all times and who was not loath on occasion to resort to bribery and corruption. The Star

Chamber had grown increasingly into a court for effecting the king's personal vengeance on his opponents and the punishments it administered became both savage and tyrannical.

During that decade Charles could usually rely on the judiciary to provide a semblence of legality for his more provocative and authoritarian policies – the issue of ship-money, for example, although in that particular instance it is difficult to say whether the judges' decision was due to their partisan approach or was a genuine effort to interpret a somewhat obscure point of fiscal law. Certainly ship-money had been levied on sea-ports and maritime areas during the Middle Ages in order to obtain funds for the navy, but Charles had extended the tax to cover the whole country and had used the money he raised for general purposes. Even if the judges of the Exchequer had concluded that ship-money was a lawful duty, the majority of the country supported John Hampden, the Buckinghamshire squire who refused to pay it. People were appalled, too, by the barbarous sentences meted out by the Star Chamber in a series of politically motivated trials. In 1632 William Prynne was ordered to have both ears removed, and to be pilloried, fined and perpetually imprisoned for the authorship of a book. In 1637 Prynne, Bastwick and Burton were mutilated on conviction for libel. A year later John Lillburn was savagely whipped and pilloried for an alleged sedition. But in spite of a growing resentment, the traditional loyalty of the British to a legitimate monarch prevented, at that stage, an outbreak of active resistance.

Charles was forced to summon a new Parliament in 1640 in order to raise money for the suppression of an insurrection in Scotland, but he dissolved it almost immediately rather than give way to its demands for governmental reforms. However, he was now faced with a full-scale Scottish invasion and again he was obliged to sink his pride and to convene another Parliament – the historically significant Long Parliament – towards the close of the same year.

The Long Parliament proceeded to impeach the Earl of Strafford, the king's principal advisor, as well as the primate and a number of the leading judges. More constructively, several measures were passed to redress some of the predominant national grievances. The House of Commons attained absolute control over direct and indirect taxation, the levying of ship-money was declared illegal, the decision of Darnel's case was reversed, the Triennial Act provided that not longer than three years should elapse between the dissolving of one Parliament and the convening of another, and a statute in 1641 abolished the Star Chamber, the High Commission, and the other prerogative courts and virtually deprived the Council of all its jurisdiction over any cases which had originated in Great Britain. But what the parliamentary party required above all was that the ministers of the government should become responsible to the Houses of Parliament as well as to the king, and should always be men who enjoyed their fullest trust and confidence. It was with that object they formulated, and forced the king to listen to, the Grand Remonstrance on his misrule and his unconstitutional conduct. In January 1642 Charles attempted to arrest five members of the Commons whom he had accused of treason. From that moment the Civil War was inevitable and a few months later the fighting actually started.

It is ironic, perhaps, that the forces of political radicalism during the Civil War were predominantly the supporters of the Puritan cult with all its narrowness and severity. The king's party, on the other hand, combined their belief in the absolutism of the monarchical will with a desire for a broadly based religious toleration. As soon as the bitter realities of the conflict became apparent the entire nation was divided into two assailing factions, which were founded partly on creed and conviction and partly on social and hereditary affiliations. The House of Commons was by no means unanimous in wanting an armed insurrection; nor was the House of Lords unequivocally committed to the royalist cause. The Lords had become a considerably larger House than it had been a generation before; it was now dominated by the Commons and had lost most of its inherent fidelity to the Crown.

The initial battles of the Civil War ended slightly in favour of the Royalists, due principally to the superiority of their cavalry. However, when Oliver Cromwell had retrained and reorganized the Parliamentary army the tide of fortune swung the opposite way, culminating in the two major parliamentary victories Marston Moor and Naseby. In 1646 Charles abandoned his defeated forces and surrendered to the Scots; at the beginning of the following year he was handed over to the English Parliament. After a period of intrigue and negotiation the revolutionary army took control; Colonel Thomas Pride was detailed to purge the House of Commons, and standing at the entrance he arrested and imprisoned about a hundred members suspected of having royalist sympathies. The depleted House then passed a spurious resolution that Charles should be brought to trial before an *ad hoc* tribunal which was to be called the High Court of Justice. The House of Lords was peremptorily abolished as a penalty for declining to endorse this proposal. Events were now following a pattern which has become all too common throughout the ages; the reformatory zeal, the idealistic fervor which had engendered the rising, were being obliterated or submerged and, in the event, the only practical result was the substitution of one form of despotism for another.

Charles I refused to acknowledge the jurisdiction of the 132 appointed members of the High Court of Justice and declined to defend himself before them. After a seven day trial the king was convicted of being a tyrant, a murderer, and a traitor to his country. He was beheaded outside the royal Banqueting House in Whitehall in January 1649.

For the next five years Britain was ineffectually and clumsily governed by the various committees of a Council of State, which were incorporated into the House of Commons but were strong enough numerically to outvote the diminishing residue of the elected members. This continued until April 1653 when Cromwell moved in with the army, and having dismissed both the Council and the Commons he instituted what was virtually a military dictatorship. Thereafter Cromwell was always attempting to recreate some form of constitutional legislature. His first House of Commons after he had seized power consisted of 140 men 'of approved fidelity and honesty' who had been selected by himself and his army council. The experiment was unsuccessful and this makeshift Parliament resigned all its authority to him at the end of the year. Cromwell's second constitutional experiment came into effect a few days later; under this he was placed in a position of supreme power with the title of Lord Protector of the Commonwealth of England, Scotland and Ireland, and was to be assisted by the personally nominated members of a new Council of State. For the next nine months

Britain experienced a period of vigorous and progressive rule, combined with imposition of a stringent code of Puritan morality on the lives of the people. A measure of religious toleration was extended to the Jews and the Quakers, but none was proffered to the Anglicans and the Roman Catholics. Cromwell convened another Parliament in September 1654; however, when the members showed themselves to be critically obstructive he adopted a style of military government in which the country was divided up into localities, each of which was put under the control of one of his major-generals.

Once again in 1656 Cromwell attempted to rule with the House of Commons; this time he found the members more compliant and the major-general system of control was abandoned. Still striving to perfect a permanent, manageable constitution, Cromwell, who had refused to assume the title of 'king', endeavoured to improve the balance and reliability of Parliament by re-creating the House of Lords. His proposal for a second chamber was rejected out of hand by the Commons, who were apprehensive, no doubt, of a diminution of their own importance and authority.

Oliver Cromwell died in September 1658, being succeeded as protector by his son Richard. But the new protector was a man of vastly different calibre from his father, and the army, without a firm hand to control them, soon ceased to be the disciplined, cohesive force on which Cromwell had always placed so much reliance. During the next eighteen months the country gradually relapsed into a state of military anarchy until, in May 1660, Richard Cromwell was dismissed by the House of Commons which then voted its own dissolution. A new Parliament assembled almost immediately and commenced negotiations for the restoration of the monarchy.

The eleven years of the interregnum had made a deep and abiding impression on the mind of the British nation. The political domination of a standing army and the enforcement of a puritanical régime with all its narrowness and its bigotry would not be easily eradicated from the memories of a freedom-loving people.

CHAPTER 14

THE CONSTITUTIONAL SETTLEMENT

Charles II received an enthusiastic welcome when he returned to England in May 1660 after his long exile on the Continent. When he arrived in London, said the diarist John Evelyn, 'the ways were strewn with flowers, the bells were ringing, the streets were hung with tapestry, and the fountains were running wine'. A month earlier in Holland Charles had issued a form of restoration manifesto, the Declaration of Breda, which had guaranteed a general amnesty, full liberty of conscience, security of property, and arrears of payment to the army. It was noticeable that the Declaration did not make any specific mention of the principal issues which had provoked the Civil War and had led eventually to the execution of his father.

Even the Royalist party did not wish for a return to absolute monarchy; they desired, rather, to reinstate the constitutional position which had existed in 1641 prior to the legislative changes introduced by the Long Parliament and to achieve a system of government based upon the co-operation of the king and his Parliament. Certain of the developments which had taken place in the recent past seemed now to be irrevocable; one of these was the altered position of the House of Commons, its independence of action, and its political control over the administration. The House of Lords was re-established – the experimental constitutions of the Interregnum had demonstrated the need for a second chamber – but the initiative and authority henceforth would be more firmly vested in the House of Commons, who were determined to resist any further abuses of the royal prerogative. In the early 1660s there was no more than a tacit understanding between Charles II and Parliament; a mutual acceptance, perhaps, of a necessity for compromise. On his side the king was willing to concede the essential function of Parliament in the process of legislation, parliamentary control of taxation, and the right of the Commons to impeach his ministers if they committed offences. He was not willing, however, to accept that Parliament was in any way entitled to direct the policy of his ministers or to call them to account for their failures and mistakes.

The Restoration was not followed by any widespread recrimination or vengeance. Fourteen of those who had been associated with the death of Charles I were executed and another twenty-five were imprisoned, but apart from these Charles II adhered to the general amnesty he had proclaimed. After the Anglican faith had been reinstated as a national religion and a new uniformity of worship had been imposed by Parliament, the Protestant Dissenters were not treated with excessive severity, and indeed they themselves joined in the general outcry which forced Charles to abandon a policy of toleration towards the Roman Catholics.

In the prevailing mood of conciliation the Cavalier Parliament granted Charles a generous annual revenue but retained the right of appropriating any further supplies to specified items of expenditure. Owing to the king's extravagance he soon encountered grave financial difficulties, and when a war broke out with the Dutch he is believed to have misapplied a part of the money voted for upkeep of the fleet and used it to subsidize the frivolous pleasures of his gay and dissolute court. In 1666 the Commons felt obliged to appoint a commission to investigate these irregularities. Charles, who was himself a covert Roman Catholic, then began to look elsewhere for funds. In 1670, by the secret treaties of Dover, he agreed with Louis XIV of France to overthow Protestantism in Britain in return for an annual pension of £200,000 a year. At the beginning of 1672 Charles, acting on his royal prerogative, issued a Declaration of Indulgence suspending all the penal laws against the Roman Catholics and the Protestant Dissenters. The moment for such a measure was ill-advised as the Catholics were still dreaded the Dissenters still despised, and the king was forced by parliamentary pressure to withdraw his proclamation. At this time Charles was still desperately short of money and, relying on their power of financial compulsion, Parliament prevailed upon the king to give his assent to the Test Act, by which every holder of an office, civil or military, was obliged to take the sacrament according to the rites of the Church of England and to make a declaration wholly inconsistent with the Roman Catholic belief. In consequence of this enactment the king's brother, the Duke of York, was impelled to resign from his position as lord high admiral.

Britain was once again becoming obsessed with its fears of Catholicism and its distrust for Louis XIV, who had at his disposal the most powerful army in Europe and who had been constant in his militant support for the Church of Rome. In 1677 an arranged marriage took place between Mary, elder daughter of the heir to the British throne, the Roman Catholic Duke of York, and her first cousin the Protestant William of Orange, Charles II's nephew; thus Britain was provided with a possible Protestant alternative if the Duke of York could be excluded from the legitimate line of succession. In such an atmosphere of tense mistrust it needed very little to create a nationwide panic, and this was effectively managed by two scoundrels Titus Oates and Israel Tonge who invented a nefarious Popish Plot to murder the king, slaughter the Protestants, and set fire to London. In the ensuing witch-hunt there were false accusations and biased trials, and much innocent blood was shed.

Charles dissolved the Cavalier Parliament in 1679. His next Parliament was dissolved three months later after it had sought to introduce legislation with the object of excluding the Duke of York from succession to the throne; however, during its short life it had managed to get on to the statute-book the all-important Habeas Corpus Act. Even after the Petition of Right the authorities had continued to defeat the purpose of the habeas corpus procedure by constantly moving their prisoners from gaol to gaol so that the writs could never be served. Indeed, this stratagem had been sanctioned by the judges in Jenks's case in 1676. The Habeas Corpus Act of 1679 imposed rigorous penalties on those who defied the will of the courts to investigate an imprisonment and also provided that a person who had been lawfully committed in custody should be given a speedier trial.

In its later stages the Cavalier Parliament had drifted into opposition to the king, principally on account of its hostility towards his religious policies, but in addition because of its refusal to accept his conception of the unfettered scope of the royal prerogative. In Charles's subsequent Parliaments the origins of the British political party system became apparent: the titles of 'Whigs' and 'Tories' were derogatory nicknames bestowed on the two main groups, the Tories supporting the transcendent power of the king's prerogative while the Whigs upheld the supreme authority of Parliament.

Charles's third Parliament was dissolved in January 1681 when the House of Commons had passed a new Exclusion Bill which was rejected by the House of Lords. There was now an ominous confrontation between the king and his ministers on the one side and the Commons on the other, but the royalist faction had an inestimable advantage in that the whole nation was so much in dread of another civil war. There was again a complete deadlock on the succession issue when Charles's fourth Parliament assembled at Oxford in April 1681, and he dissolved it without further ado. For the remaining three years and ten months of his reign he governed the country without a Parliament, relying on financial support from Louis XIV. He could argue that such a course was no longer illegal as the the Cavalier Parliaments soon after the Restoration, had repealed the Triennial Act. Charles II died of a stroke in February 1685.

The Duke of York succeeded to the throne as King James II. He commenced his reign with a new and predominantly Tory Parliament and a universal acceptance of the reality of prerogative rule, but he soon managed to offset these initial advantages by his bigotry, the impatience of his character, and his complete lack of statesmanship. He started well, however, by assuring the Privy Council that he had no desire for arbitrary power; instead he professed his intentions of upholding the law and preserving the nation 'in all its just rights and liberties'. In reality his primary objective was to re-establish Roman Catholicism as the national religion and his entire policy was directed to that end.

Immediately after his accession James II was faced with a rebellion in the west of England, led by the Duke of Monmouth, Charles II's illegitimate son, and a rising in Scotland under the Earl of Argyle. Both of these revolts were suppressed without undue difficulty and they tended to rally public opinion to the king's side, in spite of the brutal aftermath epitomized by Lord Chief Justice Jeffreys' 'bloody assize' on the western circuit. James utilized his victories over the insurgents to press Parliament for leave to keep a standing army 'to guard against all disturbances from without and from within' and he also sought to repeal the Habeas Corpus Act. When Parliament would not agree with his demands it was prorogued and, in fact, it never met again before its dissolution some seventeen months later.

At the end of 1685 James II, now unemcumbered by a Parliament, concentrated an army of 16,000 men on the outskirts of London. Already he had begun to infiltrate Roman Catholic officers into positions of military command, and in Ireland a Catholic Irish army was being organized for use in an emergency. During the following year James also purged the Bench of the judges who might be unlikely to approve of his plans. In consequence, when the judiciary was asked to adjudicate upon the king's purported right of dispensing with the law, the judges decided by eleven to one in his favour. In order to impose his will on the Church James set up a body remarkably similar to the Court of High Commission which had been abolished by the Long Parliament, and he appointed several Roman Catholics to places of authority at the universities of Oxford and Cambridge.

Now that the stage was set, James proceeded to his ultimate purpose. In April 1687 he issued a new Declaration of Indulgence granting full religious liberty to all his subjects; next he dissolved his already dormant Parliament. For a while the king considered the possibility of summoning a carefully contrived Parliament which would be compliant with his policies, but he abandoned the scheme when he began to appreciate his immense and growing unpopularity. In May 1688 he proclaimed a second Declaration of Indulgence and ordered that it should be read out in every church in the kingdom. Seven bishops published a petition in protest and were prosecuted for sedition. The triumphant acquittal of the seven bishops, coupled with the birth of a son to the queen and the prospect of a Roman Catholic line of succession to the throne, precipitated the bloodless revolution which brought to Britain a Protestant monarch and a system of constitutional government which has persisted ever since.

The replacement of James II was anything but formalistic or constitutional. A group of men, comprising leaders of both political parties and others of notability and wealth, put their signatures to a precise and dispassionate document inviting William, Prince of Orange, to come to England and to restore the laws and religion of the nation. William landed on the coast of Devon in November 1688 with a small force of infantry and cavalry and advanced towards London. James never made a serious effort to oppose the invasion and eventually deserted his army and fled to France. An election was held for a body which was to be called a 'convention', since a Parliament could only be assembled by means of a royal summons. After discussing various constitutional theories and proposals, the Convention declared that the king's past behaviour, followed by his flight from the kingdom, was equivalent to an abdication, and hence that the throne of Britain was now vacant.

Early in 1689 the Convention drew up a Declaration of Rights which was embodied eight months later in the statutory Bill of Rights, and which has been described as the closest approach Britain has made to a written constitution. Although the Declaration of Rights contained no new law, said Macaulay in his *History of England*, it contained the germ of every good law 'which may hereafter in the course of ages be found necessary to promote the public weal, and to satisfy the demands of public opinion'. It was aimed principally at preventing the recurrence of the arbitrary practices which had been employed by the Stuart monarchs. Its clauses laid down that the king might not keep a standing army in time of peace without parliamentary consent; that the election of Members of Parliament ought to be free, and that there should be absolute freedom of speech in parliamentary debates and proceedings; that the approval of Parliament was necessary before the king suspended or dispensed with the law of the land or levied taxes on his subjects; that jurors must be properly empanelled for criminal trials; that 'excessive bail ought not to be required, nor excessive fines imposed, nor cruel and unusual punishments inflicted'; and that 'for redress of all grievances, and for the amending, strengthening, and preserving of the laws, parliament ought to be held frequently. And they do claim, demand, and insist upon all and singular the premises, as their undoubted rights and liberties'.

The Convention then offered the vacant throne jointly to

William and Mary who formally accepted in February 1689, at the same time adopting the Declaration of Rights. The new sovereigns were granted an annual income out of which to pay the expenses of the royal household and the civil service. However, they were made financially dependent upon the House of Commons, as additional grants were to be made for limited periods only and were to be strictly appropriated.

The Revolution of 1689 was not accompanied by an advent of complete religious toleration. Although there was no policy of active persecution against the Roman Catholics they were still excluded from holding public offices, or commissions in the army and the navy. The Protestant Dissenters were more fortunate as they were permitted to have their own places of worship, provided that they notified the details to the ecclesiastical authorities and that they always held their services behind unlocked doors.

The Bill of Rights set the trend for much of the subsequent legislation of the reign. The Mutiny Act of 1689 permitted the enforcement of discipline in the army, but only for a period of twelve months; similar Acts were passed from year to year for the next two hundred years. The Triennial Act of 1694 limited the duration of a Parliament to a maximum of three years and provided that no longer than three years should elapse between the dissolution of one Parliament and the summoning of the next.* And the Act of Settlement of 1701 ensured the complete independence of the judiciary for the future, as judges were granted fixed salaries and it was provided that they might only be removed upon the addresses of both Houses of Parliament.

Although the revolution had finally shattered the concept of divine right and had established beyond doubt the superiority of Parliament and the supremacy of the law, there were many problems of a constitutional nature still remaining. Elections to the House of Commons were subject to bribery and manipulation, and the suffrage was ill-proportioned and limited. Above all, ministers continued to be appointed by the personal selection of the king and, generally speaking, there was no way in which they could

* The maximum duration of a Parliament was extended to seven years by the Septennial Act in 1716.

be controlled by Parliament except by the drastic and rather clumsy method of impeachment – although William, as an experiment, began to choose as his ministers leading members of both Houses who enjoyed the confidence and support of the House of Commons.

The bitter struggles between the monarchy and Parliament had neither tarnished the common law nor deflected it from a gradual process of development. Even the manifestly partisan judges, the blatantly political nominees of the post-Restoration era, had always paid heed to legal precedent and had endeavoured to formulate their judgements within the ambit of legal credibility. The courts did not profess an authority to alter or add to the common law, but only to interpret and elucidate its principles and to test its application to any given set of circumstances. Indeed the common law was viewed in such a spirit of veneration that certain eminent jurists, Edward Coke amongst them, seemed to argue that its precepts were incapable of statutory amendment and that, accordingly, any statute which purported to achieve such an object was bound to be null and void. The growth of the common law was facilitated from the middle of the seventeenth century by an improved and expanded system of law reporting, usually undertaken by highly competent professional lawyers.

The rivalry between common law and equity continued throughout the Stuart period. The chancery lawyers, unlike the common lawyers, did not ally themselves with the parliamentarians during the constitutional struggle, but tended to uphold the dominance of the royal prerogative. Chancery suits, often involving the close study of detailed accounts and other abstruse documents, were very slow and expensive compared to common law actions, and without a settled form of procedure they usually necessitated a succession of intermediate hearings of an interlocutory nature. There was a danger that the Court of Chancery would be abolished altogether by the Long Parliament at the time when it had terminated the prerogative courts, but it survived and in 1653, during a two-day parliamentary debate on the deficiencies of the Court, it was disclosed that there were at that time some 23,000 equity cases pending, some of which had lasted for over thirty years. Chancery was again under parliamentary attack after the Restoration when the House of Commons directed that a Bill should be introduced to restrain the lord chancellor's 'extraordinary jurisdiction'. The Earl of Nottingham, who was lord chancellor from 1675 until 1682, made the first real attempt to shape the rules and the axioms of equity into a logical or orderly system of jurisprudence so that the Court of Chancery could fulfil its primary function of supplementing the common law.

The barristers practising at the common law courts and those who practised at the Court of Chancery were all members of the Inns of Court. The leaders of the Bar were the law officers, the attorney-general and solicitor-general, who were the legal advisers to the Crown and one or both of whom always sat in the House of Commons. They were assisted in their work by a select body of 'king's learned counsel' retained by the Crown and ranking next in precedence after the serjeants. During the seventeenth century the king's counsel became a recognized order in legal profession and was probably equivalent in status to a serjeant. Another legal grade to emerge at this time was the solicitor. At first solicitors were considered to be of lower standing than attornies, and in 1614 the four Inns of Court decided that attornies and solicitors were both 'of an inferior nature' to barristers. Shortly after this solicitors became equated with attornies. The collegiate life of the Inns of Court almost disappeared during the seventeenth century, due to the fact that with the growth of printing students tended to buy their own books and to study privately. After the Restoration the benchers and the readers of the Inns attempted to revive the old form of scholastic training, but without much effect.

William of Orange died in 1702, having been predeceased by his wife eight years earlier. By the terms of the Act of Settlement William was to be succeeded by Anne, the younger daughter of James II, and if she should leave no issue the Crown was then to pass to the decendants of Charles I's sister Elizabeth. In fact Anne bore seventeen children but none of them were still surviving at the time of her death; consequently, in accordance with the order of succession prescribed by the Settlement Act, Elizabeth's grandson George, Elector of the Prussian state of Hanover, inherited the throne of Great Britain and Ireland in 1714.

CHAPTER 15

THE LAW IN PRACTICE

The structure of the courts system in Britain remained basically unaltered throughout the Stuart period. The House of Lords continued to try first-instance cases until its abolition in 1648, and when it was reconstituted in 1660 it again claimed an original jurisdiction both in criminal and in civil matters. Soon after the Revolution, however, it had come to be generally accepted that the House of Lords no longer constituted a court of trial, except for the hearing of impeachment proceedings and of charges of treason or felony against peers, although it still retained the right to hear appeals from the Court of Chancery and to issue writs of error against the courts of common law.

The position of the common law courts had been considerably strengthened by the disappearance of the Star Chamber, and also by the new-found independence of the judges following the Act of Settlement. Moreover, by the end of the seventeenth century the ecclesiastical courts has been deprived of most of their jurisdiction and had receded into quasi-clerical tribunals only concerned with causes which had a religious or a semi-religious connotation. The common law courts were trying civil actions in their own right, or were engaged in the supervision of the inferior courts by granting writs of error, prohibition, and certiorari or, in certain types of case, by assenting to motions for retrials.

The Court of Requests had been abolished by the Long Parliament in 1641, leaving no general courts where poorer litigants could get their minor civil actions tried either speedily or cheaply. It is true that several Small Debts Courts had been set up in London in 1606 with such an object in view, but the idea had never spread to the rest of the country.

The rules of procedure in common law were generally arranged by the individual courts, although they were all subject to a few statutory principles. The King's Bench, Common Pleas, and Exchequer still continued shamelessly and blatantly to steal each other's work, owing to the absence of any clear divisions between their respective jurisdictions*. Their motives, no doubt, were partly based upon the element of prestige, and partly upon the cruder inducement that the litigants paid their legal fees directly to the court concerned. The manner in which cases were conducted was largely governed by the formalism and rigidity of written pleadings, the preparation of which was ever becoming a more adroit and complicated art. By the beginning of the eighteenth century facts were generally proved on oath by witnesses and issues were decided according to the weight of relevant evidence.

Criminal trials during the reigns of James I and Charles I showed some small improvement over those of the Tudor era. The prosecution witnesses were usually called to give evidence rather than their depositions and statements being read to the court; the prisoner could decline to answer questions and was allowed to cross-examine and to call his own witnesses. Very little change in this procedure took place during the Interregnum, but in the years following the Restoration the standards of the religiously or politically actuated trials sank to a low ebb. 'I do not think', says Stephen, 'that the injustice and cruelty of the most notorious of the trials – the trials of the Popish Plot, or those which took place before Jeffreys – have been in any degree exaggerated.' He attributes this decline to perjured witnesses, the bias of jurors, and the gross brutality of certain judges. Nevertheless, the ordinary, post-Restoration criminal trials were relatively fair considering the age in which they took place. Sometimes the Crown was represented by counsel; sometimes it was not. Although the prisoner could cross-examine the prosecution witnesses, he had no advance knowledge of the substance of their evidence. Afterwards he was called on to make a statement in his defence and he was liable to be rigorously questioned on what he said; he was also allowed to call witnesses on oath. The judge's summing-up was extremely brief, sometimes being confined

* Each had its own chief justices (who was called the chief baron in the Exchequer). The Chief Justice of the King's Bench was known as the Lord Chief Justice of England.

to a few sentences; he had often made no record of the evidence and merely suggested to the jury that they should rely on their own notes. The worst features of the system were still that most prisoners were kept in close confinement until their trials and were given no opportunity of consulting counsel or preparing their own cases.

Moreover, there were no rules of evidence, so that the witnesses for the prosecution could mention all sorts of details which were, in fact, irrelevant and highly prejudicial; hearsay was admitted and accomplices did not require any corroboration. There was a strange custom, almost amounting to a legal principle, that every trial should be completed in one continuous sitting; the reason for this might have been to avoid the dispersal of the jury.

After the Revolution there was a marked improvement in the administration of criminal justice. The judges started to behave in a more detached and more judicial manner and rules of evidence and procedure were introduced which were more favourable to the defence. Hearsay was regarded with growing disfavour, and Sir John Holt, chief justice of the King's Bench at the time of the Bill of Rights, held that evidence of a prisoner's previous convictions was inadmissible as proof of his guilt. Holt also discontinued the practice of keeping the prisoners in manacles throughout their trials. In 1695 it was enacted that prisoners charged with treason should be shown a copy of the indictment before their trials, and further that they should be allowed to have their own counsel and to call defence witnesses on oath; in 1702 prisoners charged with felony were also permitted to have their witnesses sworn. In 1708 it was provided that a person indicted for treason should be given a list of the prosecution witnesses and the jurors at least ten days before his trial commenced.

Throughout the Stuart period new offences were continually being created by statute and the penalties for a number of existing crimes were being stiffened. High treason was extended intermittently to cover the special circumstances of the moment. The law was developed in relation to forgery and to preserving the purity of the coinage. Street-robbers, housebreakers who caused fear, and thieves who stole from specified buildings were all deprived of Benefit of Clergy. To buy or to receive goods knowing them to be stolen became a statutory offence and various crimes were introduced relating to damaging private property. In the second half of the seventeenth century laws were passed to punish those who traded on a Sunday, and a drive was started against lotteries and public gambling.

After the Restoration the jury finally lost the character of witnesses and became independent assessors of the evidence; indeed, an Act passed in 1705 provided that jurors need no longer be residents in the actual locality of an alleged crime so long as they came from the county in which the place was situated. The Crown could still indirectly influence a jury's decisions as the jurors were selected by royal officials; both Charles II and James II often availed themselves of this method of controlling verdicts when they had a special interest in the outcome of a trial. Even after the abolition of the Star Chamber, jurors were still liable to punishment if they refused to convict a prisoner when they had been directed to do so by the judge. This continued to be the position until Bushell's Case in 1671. Edmund Bushell had been the foreman of a jury at the Old Bailey which had declined to convict the Quakers Penn and Mead on a charge of unlawful assembly, although the Recorder of London had kept them locked up for two days and two nights without food or drink in an effort to make them change their minds. Eventually the twelve jurors were fined for their obduracy and when they refused to pay they were committed to Newgate Gaol. Bushell and several of his fellow-jurors then brought habeas corpus proceedings in the Court of Common Pleas. In a historic judgement the court vindicated the behaviour of Bushell and his colleagues and laid down the principle that at a trial by jury the jurors remained 'the only competent judges' of the facts in issue. With the Revolution of 1689 the fining and imprisonment of jurors came to an end. From then on the only way of correcting a patently wrongful acquittal was by ordering a retrial. At the beginning of the eighteenth century the courts were developing the power of discharging juries which could not agree, rather than coercing them into returning a verdict.

The increase in the number of felonies during the Stuart period brought about a corresponding increase in the number of death sentences passed by the courts. 'What a lamentable case it is', Coke wrote in his *Institutes*, 'to see so many

Christian men and women strangled on the cursed tree of the gallows'. The prisoners were literally strangled in front of vast, jostling crowds who were given a public holiday for the occasion. An account of the hanging of three men for murder in 1682, as reported in *State Trials*, described the scene as the prisoners waited in the cart while the final preparations were being made. 'When they had stood about a quarter of an hour under the gibbet, after being tied up', the account goes on, 'they were asked when they would give the signal for being turned off; they answered they were ready; so a little while after, the cart was drawn away and thus ended their lives'. A great many people claimed Benefit of Clergy when it was available, but the list of non-clergyable offences was being continually extended. In 1622 women were permitted to claim Benefit for a limited number of offences, and in 1692 they were enabled to make the claim on a first conviction for any clergyable felony. In 1705 the necessity for reading the relevant lines of the 'neck verse' from the 51st Psalm was abolished and prisoners of both sexes were allowed to memorize the words. The growth of transportation also enabled a great many convicted felons to escape with their lives. The term 'transportation' was first used in a statute during Charles II's reign; this permitted the king to grant pardons to prisoners convicted of certain offences on condition that they consented to being transported overseas. The Webbs have commented that the sale of convicts to contractors who shipped them to the plantations of Maryland and Virginia virtually became another branch of the slave-trade.

The pillory was used increasingly as a punishment for political offences, the helpless prisoners often having to endure the abuse and molestation of a hostile crowd. Men locked in the pillory frequently suffered severe injuries and some were even killed. Yet torture was not permitted by British penal code. There is no law to warrant the use of tortures in this land'; said Coke, 'nor can they be justified'. And in 1628 the judges advised Charles I that a prisoner 'ought not by law to be tortured by the rack, for no such punishment is known or allowed by our law'.

The justices of the peace remained the cornerstone for the enforcement of the law. They were nominally selected from 'the most sufficient knights, esquires and gentlemen of the law', and had to be resident within the county of their commission, possessing a freehold there worth at least £20 a year. From earliest times there had been allegations of corruption against the justices, for they were authorized to collect fees from applicants in relation to most of the functions they performed. These accusations increased during the seventeenth century when a succession of justices were appointed who possessed no other qualification than that of being supporters of the governments then in power. The newcomers were mostly men of humble origin and they frequently replaced men of a far abler stature; they were known as 'justices of mean degree' and some of those selected by Charles I and Charles II were described by Smollett as 'men of small fortunes, depending on the court'. Other terms were coined at that time like 'basket justices' and 'trading justices'. Basket justices were principally found in country districts and it was said that they left a basket handy for receiving the offerings of those who were due to appear before them, both in civil and in criminal matters. Trading justices operated mostly in urban areas where there were no local squires and there was no parochial life. They comprised small shopkeepers and tradesmen who regarded their judicial duties as a means of livelihood and they used every artifice to increase the volume of their work.

Cromwell tried unsuccessfully to improve the standards of the justices by introducing a completely new commission in 1651. After the Restoration the Commons declared that it would be greatly beneficial 'that gentlemen of quality should be restored to the Commissions and Lieutenancy and that men of small estates be neither continued nor put into the said Commissions'. Again, little was achieved for in 1704 the House of Lords were complaining that there had been recent appointments of justices who 'did not deserve so great power', and further that 'many gentlemen of good estates and ancient families' had been dismissed from the commissions for no adequate reason.

Although the principal work of the justices of the peace was performed at Quarter Sessions their other duties were still of considerable importance. In James I's reign they were directed to form themselves into regional divisions so that they could all be responsible for specific areas. They also continued to carry out preliminary investigations, playing the role of detectives more than judicial officers, and giving evidence at the subsequent trials of the offenders which in a later age would have come more appropriately from the police officers in charge of the cases. As few towns had official buildings for the holding of Quarter Sessions, they were usually held in the largest available room at a local inn. The justices in Quarter Sessions still shouldered the main responsibility for local government, assisted by the lord lieutenants and the sheriffs, and delegating particular functions to the high constable, the petty constables, and the overseers and churchwardens of the parishes. This system worked out fairly efficiently – especially up to the Civil War – and was always kept under the constant supervision of the judges of assize. In the years following the Restoration the justices took over the complete administration of the operation of the Poor Laws and the appointment of the overseers of the poor. On the opening day of every Quarter Sessions the justices received the presentments of the constables, and the grand jury considered the Bills of Indictment, deciding in which cases there were sufficient evidence to proceed with the trials. The grand jurors were mostly professional men, merchants, landowners and well-to-do farmers; they were people of substance, said Blackstone, but were not usually 'gentlemen of the first figure in the county'. They performed their somewhat arduous duties without any form of remuneration.

The deficiencies in the British policing system were becoming more and more evident during the Stuart period, especially in the cities and towns where, according to a contemporary tract, 'scarce any durst walk in the street after nine at night'. There were no experienced officers to supervise the amateur petty constables and watchmen; even the high constables, whose duties included the direction of the watch, were only temporary unpaid officials appointed by Quarter Sessions, and a great many of them were either incompetent or corrupt. Oliver Cromwell subjected the nation to a military dictatorship relying on his army for the preservation of order, but on the Restoration the old chaotic lawlessness returned, aggravated now by the mass of vagrants and disbanded soldiers who were overrunning the country.

Criminal prosecutions were still initiated by private individuals at their own risk and expense. To encourage the public in the fulfilment of this necessary duty the Government introduced the Tyburn Ticket in 1669. The Tyburn Ticket was, in fact, a certificate which was awarded to any person who prosecuted a felon to conviction and it ensured the holder perpetual immunity from any ward or parish duties. It could be sold by the recipient once and once only and this gave it considerable financial value. In 1692 a further effort was made to stem the growth of crime by an Act which provided that as the roads of the kingdom had become 'more infested with thieves and robbers than formerly', anyone who apprehended a highwayman might keep his horse and his equipment, as well as receiving a payment of £40 from the State. Free pardons were offered to accomplices who turned 'King's Evidence' against their former colleagues.

At the commencement of this period the Star Chamber had exercised a close control over the law of libel and over the printing and publication of books. The Council was particularly concerned with any libels which might endanger the welfare or security of the State, such as sedition, heresy or blasphemy, but it also sought to discourage personal insults which might result in breaches of the peace and duelling. At the same time the common law was developing its jurisdiction over defamatory statements by a defendant which had caused material damage to the plaintiff. Only the officially sponsored Stationers Company, or some other person with a special licence from the Crown, was allowed to print or publish a book. An Act in 1637 imposed stringent penalties for the publication of unlicensed literature, and under the Commonwealth similar regulations were equally strictly enforced. The Restoration brought about no appreciable improvements in the situation, the sole alleviation being that thenceforth the licensing acts were limited to a specific duration, but were renewable nevertheless at the moment they expired. This continued to be the position until 1694 when the House of Commons refused to renew the then existing Act and the whole discredited system for the compulsory licensing of publications came to an abrupt finish. From that time forward the printed word was merely governed by the restrictions applicable to the ordinary law of libel. The modern principles of defamation were then beginning to take shape with the division of libels into two categories; firstly criminal libels, the substance of which was the likelihood of a breach of the peace; and secondly civil libels, which were dependent on the damage, financial or otherwise, inflicted upon the plaintiff. A further distinction emerged between defamation in a verbal or transient form, which was called slander, and defamation in a written or permanent form, which was called libel; each was governed by different legal considerations.

Over the whole of this period there were few changes in land law, except that early in the reign of Charles II the remaining feudal tenures were converted into free tenures and the ancient services which were due from the Crown's tenants became purely nominal. As far as wills were concerned the formal requirements were simplified and the distribution of the effects of an intestate husband between his widow and his children was rearranged on a fairer and more logical basis.

The ecclesiastical courts retained their jurisdiction over matrimonial matters but a new form of absolute divorce by private Act of Parliament was originated after the Restoration. However, the procedure was intricate and costly and had only been employed on five occasions up to the death of Queen Anne. There was no improvement in the legal status of married women; they could not own any personal possessions nor could they control their real property, although the Court of Chancery allowed their friends to hold it in trust on their behalf.

British interest overseas continued to develop under the Stuarts, and successive governments endeavoured to regulate foreign trade in a manner which was most conducive to the prosperity of the nation. As they had very few civil servants to implement their mercantile policies, they placed their reliance upon the privileged companies which operated royal monopolies in specific regions. After the Revolution the Crown lost the right of granting monopolies to companies and most of the existing incorporated charter companies either renounced their exclusive rights or gave up business completely. Internal commercial policy, too, was largely controlled by individual bodies such as charter companies and boroughs – and earlier in the period by the surviving guilds – which were made responsible for the enforcement of the relevant statutes and proclamations, largely designed to ensure the efficiency and honest workmanship of the various crafts and industries.

Until the penultimate year of his reign, James I, continuing the custom of the Tudor monarchs, had treated the granting of monopolies as being principally a source of royal income. All this was changed by the Statute of Monopolies in 1624, which declared that all monopolies 'grievous and inconvenient to the subjects of the realm' were void, but excepted grants of letters patent for fourteen years 'for the sole working or making' of a new invention. The Act further provided that patents and monopolies should come within the jurisdiction of the common law courts rather than that of the Council. A statute in the reign of Anne stated that books and other writings were being reprinted and published without consent of the authors 'and too often to the ruin of them and their families'. The Act went on to introduce a renewable copyright of works of art lasting for fourteen years.

The campaign against vagrancy was waged as firmly as ever both under the Stuarts and during the Commonwealth. An Act in 1609 urged that the Elizabethan legislation relating to 'rogues, vagabonds and other wandering and idle persons' should be more rigorously enforced, and complained that houses of correction were not being effectively operated and that many men with families 'do themselves run away out of their parishes and leave their families upon the parish'. A Commonwealth statute in 1656 recited that 'the number of wandering, idle, loose, dissolute and disorderly persons is of late much increased' with a resultant growth in crimes of violence and dishonesty; this Act extended the definition of a 'rogue and vagabond'. In the same year it was made an indictable offence for a person to have 'no visible estate, profession or calling' corresponding to his rate of expenditure. A statute in 1662 introduced the principle of 'settlement' which was to bedevil the Poor Law system for a century after. The Act stated that the continued increase of the poor was due to defects in the law, and that owing to the scarcity of employment and relief in so many parishes where paupers were supposed to reside, these people drifted away to parishes which had more to offer. It was enacted that justices of the peace could remove any person coming into their parish and living in a dwelling worth less than £10 a year, within forty days of his arrival; they could then return him to the parish where he was last legally settled 'as a native, householder, sojourner, apprentice or servant', unless he was able to offer security for being allowed to stay. A member remarked in the House of Commons that under this Act 'the poor are hunted like foxes out of their homes'. As it became customary for newcomers in a parish to conceal themselves until the initial forty-day period had elapsed, a statute in 1685 provided that the time would only start to run when they had reported their presence to a parish officer.

Side by side with this legislation, the methods of treating and punishing 'incorrigible rogues, vagabonds and sturdy beggars' were becoming progressively harsher. An Act which was passed a year before the death of Queen Anne consolidated all the former statutes and provided that vagrants who were being compulsorily returned to their parishes of settlement should be whipped in every county through which they passed. This measure accorded with the national outlook on idleness, poverty, and vagrancy.

Part VIII

THE HANOVER PERIOD

(1714–1837)

CHAPTER 16

THE REFORM OF PARLIAMENT

When George I ascended the British throne in 1714 the constitutional status of the sovereign had been changed significantly by the tide of events during the previous twenty-six years. Legislation had imposed various limitations both on his independence and his powers. He was bound to adhere to the Anglican faith; he required parliamentary sanction to levy taxes, to raise an army, to suspend a law, or even to leave the country; he could choose his ministers but he was forbidden to create new ministerial posts; and although he appointed judges, he was unable either to dismiss them of his own volition or to interfere with their decisions. Theoretically he could reject a Bill which had been approved by Parliament, but in practice no monarch has refused to grant the royal assent to any measure which has been passed by both Houses since the beginning of the Hanover period. However, the king could still exert a considerable influence over men and over affairs. On the material plane he controlled the expenditure of the civil list, and on the personal, his active support continued to count for a great deal. As Granville, the eighteenth-century statesman, once remarked, 'Give any man the Crown on his side and he can defy everything'.

The Privy Council had ceased to be the sovereign's principal consultative committee and had been deprived of its entire administrative function. It was now a mere ratifying body for the formal expression of the royal endorsement on occasions when this was required. The centre of authority had moved to the Cabinet, a select group of persons which did not have then, and has never since had, any recognized legal basis within the British constitution. In its early days the meetings of the Cabinet were attended by the leading members of the government, the judiciary, the Church and the royal household; they were presided over by the monarch and they settled many matters of national policy. The Cabinet did not possess a fixed composition, a regular meeting-place, an office, or a staff, and no record was kept of its discussions. Soon after the start of the Hanover period the larger and more formal meetings of the Cabinet were replaced by purely political consultations between the more important ministers. George I presided at cabinet meetings for a few years, even though he could not understand English; after 1718 he ceased to attend – a precedent which was followed by his successors. The office of prime minister evolved somewhat later than the origination of the Cabinet, but it had the same absence of constitutional foundation. There was no collective responsibility of the ministers in a government; each was responsible for his own department and was virtually independent of his colleagues. The senior ministerial appointment was the first lord of the Treasury, but the resignation of the holder of that office did not necessarily bring down the whole ministry. None of the three dominant first lords of the Treasury during the eighteenth century, Walpole, Newcastle and Pitt, was ever officially called the prime minister, though North and Addington (in 1801) were known by such a title.

In the aftermath of the great constitutional struggles under the Stuarts the reputation of Parliament stood high at the commencement of the Hanover period, and very little criticism was directed against the form or the efficacy of the parliamentary institution during the reigns of George I and George II. Nevertheless, the two Houses were wholly unrepresentative of the bulk of the nation, comprising as they did a cross-section of the especially privileged classes, the large landowners, the country gentlemen, the eminent lawyers, the prelacy, and the rich merchants. The populace were experiencing a mood of political apathy; the principal issues of the former era were apparently settled; it only remained to enjoy the stability and progress which lay ahead. In any event, an intelligent interest in the business of Parliament was almost impossible as the proceedings were private and neither the speeches of the members nor the ways in which they voted were ever officially disclosed.

Although the House of Lords had lost its former predominance, it still retained a position of considerable constitutional significance, not only as the Upper House, but also as a chamber having an almost equal responsibility with the House of Commons for instituting or rejecting any proposed measures of legislation.* The numerical strength of the Lords was usually about 222, which included a total of 26 bishops. The peers were mostly men of vast wealth, possessions, and prestige who were utterly out of touch with the problems confronting the lesser orders of society.

The House of Commons represented a slightly wider range of interests but here again the substantial property-owners held the lion's share of the seats. The overall strength of the House was 558, being made up of 92 members for the English and Welsh counties, 417 for the English and Welsh boroughs, and 49 Scottish members. The majority of the county members were landed squires who had been chosen by the principal family, or by a group of the most influential residents in their constituencies and had been elected on a 40/- freehold suffrage. They tended to regard themselves more as regional representatives than as the delegates of national constituent assembly and their outlook was frequently narrow, parochial, and reactionary. For the most part the borough members too belonged to the landed gentry, but they included a sprinkling of lawyers, merchants, naval and military officers and government officials as well. Many borough seats were controlled by peers, squires or other powerful personages in the locality; in fact it was said that at that time no less than 205 of the borough seats were at the personal disposal of some 111 patrons. There was no general method of franchise in the boroughs. Sometimes the members of Parliament were elected by householders, sometimes by the owners of specific properties, sometimes by the local freemen, and sometimes by the members of the corporation. Parliamentary voting was open rather than by ballot and elections were subject to a mixture of bribery and duress. Votes were freely bartered for money, pensions, and patronage appointments, the ministry in power being in a particularly favourable position to hand out this form of electoral largesse. The tide of political corruption ran to its lowest ebb under Robert Walpole and the Duke of Newcastle.

* Financial Bills could not originate or be amended in the House of Lords.

In spite of all the chicanery at election-time the members of Parliament adopted an attitude of sturdy independence towards the policies of their political parties and the opinions of their leaders. The king could appoint his ministers but he could not sustain them in office if they did not enjoy the confidence of the House of Commons. This self-reliance of the individual members was partly the cause of their objecting to any abrogation of the absolute privacy of their debates, for, as an ex-minister said in 1738, the disclosure of their speeches would make the members 'accountable without the doors for what they said within'. But the growing interest of the public in parliamentary affairs somewhat later in the century led at least four journals to publish regular accounts of the principal debates, seeking to avoid breaches of privilege when they did so by using fictitious names to thinly disguise the identities of the various speakers. After the year 1771, when the editors of three newspapers were summoned to the bar of the House for reporting parliament proceedings, both the Lords and the Commons quietly resigned themselves to the inevitable. Lord North, who was first lord of the Treasury from 1770 until 1782, even used to encourage journalists to attend the House when he desired publicity for a debate, and members habitually handed out copies of their speeches to the Press. General elections were infrequent, as by the Septennial Act in 1716 the natural life of a Parliament was extended from three to seven years; all Parliaments came to an end automatically on the death of the monarch.

The day-to-day transactions of national administration were considered to be a royal rather than a parliamentary responsibility, and both the Civil Service and the Diplomatic Service were directly answerable to the king and were paid by him from the civil list, the fixed income which he had been granted on his accession to the throne. The king's personal control over the counties was being rapidly minimized: he still appointed the lord lieutenants and the high sheriffs, but the duties attaching to both these offices were now largely honorary. Although the lord lieutenant was the nominal commander of the county militia in any emergency, and was entitled to preside over the justices of the peace at Quarter Sessions, his actual responsibilities went no further than appointing the clerk of the peace and recommending candidates for the local magistracy. The high sheriff's chief functions were to attend the judges on circuit, and to sit on the bench at the County Court, a task he usually allocated to his under-sheriff.

The struggles of the Stuart period had left their imprint on the mood of the nation. On the one hand there was a reaction against the excesses of Puritanism, a moral and intellectual relaxation and a glimmering awareness of the problems of social progress; on the other, there was a chauvinistic pride – a smug and implacable arrogance with regard to the British polity. Ignoring the insecurity and impotence of the masses, the Earl of Chatham could proudly declaim, 'the poorest man may in his cottage bid defiance to all the forces of the Crown. It may be frail – its roof may shake – the wind may blow through it – the storm may enter – the rain may enter – but the King of England cannot enter. All his force dares not cross the threshold of the ruined tenement'. And in spite of the harassment of the poor and the intolerant brutality of the vagrancy laws, a lord chief justice, after asserting that the detention of an African in a slave-trading ship in the Thames was unlawful, went on to say, 'The air of England is too pure for any slave to breathe. Let the black man go free'. Britain in that era possessed no social conscience. Poverty and unemployment were condemned as self-induced afflictions and class divisions were regarded as the rigid demarcations between differing species of humanity. Even the compassionate Henry Fielding denounced the extravagant habits of the lower orders and spoke of the ways in which 'the very dregs of the people' would aspire 'to a degree which does not belong to them – and abandon themselves to idleness'.

The reputations of successive governments during the reigns of George I and George II were utterly debased by the corrupt leadership of Robert Walpole, Henry Pelham, and the contemptible Duke of Newcastle. George III was perhaps voicing the general opinion of his people when he said, on coming to the throne in 1760, 'As to honesty, I think, all sets of men seem equally to have thrown that aside'. Of all the foremost politicians only William Pitt, later the first Earl of Chatham, had been widely respected for his fearless integrity and for the ethical principles he was seeking to re-instill into public life.

During the second half of the eighteenth century, Britain was surging ahead with her industrial revolution, an advancement in mechanization and techniques which was to lead eventually to her virtual economic domination of the rest of the world. In 1761 James Brindley constructed his first canal, the forerunner of a great network of internal waterways which provided an essential form of transport until the improvement of road surfaces and the advent of commercial steam. In 1767 James Hargreaves invented his mechanical 'spinning jenny', and a year later Richard Arkwright perfected a more sophisticated machine for the same purpose. James Watt brought out his improved steam engine in 1768, and Samuel Crompton transformed the process of cotton manufacture in 1784 when he successfully operated his automatic spinning mule. With the mass-production of cheap cotton, the ever-increasing output of coal and iron, and the improvements in machinery, British exports expanded from just over fourteen million pounds sterling in 1760 to just under thirty million pounds sterling in 1800. With the consequent increase in wealth and prosperity there arose a new social class of wealthy merchants and manufacturers who began to occupy a place of privilege quite apart from the traditional landowning aristocracy.

At the end of the eighteenth century a cogent school of radical reformers was becoming a potent force in British political affairs. They extended their criticisms to the legal system, the methods of suffrage and the composition of Parliament, the infamy of the slave trade, the brutalities of the penal code, and the constraints still placed upon the Roman Catholics. At the moment when their arguments were gathering strength the French Revolution broke out and put back the cause of reform in Britain for at least three or four decades.

The French Revolution precipitated a head-on clash between the reactionaries who were opposed to any changes whatsoever in the British law or constitution, and the radicals who were seeking a wide range of far-reaching reforms. The Whig party was immediately split, one faction siding with Charles Fox in their belief that what was happening in France was an honourable uprising which would result in the establishment of free institutions throughout that country, and the other group, under Edmund Burke, realizing the full magnitude of the struggle, the latent tyranny and vengeance, the usurpation of order, and the dangerous pollution of anarchical precepts. Meanwhile William Pitt the Younger, the first lord of the Treasury from 1783 to 1801, viewing the matter with practical realism, saw the preoccupation of the French as a merciful relief from their all-too-customary moods of militancy and aggression. However, as more and more news emerged from France of the atrocities, the bloodshed, and the destruction which were being perpetrated in the name of the new order, the revolution was seen in a different light even by Fox and the other Britons who formerly had been so sympathetic towards it. Moreover, there was a widespread alarm amongst the British upper classes at the subversive violence of the French peasantry and at the proclamation of the French National Assembly promising support for the people of any nation who were struggling for liberty against their own governments. The tide of events not only brought Britain and France into open conflict, but also caused the British Government to adopt a domestic policy of illiberal oppression in which every suggestion of reform was branded as treachery or sedition.

When William Pitt died in January 1806 the Whig 'Ministry of All the Talents' came into being under Lord Grenville with Charles Fox as foreign secretary. Despite the death of Fox, by far their ablest member, during the autumn of the same year, the Government pressed ahead with their policy of reform. Their most striking achievement was an Act for the abolition of the slave trade, in the passage of which through the Commons they were actively supported by a small group of zealous evangelical Christians led by William Wilberforce. But when they attempted to bring about the emancipation of the Roman Catholics they encountered such a measure of opposition from the king and from a majority in both Houses that they were forced to abandon the proposal. Upon George III demanding a written undertaking that this issue would never be raised again, Grenville and his ministry decided to resign rather than to provoke a delicate constitutional confrontation.

The Napoleonic Wars eventually came to an end with the total defeat of the French army at the Battle of Waterloo in 1815. Britain, however, had no opportunity of basking in the full glory of her victory as the disruption of her industries, due to the sudden transformation to peacetime conditions, coupled with a disastrous harvest in 1816, caused a severe economic depression throughout the country. Unemployment rose alarmingly and wage-rates declined to starvation levels. Bands of workless, desperate, and destitute wandered from door to door demanding money, shelter, and provisions. Presently there was intermittent rioting and recurrent acts of vandalism; machinery was smashed in the factories and hayricks were burnt down on the farms. The authorities responded with the use of troops and repressive violence, habeas corpus was suspended, and legislation was rushed through Parliament enforcing new provisions against seditious assemblies and the subversion of the the law. Political agitators seized this opportunity to fan the flames of violence with impassioned tracts and inflammatory speeches. For a moment the British seemed to be poised on the threshold of a bloody revolution, from which they were saved in all probability by their memories of 1688, and by the first empirical steps they had taken towards the establishment of a democratic form of constitution.

By the beginning of the 1820s Britain was regaining her former prosperity and the clamour for parliamentary reform, which had been one of the popular grievances during the years of depression, had lost a great deal of its ardour. Nevertheless, when Robert Peel became home secretary in 1822 he fully realized that the time had come for modifications and changes in law to meet a new situation brought about by the sustained progress of industrial development. During Peel's two terms at the Home Office, from 1822 to 1827 and from 1828 to 1830, he initiated a large number of liberal enactments, many of which reflected the theories of such eminent radicals as Jeremy Bentham and Samuel Romilly. Perhaps the most notable of these measures was the Catholic Emancipation Act of 1829, which repealed the provisions requiring a declaration against substantiation as a condition precedent to sitting in Parliament or holding office under the Crown: henceforth Roman Catholics were enabled to enter Parliament and they became eligible for all civil and military appointments with a few specified exceptions.

Chatham had said in 1770, 'Before the end of this century either Parliament will reform itself from within or will be reformed with a vengeance from without'. In fact the end of the century came without any appreciable parliamentary reforms, although William Pitt had repeatedly criticized the existing system of representation. As a result of the union with Ireland in 1801, twenty-eight Irish peers and four Irish bishops were added to the membership of the Lords, and a hundred Irish members were added to the Commons, increasing the size of that chamber to 658. Various plans for reform were discussed during the early part of the nineteenth century but none of them ever made any headway.

George IV died in 1830, being succeeded by his brother William IV. According to custom, a general election was held on the accession of the new monarch, and suddenly parliamentary reform became the burning issue of the day. The reformers were certainly in a position to make out a strong case. The record of the House of Lords in the field of progressive legislation had been, and would continue to be, lamentable; both prelates and peers were resolutely opposed to the removal of social abuses and to the onset of humanitarian enlightenment. As for the House of Commons, it was said in 1827 that 276 of the seats were still at the disposal of landed patrons; in addition, the haphazard dimensions of the constituencies bore no relationship to changes which had occurred in the population and in the comparative importance of various localities. At the 1830 election the Duke of Wellington, leading the Tories, took the view that parliamentary representation was perfect and could not be improved. On the other hand, Earl Grey, the leader of the Whigs, made it quite clear that should he be invited to form a ministry he would introduce a Bill for parliamentary reform. In the event, the Whigs were returned to power, but their first few months in office were marred by rioting and strikes, due partly to abysmal wage-rates and partly to a general atmosphere of social discontent.

At the beginning of 1831 the Government set up a committee to draft a measure for reforming the House of Commons. The necessary Bill was speedily prepared. It disenfranchized a large number of boroughs and reduced the representation of many others, at the same time creating new constituencies in certain towns and increasing the representation in some of the counties. Further, the basis of suffrage was to be broadened, voting was to be by ballot, and the maximum duration of a Parliament was to be reduced from seven to five years. The nature and extent of these proposals took both the Whigs and the Tories by surprise; nor were the critics appeased by the assurances of Viscount Althorp, the chancellor of the exchequer, that the intention was, while augmenting the democratic proportion of the representation, to preserve the aristocratic share 'by increasing the influence of the great landed proprietors in the counties'. The debate on the second reading lasted for seven nights and culminated in a packed House carrying the Bill by a single vote. The excitement was growing throughout the nation. Macaulay remarked, 'The danger is terrible. The time is short'. But the triumph of the reformers was short-lived. The Tories combined with the dissident Whigs to defeat the Government in committee and the king agreed to dissolve Parliament.

The mood of the nation was overwhelmingly behind the Government and at the ensuing general election they secured an even bigger majority than before. The second Reform Bill, a slight modification of the first, passed its second reading in the Commons in September 1831. A month later it was soundly rejected by the House of Lords, twenty-seven of the bishops voting with the opposition. In spite of this setback the ministry consented to remain in office on an assurance from the king that he would support a similar Bill in the following session. Macaulay's forebodings were now borne out. Riots occurred up and down the country, mass meetings were held demanding parliamentary reform, and the country seemed again to be on the brink of a civil war. The third Reform Bill, with further minor amendments, was carried in the Commons by a substantial majority. As the result of a considerable amount of lobbying by the Government, and a threat by the king to create a sufficient number of new and acquiescent peers, the Bill was forced through the Lords in the spring of 1832.

The Reform Act completely altered the composition of the House of Commons and also introduced a much wider basis of suffrage. Fifty-six boroughs were wholly disenfranchized and thirty more had their representation decreased. Forty-four new urban constituencies were formed, returning a total of sixty-four members, and the county representation was increased from 92 to 159. Franchise in the boroughs was granted to occupiers of houses of an annual value of £10, and in the counties certain classes of copyholders, tenants and leaseholders were added to the owners of 40/- a year freeholds. The overall effect of the Act was to leave the strength of the House at 658 and the permissible life-time of a Parliament at seven years; a total of about 217,000 voters was added to the electorate of England and Wales. A large proportion of the voting strength in the towns had been acquired by the middle classes but the lower classes were still excluded from power. However, the influence of the aristocracy was still very great and in 1833 nearly 500 members of the Commons were said to belong to the landed gentry.

It was too much to hope that Parliament could be cleansed from corruption at one stroke. Certain borough seats remained at the disposal of patrons; the habits of bribery and coercion at election-time would die hard; and open voting was constantly subject to abuse – indeed it had only been retained by Lord Grey because he feared that voting by ballot might deprive the landed interest of much of their influence at the polls. Nevertheless, the Reform Act marked a turning-point in British parliamentary history; it drew the legislature in a closer relationship with the moods and attitudes of the nation, and it laid a foundation for the democratic development of the constitution in the years ahead. Both Houses had now accepted the right of the public to follow their proceedings – in 1834 the Commons sanctioned the creation of a reporters' gallery in their chamber and from 1836 the division lists were published after every vote. But the spirit of reform went far wider than the Houses of Parliament. The official control of sinecure appointments was gradually disappearing and the Civil Service was gathering a permanence, a professional competence, and an immunity from political or personal dependency.

Grey retired from political life in the summer of 1834 and the ministry was taken over by Lord Melbourne. The new prime minister was soon involved in a constitutional difficulty with the king. In November of that year Lord Althorp, the leader of the House of Commons, inherited his father's earldom, and William IV accepted Melbourne's resignation rather than agreeing to his proposal that the leadership of the House should pass to Lord John Russell.

This is believed to have been the last occasion on which a British sovereign has ever actively interfered in a change of ministry.

A minority government was formed under Sir Robert Peel in December 1834, but after another four months Melbourne was once again returned to power. He was still the prime minister in June 1837 when William IV died, to be succeeded to the throne by his eighteen-year-old niece Princess Victoria.

CHAPTER 17

THE ENFORCEMENT OF THE LAW

By the beginning of the eighteenth century the ancient communities of the manor, the township, and the hundred were obsolescent and had been replaced by the parish as the unit of local government. Parish business was transacted by the vestry, which met annually at Eastertime to sanction the rates and to appoint parochial officials such as the churchwardens, the overseers of the poor, and the surveyors of the highways. Some vestries were open and could be attended by all the ratepayers in the parish; others were closed and had fallen into the hands of a small group of the principal citizens in the neighbourhood. The tradition of compulsory but gratuitous service still applied to all the parish officers, who were supervised in their duties by the justices of the peace. During this period the municipal administration attained a high degree of independence from the control of the national executive, Parliament, and the central courts, although it was still subjected to the general surveillance of the itinerant judges and the courts of common law which by the use of prerogative writs compelled the local officials to carry out their functions and at the same time prevented them from exceeding their jurisdictions. Both the county Quarter Sessions and the individual parishes assumed the power of making bye-laws applicable within their own regions.

This casual, amateur style of local government was ill-suited for the populous and rapidly developing urban areas. The Webbs in their history of statutory authorities have given a graphic description of the conditions which might be found at that time in the suburbs and the towns. Houses were springing up like mushrooms and there were neither building regulations nor planning controls. The rain poured down from the rooftops to the streets, which were 'unpaved, uneven and full of holes in which the water and garbage collected'.

There were cowsheds and slaughter houses in the principal thoroughfares, pigs roamed the streets, and every yard and alley contained pigeons and poultry. On moonless nights, apart from an occasional lantern swinging above a doorway, the streets were in total darkness. During the second half of the eighteenth century, in order to meet the necessities of the time, bodies of voluntary improvement commissioners were formed to direct the policing, paving, lighting, and cleansing of the streets, and the naming and numbering of houses. It is not surprising that the justices of the peace who had gained considerable influence over the management of parish affairs should have also provided the chief strength on the improvement commissions.

'A history of the eighteenth century which does not place the justice of the peace in the very foreground of the picture', Maitland has written, 'will be known for what it is – a caricature.' During the reigns of George I and George II most of the landed gentry were members of the Commission of the Peace but the active work was usually undertaken by a small number of the minor squirearchy. Early in the reign of George III the composition of the Commission began to change: the great landowners started to play a more energetic role and the justices of lesser substance receded from their former prominence. The country gentleman rigorously opposed the admission to the Commission of those who were engaged in industry or trade, but they raised no objections to members of the clergy who were being appointed with ever-increasing frequency. The property qualification for a justice, which had stood at £20 a year since 1439, was raised to £100 a year in 1732.

The justice of the peace, in theory, was always on duty, either waiting for cases to be brought before him, supervising the work of the parish officers, or investigating criminal offences within his own neighbourhood. The Newgate Calendar reports innumerable instances in the eighteenth century where suspected offenders were 'carried before a justice' for examination. The powers of trial and punishment of a single justice were wide and various. 'Speaking very generally', says Stephen,

> it may, I think, be said that the general character of statutes giving summary jurisdiction to magistrates was for a great length

> of time to enable them to deal with matters of small importance, more particularly with offences in the nature of trifling nuisances or disturbances of good order, jurisdiction in cases of more serious crime being reserved for juries.

The statutes creating summary offences were being constantly augmented, sometimes with the provision that the trial must take place before two justices of the peace sitting together. In many counties it became customary to arrange regular meetings for the transaction of the criminal and administrative business which required the attendance of more than one magistrate; these meetings, which were not authorized by law, were known as Petty Sessions. There was still no set procedure for summary trials before justices of the peace and in all probability there had been little or no improvement over the methods which had been applied in the seventeenth century.

When magistrates conducted a preliminary enquiry with a view to committing a defendant for trial at Quarter Sessions or at Assizes they did not normally allow him to be present while they were taking depositions from potential prosecution witnesses. In 1824 a judge sternly rebuked a bench of justices who had allowed a report to be published by the Press of their preliminary enquiry into a charge of murder. They had been at fault, he declared, in allowing any persons to enter their apartments for the purpose of taking notes of these proceedings, for a committal enquiry was an inquisitorial rather than a judicial function and the depositions were being prepared solely for the benefit of the trial judge. He continued, 'the prosecutor or his solicitor might have access to them, but not the party accused. For what would be the consequence if the latter had access to them? Why, that he would know everything which was to be produced in evidence against him – an advantage which it was never intended should be extended to him'.

At the start of the Hanover period, the justices at Quarter Sessions made very little distinction between their criminal and their administrative work, but it gradually became customary to carry out the criminal side of their duties in public and the administrative side in private. Only the more important and more active magistrates used to attend at Quarter Sessions, which continued to assemble at the shire hall or at the principal tavern in the county town. The benches which sat for the criminal work were relatively small; in most counties, apart from those in the vicinity of London, they usually consisted of no more than three or four justices. In fact Quarter Sessions possessed a very wide criminal jurisdiction which extended theoretically to all offences other than treason, but a custom arose during the eighteenth century that any crimes which were capitally punishable should be tried by a judge at Assizes. The justices could also transmit to Assizes any cases of especial difficulty.

Although the magistrates in the country areas were in general free from corruption at this time, the depravity of some of the urban justices, especially those in the Commissions of Middlesex and Westminster, knew no bounds. The whole system was utterly incapable of adaptation to the conditions of an expanding and densely populated town where there was no local squirearchy, no environmental stability, and where the job of a magistrate, if properly performed, would have been expensive, exacting, and dangerous. In consequence the Commissions became filled with avaricious, unprincipled adventurers. 'The justices of Middlesex', said Burke, 'were generally the scum of the earth – carpenters, brick-makers and shoe-makers; some of whom were notoriously men of such infamous characters that they would have been unworthy of any employment whatever, and others were so ignorant they could scarcely write their own names.' Laetitia Hawkins, the daughter of a well-known chairman of Middlesex Quarter Sessions, expressed the view that the Westminster magistrates were a disgrace to those who had the power of appointing them. And Smollett, writing of trading justices as a whole, described them as being 'men of profligate lives, needy, mean, ignorant, and rapacious, and often acting from the most scandalous principles of selfish avarice'. Yet Sir Thomas de Veil, a foremost Westminster magistrate, was probably right when he said that such people, in the prevailing circumstances, were 'a kind of necessary evil', for if they had not existed 'the laws could not well be put into execution'.

There were plenty of opportunities for bribery and graft when the justices were performing their administrative duties and even more, perhaps, when they were carrying out their criminal function. Swift alleged that there were certain magistrates in London to whom all the local prostitutes 'pay contributions for shelter and protection from the laws'. The system whereby a magistrate received fees for so many of the tasks connected with his office was an open invitation to dishonesty. An arrested person even had to pay a fee to the justice who granted him bail. Townsend, the Bow Street runner, has told of a certain London magistrate who derived his main income out of bail. 'The plan used to be', said Townsend, 'to issue warrants and to take up all the poor devils in the streets, and then there was the bailing of them, 2/4, which the magistrate had; taking a hundred girls, that would make, at 2/4, £11–13–4. They sent none to gaol, for bailing then was better.' In the opinion of Doctor Johnson any upright magistrate in the Metropolis became 'odious for doing good' and had to withstand 'the secret malevolence and clamorous invectives' of his colleagues.

There is no doubt that the justices in many areas were frequently in a great deal of personal danger. A cabinet minister wrote in 1756, 'It often happens that the very magistrates themselves in the country are deterred from pursuing or apprehending common villains for fear, as they say, of having their houses burnt or some such injury'. The town justices were also expected to be in the forefront whenever the military were called in to break up a riot. By the terms of the Riot Act of 1715, where twelve or more persons were 'unlawfully, riotously, and tumultously assembled together', a justice could make a proclamation ordering them to disperse, and if they did not do so within an hour, not only had they committed a felony, but they could be dispersed by force, even if some of them were injured or killed in the process. For many years after the passing of the statute there was an erroneous but a widely held belief that troops were not entitled to break up an unlawful assembly unless a magistrate had read out the relevant proclamation first. This was the cause of a great deal of uncertainty and confusion, especially during the Gordon Riots in 1780.

In their efforts to maintain law and order the justices could expect very little assistance from the peace officers either in the towns or in the country, as national opinion remained steadfastly opposed to the establishment of a well organized or a professional police force. The high constables, who were mostly drawn from the middle class, occupied an intermediate position between the justices and the petty constables. A very experienced London magistrate, Patrick Colquhoun, wrote in 1803 that the high constable's duties were to superintend and direct the petty constables in his hundred, to notice and report all offences therein, and to ensure that there were sufficient constables present 'to maintain good order and decency during the execution of malefactors or the punishment of offenders'. Although high constables were nominally unpaid, most of them found ways of reimbursing themselves by the receipt of bribes and by the exaction of illicit fees. The duties of petty constables, according to Colquhoun, were to 'regularly perambulate their districts, once at least in twenty-four hours, and visit alehouses once a week to see that no unlawful games are being played and that labouring people are not suffered to lounge and tipple until they are intoxicated'. When a riot was developing the constable 'must repair to the nearest justice and repair instantly to the spot with his stave and there put himself under the direction of any magistrate in attendance'. The onerous nature of the constable's work, the lack of remuneration, and the risks involved, especially in urban areas, made it the most unpopular of all the parish duties.

The towns were supposed to have the additional protection by night of watchmen patrolling the streets, though every parish had a complete discretion whether to employ them or not. In any event, they were hardly an impressive body of men owing principally to their very meagre scale of payment. Watchmen, said Henry Fielding, who were meant to guard the inhabitants against thieves and robbers, 'are chosen out of those poor, old, decrepit people who are for want of bodily strength rendered incapable of getting livelihood by work'. Colquhoun has suggested that they were often recruited from the 'old and infirm' with the object of keeping them out of the workhouse, 'so saving the expense of keeping them'.

With such totally inadequate policing arrangements it was inevitable that Britain, now a growing industrial nation with a steadily mounting population, should become ever more vulnerable to the depredations of the criminal and the violence of the mob. Footpads and housebreakers roamed the streets of the large towns after nightfall and thieves and pickpockets abounded in the daytime. The situation in London was especially bad. Fielding warned in 1751, 'The streets of this town and the roads leading to it will shortly be impassable without the utmost hazard'. People were forced to impose a voluntary curfew on their movements, and in some areas the residents and shopkeepers installed man-traps and organized their own security patrols. This was also the era of the highwayman. The possibility of a hold-up was so great that travellers on coach journeys habitually carried in a separate pocket a purseful of money which they could easily produce if necessary. As for the mob, Henry Fielding described it as 'that large and powerful body which forms the fourth estate of this community'. On the slightest instigation the rabble would run wild, burning, wrecking, and pillaging property, and ruthlessly assailing all who stood in their way. During the Gordon Riots in 1780 the mobs were rampaging through the streets of London for just over a week and eventually were only suppressed by a resolute military operation against them.

Faced with the near-impossible task of attempting to contain the mounting wave of crime and disorder with their inadequate resources, the executive resorted to a series of makeshift expedients. They placed their principal reliance on financial inducements – Tyburn Tickets and blood money rewards for the successful prosecution of offenders. A set scale of payments was introduced for persons who apprehended criminals and prosecuted them to conviction, varying in amounts from the sum of £40 in the case of highwaymen, street-robbers, burglars, and coiners, down to £10 for horse-thieves and shoplifters. A statute in 1722 offered recompense to those who were injured, and to the dependents of those who were killed in detaining people for certain offences. Other statutes gave judges a discretion to grant the prosecutor his costs, and if he or his witnesses were poor to make them an allowance in token of their time and trouble. Further, informers were amply remunerated and criminals were offered free pardons in respect of all offences except murder and treason if they assisted in convicting their former accomplices by 'turning King's Evidence' against them.

One of the most sinister effects of this system of bribery and rewards was the emergence of the freelance thief-taker, some of whom made their entire living from the receipt of prosecution payments. There were many instances of thief-takers inventing an offence and then giving perjured evidence against an innocent defendant, often resulting in his execution. Others, like the notorious Jonathan Wild, combined the business of catching criminals with the large-scale practice of crime on their account. Wild's most profitable enterprise was instigating thefts and later undertaking to arrange for the recovery of the stolen property. Owing to the ineffectuality of the police the victims of burglaries and robberies often negotiated privately for the return of their goods, giving an undertaking not to report the transaction to the authorities. This custom was becoming so prevalent that in 1717 it was enacted that any person who received money for helping an owner to recover stolen property would commit an offence, unless he caused the thief to be apprehended and gave evidence against him at his trial. In 1752 it was made an offence to advertise a reward for the return of stolen goods coupled with a promise that no questions would be asked.

When Henry Fielding, as a justice of the peace for the City of Westminster, took up residence in Bow Street at the end of 1748 it was an event destined to have far-reaching results for the future of the British magistracy and the future of the British police. Sir Thomas de Veil, the well-known and flamboyant London justice, had lived in the same Bow Street house for six or seven years before his death in 1746, and had arranged a part of the ground floor, which he used as his official office, in the style of a formal courtroom. The exact scale of de Veil's activities is still obscure but it is believed that he was employed by the Government both on Secret Service work and on other confidential duties. When Henry Fielding became an active magistrate he was only forty-one years old but he seemed already to have reached the end of his turbulent career. His vogue as a popular satirical dramatist had been abruptly and intentionally terminated by Walpole's Licensing Act in 1737, his progress at the Bar had been curtailed by his declining health, his first novel had been received without acclamation, he was virtually destitute, and his personal reputation had been smeared by scandal and derision. Fielding, in fact, was offered the appointment by the anti-Walpole ministry largely as a rather murky reward for his political services, because, as the Duke of Bedford, the home secretary, explained, 'he could not indeed say that acting as a principal justice of the peace in Westminster was on all accounts very desirable, but all the world knew that it was a very lucrative office.'

Henry Fielding discovered that his predecessor at Bow Street had been collecting fees amounting to about £700 a year of what he later described as 'the dirtiest money on earth'. Fielding managed to reduce this amount to a little more than £300 annually, which he treated as being the legitimate income of his clerk. As for himself, he persuaded the Government to give him a small salary which he would regard as his sole remuneration. In a short while Fielding had completely reorganized the Bow Street office. Using his experience as a barrister, he conducted the judicial side of his duties in strict conformity with proper legal procedures, and he tried his cases on the same principles as those which applied in the higher courts. As far as policing arrangements were concerned, he placed no faith in the ordinary petty constables and watchmen, but recruited his own group of six full-time thief-takers. Fielding's original thief-takers, the forebears of the Bow Street Runners, soon became a highly proficient little squad, greatly feared and greatly respected by the underworld at large; they relied entirely on blood money payments for their livelihood.

Henry Fielding made a close study of the causes of crime and the habits of the criminal – indeed, in 1751 he published an informed treatise on the subject. The system of policing he adopted at Bow Street was as practical as it was elementary. He advertised in the Press that 'All persons who shall suffer by robbers, burglars etc.' should notify his office immediately, where his thief-takers were waiting at instant readiness to go out and investigate. Careful records were kept at the office of the details of offences and the descriptions of suspects. Lists of stolen property were notified to pawnbrokers, innkeepers, and the managers of stables. Above all, every member of the public was urged to join in the fight against crime. Fielding's methods were so successful that in 1753 the Government invited him to submit a plan for the suppression of the outbreak of lawlessness in London. He drew up a scheme which would cost £600, 'at which small charge', he said, 'I undertook to demolish the then reigning gangs'. In the event he was true to his word.

After Henry Fielding's retirement the Government continued to pay salaries to the magistrates at the Bow Street office and also assumed responsibility for the maintenance of the Bow Street thief-takers. Sir John Fielding, Henry's blind half-brother who took over from him, maintained and extended the existing arrangements for the apprehension of criminals. Sir John acknowledged no limits to the Bow Street jurisdiction; he treated the office as the police headquarters for the whole country and he established himself as a special executive-consultant to the home secretary on all matters appertaining to the preservation of law and order. In 1763 Sir John was allowed to form a body of eight horsemen for the purpose of patrolling the turnpike roads in the immediate vicinity of London during the hours of darkness. The experiment lasted for almost a year before being abandoned by the Government on account of its expense.

The Middlesex Justices Act of 1792, which was strenuously opposed by Fox and Sheridan but supported by William Pitt, authorized the establishment within the Metropolis of seven 'public offices' on the Bow Street model. The king was to appoint at each office three 'fit and able' police magistrates who would be paid an official stipend and would be prohibited from taking any fees. Each office was also to have a staff of six salaried constables. It was inevitable in that period that the appointment of the first stipendiary magistrates should be largely influenced by patronage and graft. 'It was the practice', said Peel at a later date, 'to select individuals to fill the office who, I must say, were utterly incompetent to discharge the duties which devolved upon them.' Gradually, however, as the salary was increased the standard improved, and although there was no statutory requirement that police magistrates should be legally qualified, from the year 1812 it became customary only to appoint barristers of at least three years' standing. By the early years of the nineteenth century the public offices were achieving a considerable reputation; indeed many large towns, especially in the mining and manufacturing areas, were applying to the home secretary for permission to adopt the metropolitan system and to have stipendiary magistrates of their own.

In 1790, ten years after the death of Sir John Fielding, the Bow Street police force was considerably enlarged by the formation of a foot patrol consisting of sixty-eight heavily armed men. They were not in uniform and were on duty from dusk until midnight patrolling the streets of the capital and the roads leading into it. In 1805 Sir John Fielding's abortive horse patrol was revived on a much larger scale as a uniformed para-military body with a strength of two officers and fifty-two men. The new horse patrol operated by night under the direction of the Bow Street magistrates. Their special task was safeguarding the roads in the vicinity of London from the depredations of the highwayman. The number of Bow Street Runners never seems to have risen above eight. They were the only skilled detectives in the country and were utilized for many different assignments including criminal investigation, the protection of the monarch, and the security of the Post Office and the Bank of England; they were also available for hire to any private individual who required their services.

The blood money system had become thoroughly discredited and in 1818 all the statutes offering rewards for the apprehension or conviction of criminals were repealed; the courts were authorized, however, to pay the expenses involved in the arrest and prosecution of a felon. Despite the upsurge of lawlessness throughout the country and the intermittent outbreaks of disorder and rioting, all classes of the British public remained adamantly opposed to the creation of a professional police force. A parliamentary committee in 1818 expressed the view that such a body would be 'odious and repulsive', and another commission four years later feared it would entail too great a curtailment of personal freedom. When Robert Peel was home secretary he persisted with a scheme for the establishment in London of a regular police force which would be 'consistent with the character of a free country'. As a preliminary step he set up in 1822 a uniformed Bow Street day patrol of three inspectors and twenty-four men, and then in 1829, after a parliamentary committee had reported that it was absolutely necessary 'to devise some means to give greater security to persons and property', he introduced his Metropolitan Police Improvement Bill. Peel conceived the new police as a major elaboration of the Bow Street patrols; they were placed under the control of two police magistrates and their headquarters was styled as an additional public office. Initially the

Metropolitan Police numbered just under one thousand men and operated within a radius of about seven miles from the centre of London, but it expanded rapidly both in strength and in territorial jurisdiction. After some hesitation Peel decided that his police should wear a uniform. However, any military aspect in their appearance was carefully avoided and the constables carried no weapons apart from their batons.

The parochial police in the Metropolis were gradually disbanded as the new force took over their districts, but the Bow Street Runners and the stipendiary constables at public offices were retained to handle the work of criminal investigation. The horse patrol stayed under the control of the chief magistrate at Bow Street until 1836 when it became the mounted section of the Metropolitan Police. The first two magistrates in charge of the Metropolitan Police – they were given the designation of 'commissioners of police' – were men of outstanding quality who moulded their men into a corps of highly efficient citizen-constables, as conscious of their civic responsibilities as they were of the powers and duties in preserving the law. The hostility of the public towards the new police continued unabated, giving rise to a succession of fake or exaggerated reports about their bad behaviour. This was partly due to a genuine fear that a centrally organized police force could so easily become an instrument of tyranny. It took time for the nation to realize that the Government had no intention of using it for such a purpose.

The transformation of the magistracy and the police in London had no immediate repercussions on the rest of the country. Towards the beginning of the nineteenth century the diligence and integrity of the justices of the peace had undergone a marked improvement and in the counties, where mistrust of the national executive was still strong, there was no inclination to exchange the unpaid justices, with local allegiances, for stipendiary magistrates who would probably be closely linked with the home secretary. Moreover, it was recognized that Quarter Sessions had attained a much higher degree of competence in performing both their judicial business and their conduct of county affairs. The work of local government, however, was becoming far too complex to be carried out by part-time justices, and between the years

1815 and 1835 they lost most of their administrative functions either to newly created statutory bodies or to the dominant responsibility of the Home Office. Notwithstanding these important changes, the ancient power of the justice of the peace in the realm of law and order was in no way diminished.

CHAPTER 18

THE SUPREMACY OF THE LAW

During this period, according to Holdsworth, the supremacy of the law became a reality. 'A spirit of legalism', he has written, 'pervaded the English government both central and local, and was reflected in the attitude of all Englishmen, from the highest to the lowest, towards their rulers.' The comprehension of the law by practitioners and students alike owed a great deal to William Blackstone, the first Vinerian Professor of Law at Oxford University, who between 1765 and 1769 published his four massive volumes of *Commentaries on the Laws of England*. Not only in Britain itself, but also in America and in the British colonies, Blackstone's commentaries were accepted as a definitive exposition of the Eglish law.

The name of Jeremy Bentham is of equal significance in the devolution of legal history with the name of William Blackstone; both men were concerned, however, with a different aspect of the law, Blackstone as the erudite exponent of principle and Bentham as the abstract visionary of reform. Their outlook and their judgement had been separated by a series of disruptive occurrences, the French Revolution, the Napoleonic Wars, and the economic transformation of Britain occasioned by the upsurge of industrial expansion. Bentham, in fact, endeavoured to subvert much which Blackstone had revered, for he was no respector of the inviolability of precedent nor of the sanctity of tradition. The English law was more than ready for a person of Bentham's restorative genius; at this time it still bore a medieval imprint and it was, as Maitland has described it, 'full of decaying husks'.

Above all Bentham advocated the modernization of the whole legal system. He was critical of the expense of litigation and the absence of local courts. He deplored the rigid absurdities of pleading, the use of fictions and technical jargon, and the separation of the courts of equity and common law. He wanted greater publicity for legal proceedings and the total abolition of the payment of officers of justice by fees. He upheld the merits of the jury of trial but condemned the secret enquiry by the grand jury. Reform, in Bentham's view, should be brought about by direct parliamentary legislation and should not be left to a more liberal interpretation by the judges. Before his death in 1832 Bentham had influenced a number of improvements in the legal procedure and in the penal code. The aftermath of his reasoning and the impact of his beliefs continued to shape the development of the British system of law for the greater part of the nineteenth century.

Following the revolution of 1688 the courts had come to be regarded as the guardians of the rule of law, the independent arbiters between the executive and the subject, and the protectors of civil liberties. During the reigns of the first two Georges the majority of the judges were honest and professionally competent, although there were a few of doubtful probity who used the prevailing fee-system for the purposes of self-enrichment. The security of judges' appointments was now undisputed: until the beginning of the reign of George III they could remain on the Bench for only six months after the death of a sovereign, but it was then enacted that the sovereign's death would no longer terminate their tenure of office. During the eighteenth century there was comparatively little legislative activity on the part of Parliament, due partially to a fallacious regard for the impeccability of the law, and it was left to the judges to mould the sequence of judicial decision. In 1815 a commission was appointed to study the duties and salaries of the judges. As a result of their report the fee-system was abolished in 1826 and the ordinary judge's salary was increased from £2,400 to £5,500 a year. The chief baron of the Exchequer was thenceforth paid £7,000 a year, the chief justice of Common Pleas £8,000, and the chief justice of the King's Bench £10,000.

During the eighteenth century the King's Counsel assumed precedence at the Bar over the serjeants, and judges ceased to be appointed solely from the serjeants' order, although they were still required to be members of the Serjeants' Inn. The King's Counsel, the barristers, and the bar students all belonged to one of the four Inns of Court, as during this period the Inns of Chancery declined into oblivion. The control of the Inns of Court became firmly vested in their respective benchers, who called students to the Bar and maintained discipline amongst their members. The benchers no longer arranged for the education of the students and they were left to plan their own courses of study. At the end of the eighteenth century the only requirement for a call to the Bar was that a student had 'kept terms' for five years by eating the prescribed number of dinners in the hall of his Inn. Solicitors and attornies were now completely merged into a single unified branch of the legal profession. Their governing body was first called the 'Society of Gentleman Practisers in the Courts of Law and Equity', but later this was changed to the simpler title of The Law Society. The principal functions of the society, which built its own hall in 1825, were the discipline of its members, the protection of their interests, and the supervision of their relationship with the Bar.

The House of Lords continued to exercise first instance jurisdiction over peers accused of treason or felony and to try impeachments brought by the House of Commons. It had also become established as the highest appellate tribunal in civil matters from the decision of any of the English, Scottish, or Irish courts. The impeachment procedure was falling into desuetude. The last four occasions on which it was used were in 1724, 1746, 1787, and 1805, and each of these cases was concerned with a serious charge against the criminal law. When the Lords was sitting in a judicial capacity every peer had the right to attend, and during the eighteenth century it was customary for the House to seek advice from the judges or the law officers. After 1784 the cases in the Lords were regularly reported and a convention began to emerge that only the legally qualified members should take part in judicial proceedings. The Privy Council remained the highest appeal court, both in criminal and in civil matters, for the British possessions beyond the seas. A statute in 1833 provided that cases would no longer be tried by the whole Privy Council but would be heard in the future by a special judicial committee composed entirely of judges.

The struggle between the Court of Chancery and the courts

of common law persisted right through the Hanover period. 'A man who owes a sum of money which it is not aggreeable to him to pay', said Bentham, 'fights a battle so long as he can on the ground of common law, and when he has no more ground to stand upon, he applies to a court of equity to stop the proceedings in the common law court'. There were many actions in which the plaintiff was uncertain whether his remedy lay in law or in equity and he might well commence his action in front of the wrong tribunal. The principal faults of the equity system were still its slowness, its technicality, and its expense; many subsidiary officers in the Court of Chancery were paid by fees and they deliberately protracted the formalities in a suit for this reason. Lord Hardwicke, who was lord chancellor from 1737 until 1756, shaped the principles of equity to a settled and methodical pattern, a process which was completed by Lord Chancellor Eldon at the beginning of the nineteenth century. In an era of reform there were two commissions of enquiry into the working of the Chancery Court in the 1820s, but their reports were followed by no immediate modifications. However, in 1833 the appointment of chancery masters was transferred to the Crown and it was enacted that they should be paid by fixed salaries instead of by fees. The common law, like equity, had failed completely to adapt itself to changing conditions, although the Earl of Mansfield, the lord chief justice of the King's Bench who had dominated legal thinking for almost the whole of the half-century from 1750 to 1800, had done his best to furbish it with a reasonably contemporary outlook. Numerous commissions were set up in the first part of the nineteenth century to investigate the archaisms of the common law, and six separate reports on the subject were published between 1829 and 1834.

The authority of the ecclesiastical courts was further curtailed in 1823 when their right to try cases of perjury was removed; they still retained jurisdiction in matrimonial and testamentary matters, and in certain cases of incest and defamation. The ancient County Courts continued to deal with civil actions where the amount involved was less than £2, and by the end of the Hanover period more than a hundred 'Courts of Requests' had been established by statute for the recovery of small debts. The work of the Coroner's

Court was now practically confined to the holding of inquests in cases of deaths in suspicious circumstances, and occasionally for deciding the ownership of treasure trove.

It was generally considered at this time that the British procedure at criminal trials* was fairer to the defendants than any of the systems which were followed on the continent of Europe, mainly because of the publicity of the proceedings, the absence of torture, and the bias in favour of individual liberty. The trials of that period, however, if judged by the standards of the present day, fell far below the basic requirements of justice. A criminal trial was still supposed to be finished at one continuous sitting, although this does not seem to have applied so strictly to indictments for misdemeanour; the right of a court to adjourn overnight in cases of treason and felony was not finally established until 1794. The defendant had no knowledge of the evidence which was going to be produced against him until the prosecution witnesses actually gave their testimony. Until 1836 defendants indicted for felonies were not allowed to be represented by professional advocates. This harsh rule was mitigated by the judges during the eighteenth century as they usually allowed the prisoner the assistance of a barrister to examine and cross-examine witnesses and, in fact, to do everything for him except make a closing speech to the jury. The Prisoners' Counsel Act of 1836 allowed a defendant charged with felony to be fully represented; it also enabled all persons committed for trial to inspect the depositions which had been taken against them. The defendant could not give evidence at his trial. Strangely enough, this was seen by Bentham as one of the greatest safeguards afforded to the accused as no questions could be put to him which might lead to proof of his guilt. Lastly, unless there was some obvious defect in the official record which would provide grounds for a Writ of Error, there was no appeal either against the verdict of the jury or the sentence of the court. It had become the unofficial practice of the judges, however, if they had any doubt as to whether the law had justified a conviction, to respite judgement and to discuss the matter with their fellow-judges in the Serjeants' Inn. If the consensus

* Trial by battle, after centuries of disuse, was formally abolished by statute in 1819.

of judicial opinion was that the conviction had been improper, it was then arranged for the prisoner to be granted a free pardon.

Blackstone, Henry Fielding, and Patrick Colquhoun all thought that the eighteenth-century juries, in their new-found independence, tended to acquit deliberately against the weight of the prosecution evidence, and the three of them agreed that this may have been due to a general revulsion against the brutality of the penal code. A jury was not allowed to separate after they had retired to consider their verdict and they were still forbidden to eat or drink whilst they were deliberating. They were confined, said a writer in 1730, 'in one room without meat, drink, fire or candle', until they had reached a verdict. An observer sent by the French Government in 1822 to study the administration of British criminal justice reported that the British did not wish to punish every crime for fear that the frequency of executions should weaken their example. In consequence, he said, they 'dismiss unpunished those whose guilt is not proved by the most positive testimony'. By this time several tenets had become accepted in the British criminal procedure which were immensely favourable to the accused. His bad character or his previous convictions could not be put in evidence by the prosecution, and if he had made a confession it was not admissible unless it was shown to be voluntary and free from the taint of duress. Above all, there was a presumption of innocence. 'I think it is probable', Stephen has written, 'that the length to which this sentiment has been carried in our criminal courts is due to a considerable extent to the extreme severity of the old criminal law, and even more to the capriciousness of its severity and the element of chance which . . . was introduced into its administration.'

With a people so mistrustful of their executive as the British, the grand jury system was generally regarded as a national protection. It was, said Henry Fielding, a privilege which distinguished the liberty of the subject, for no one could be convicted, or even tried, for any capital offence at the suite of the Crown. Nevertheless, the costs of prosecuting felons were gradually being thrown on the public purse: after 1836 half the expense of a prosecution was borne by the county and half by the Exchequer. Both Bentham and Colquhoun had even advocated that special counsel for the

Crown should be appointed to handle all prosecutions relating to public wrongs.

The British penal system was aptly known as the 'Bloody Code'. In 1800 there were more than 160 offences punishable by hanging and without Benefit of Clergy, although the majority of persons who received a capital sentence were subsequently granted a royal pardon and were transported overseas. In the first quarter of the nineteenth century Romilly and Mackintosh, two disciples of Jeremy Bentham, agitated in Parliament for the mitigation of punishment and, despite the opposition of the House of Lords, succeeded in reducing the number of offences to which the death penalty applied. Robert Peel, who abolished the nonsensical doctrine of Benefit in 1827, was by no means unsympathetic to the cause of penal reform and once described the British criminal law as being 'more severe on the whole than in any country in the world'.

Early in the eighteenth century transportation had begun to occupy a prominent position in the penal system. A statute in 1717 provided that prisoners convicted of certain clergyable felonies could be transported to the American plantations, where labour was extremely short, for a period of seven years. For some non-clergyable felonies a prisoner could be conditionally pardoned and ordered to be transported for fourteen years. From then on a large number of statutes were passed making various offences punishable with specific sentences of transportation. After the American colonies had declared their independence in 1776 transportation to the plantations was no longer possible and an Act was hurried through Parliament introducing a new type of sentence – a term of imprisonment with hard labour to be served in England. Owing to shortage of accommodation in the existing gaols a large number of convicts were then imprisoned in old warships, known as hulks, and were given the initial task of clearing the soil and gravel from the beds of navigable rivers. Meanwhile a plan was prepared for the establishment of a chain of penitentiary houses throughout the country, but before any headway had been made transportation was recommenced, this time to the newly discovered continent of Australia. The first convict fleet sailed for New South Wales in 1787, and an auxiliary penal settlement was set up in Van Dieman's Land in 1803. From that time forth the regular shipment of prisoners continued with little thought of the social, economic, or political consequences in the developing Australian colony. After twenty or thirty years transportation was meeting with mounting criticism, especially amongst the free settlers in New South Wales, and in 1837 a select committee of the House of Commons recommended the discontinuance of the whole scheme and the substitution of terms of imprisonment with hard labour to be served in prisons in Britain.

The historian W. E. H. Lecky has spoken of the 'great wave of philanthropic enthusiasm which proceeded from the Evangelical movement' during the latter part of the eighteenth century. Nowhere was this sentiment more manifest than in the agitation for penal reform. In 1764 the Italian writer Beccaria published his *Essay on Crimes and Punishments* in which he deprecated the cruelty and incoherence of the prevalent penal policies. John Howard brought out his exhaustive study of the conditions in the prisons in England and Wales in 1777, drawing attention to the over crowding, the extensive use of irons, the extortionate fees, the squalor, the drinking, and the idleness. A Government committee reported in 1811 that many offenders could be reclaimed by a form of imprisonment with a régime based upon 'seclusion, employment and religious instruction'. When Peel was home secretary in 1823 he introduced a Prison Act which abolished the payment of fees to gaolers and the general use of irons; women prisoners were henceforth to be separately confined and to be supervised by female wardresses; and rules were prescribed for the classification of prisoners and for the regulation of their clothing, health, labour, and education. These modifications and improvements owed a great deal to the selfless perseverance of Elizabeth Fry and the Quaker society for the 'Reform of Prison Discipline'. American prison methods were attracting much attention at this time and the British Government sent over a special representative to report upon them. He returned from his investigations in 1834 greatly impressed by what he had seen and having become an ardent disciple of a form of modified solitary confinement. In 1835 a statute was passed providing for the appointment by the home secretary of a team of prison inspectors empowered to standardize conditions in all the prisons in Britain.

During the course of the eighteenth century the burning of prisoners alive, cutting off their hands and ears, and slitting their nostrils, were either abrogated by Parliament or else allowed to fall into abeyance. Some of the most barbaric features of hanging, drawing, and quartering were dispensed with in 1814. Corporal punishment for women was abolished in 1820, the pressing of prisoners who refused to plead in 1827, the gibbeting of executed murderers in 1834, and the use of the pillory in 1837.

The spirit of personal liberty, wrote Blackstone, was deeply implanted in the British constitution; it was, he said, rooted in the very soil of Britain. More and more during the Hanover period people were looking to the courts to uphold their individual rights. Habeas corpus remained the great bulwark against unlawful detention, and the private citizen could also bring actions for trespass or false imprisonment against a justice of the peace who had exceeded his jurisdiction. Even the leading ministers of the Crown were confined to the power and authority permitted them by the law. In 1763 John Wilkes obtained £1,000 damages against a home secretary who had authorized his house to be entered and his private papers to be seized. In a series of cases at that time concerned with Wilke's publication of No. 45 of the *North Briton* it was decided that general warrants not naming any specific persons were illegal, and that a secretary of state had no instrinsic power of arrest.

Up to the closing years of the eighteenth century the Government continued to initiate prosecutions for seditious libel in order to stifle adverse criticism of their policies. An important dispute arose as to the right of a jury in trials for libel – in particular in trials for seditious libel. The majority of judges shared the view of Lord Mansfield that the jury could only decide, as a matter of fact, if the defendant had published the statement in question. The judge had to rule, as a matter of law, whether or not the statement constituted a libel. Jurors resented this limitation of their verdict and in several celebrated state trials between 1750 and 1790 they deliberately ignored the judge's direction and acquitted a defendant because they thought his words were justified or were not seditious. Fox's Libel Act in 1792 gave a jury the right to return a general verdict determining the guilt or innocence of the accused; the statute applied solely to cases of criminal libel but in the course of time a similar principle was extended to civil libel actions. Even after 1792 Government-inspired prosecutions still took place for seditious libel and for defamation of the king or his ministers. However, towards the end of the Hanover period these became comparatively rare in the new and more tolerant atmosphere which was then beginning to dawn.

The personal status of the people of Britain, their proprietorial rights, and their commercial transactions, were being subjected ever increasingly to the general surveillance of the courts. Lord Hardwicke's Act in 1753 forbade the solemnization of a marriage without the granting of a licence or the publication of banns, thus making a formal ceremony essential to every valid marriage. A statute in 1823 laid down new rules applicable to these formalities, and another in 1835 prohibited marriage within the degrees of relationship which had formerly ranked as canonical disabilities. A year later an Act was passed for the benefit of Dissenters, making possible a valid marriage without any religious ceremony at all. With regard to divorce the theory of the British law followed the doctrine of the Church of Rome, treating all non-voidable marriages as being indissoluble, but countenancing a form of judicial separation. A complete divorce was only obtainable by private Act of Parliament, which involved great expense and considerable delay. It was necessary first of all to procure a divorce *a mensa et thoro* in the ecclesiastical courts, and if the petition was founded on the wife's adultery the husband must have been awarded damages against the adulterous lover in a civil action. The case was then heard in the House of Lords which thoroughly investigated the matter, hearing the evidence of witnesses and the arguments of counsel. Between 1715 and 1800 a total of 134 bills of divorce were granted; the number granted between 1800 and 1850 was 90.

The improvements which were continually taking place in methods of land cultivation had resulted in considerable profit to the farmers, and also to the British nation which was enabled thereby to feed its greatly expanding population. The agricultural industry was becoming firmly organized on a capitalistic basis, with a number of statutes controlling various aspects of its development. The inclosure of wasteland, which continued actively until about 1820, enlarged the property already held by the upper classes and the wealthy members of the community, and destroyed the yeoman-farmer and a large proportion of smaller farmers as well. It also accelerated the drift of the rural population to seek employment in the towns.

There was still a twofold jurisdiction over wills, the ecclesiastical courts dealing with the administration and the granting of probate for devises of personalty, while the courts of common law controlled devises of real estate, no probate being necessary as the will itself was a sufficient document of title. A valid will could be made by a male of fourteen and by a female of twelve. A number of alterations were brought about by the Wills Act of 1837, which provided that all personal property and all real property, whatever the tenure, could in future be devised by will. The minimum age for making a will was raised to twenty-one, and a requirement was introduced that every will must be signed by or on behalf of the testator in the presence of two witnesses.

In the field of commerce, ordinary business partnerships were at an immense disadvantage compared with companies incorporated by charter. A partnership, possessing no independent legal status, could only sue or be sued in the names of the partners. Each partner was personally liable for the whole of the partnership's debts, and a partnership was prohibited from raising any transferable stock. Because the acquisition of an original charter was such a slow and costly transaction a practice grew up for a newly forming company to purchase an obsolete charter from one of the many companies which had declined as a result of the abolition of Crown monopolies for foreign trading. This process, and the disposal of transferable shares without a valid charter or the authority of an Act of Parliament, was declared illegal by the Bubble Act in 1720. After that for more than a hundred years the commercial lawyers were exercising their utmost ingenuity in contriving stratagems to ameliorate the position of the unincorporated business associations. It was not until 1834 that, by the Trading Companys Act, the Crown was given the right to bestow on any company all the privileges of incorporation, except the limited financial liability of its members, without the actual granting of a charter. By a further Act in 1837 companies could be formed in which the liability of the members was restricted to an amount which had been specified in the formation documents.

It has already been seen that an Act in the reign of Anne had given statutory copyright to the authors of published books. The Artists Copyright Act of 1735 extended a similar protection to the makers of prints and engravings. This statute was passed in the interests of William Hogarth who was suffering considerable harm from the issuing of inferior copies of his works. Copyright was also applied to works of sculpture in 1814, and in the same year the author's copyright was lengthened to twenty years – if the author was alive at the end of that period his copyright continued for the rest of his life. The copyright of plays derived from an Act in 1836; paintings and musical compositions, however, remained unprotected.

Trademarks seem to have originated in the signs which merchants attached to their shops and later to their wares. The first reported case in which they were accorded legal sanction took place in 1783 when Lord Mansfield held that it was an actionable fraud for one merchant to use the name or the mark of another. During the eighteenth century, too, the law of patents became firmly established, safeguarding an original invention or a new process from imitation and unfair competition.

The role of the justices of the peace in labour relations had radically altered by the time of the accession of George III, and they were no longer concerned with the coercion of workers into compulsory service, but rather with adjudicating in disputes between employers and employed. An Act in 1746 gave jurisdiction to one or more justices to hear complaints arising between masters and an extensive category of 'servants'. On the complaint of a servant in relation to his wages, the magistrates could compel the master to pay any sum which they found to be due. On the complaint of a master regarding 'any misdemeanour, miscarriage or ill behaviour of the servant in his or her service or employment', the magistrates might deduct a part of the wages due to the servant, dismiss him from his employment, or sentence him to a whipping and detention in a house of correction. A statute in 1823 gave the magistrates even wider powers.

An Act in 1814 repealed the long-standing statute of Elizabeth which had enforced a seven-year apprenticeship upon everyone who wished to practise any 'trade or mystery'. Thenceforward apprenticeship became a purely voluntary institution.

The growth of the manufacturing industries gave rise to a large increase in the number of secret societies amongst the mass of employees who were herded together in the factories and towns. The situation was considered so menacing that the Government passed the Combination Acts of 1799 and 1800, by which it became a summary offence, triable by one justice and punishable with three months' imprisonment, for any persons to band together with the object of exerting pressure on their employers. A combination in restraint of trade was already an indictable conspiracy at common law but it was hoped that the creation of the new statutory offences would serve to strengthen the hand of the authorities. In the event the working classes having sensed their power were not to be deterred by the threat of any criminal proceedings. It is strange, as the Webbs have pointed out in their study of the trade union movement, that trade unionism in Britain did not arise 'as a protest against intolerable oppression'. On the contrary, it gained its impulsion in the early days from those sections of the wage-earners who were comparatively well paid and independent. It had soon become apparent that this new-found cohesion of the labour force would not be easily crushed, and in 1824 a parliamentary committee urged that masters and servants negotiating rates of pay and hours of work should be 'at perfect liberty to make such agreements as they mutually think proper'. This proposal was embodied in a statute a year later and the combination laws were repealed. At once there was such a surge of strikes, rioting, and violence that another Act was hurriedly passed restoring the common law prohibition on combinations, with the special exception of associations for the regulation of wages or hours of labour. Thus the trade unions, whilst basically remaining unlawful associations, did receive a partial form of recognition from the legislature.

In the eighteenth century it would have been considered an intolerable intrusion for Government to have interfered with conditions of private employment. However, in 1802 an Act was passed by Parliament regulating the cleanliness, clothing, and working hours of children in the mills and factories. A large number of pauper children from the south of England had been flocking to the northern factory areas where the unsupervised, sweated labour and the overcrowded, unhygienic accommodation had resulted in continual outbreaks of epidemic diseases. An Act in 1819 attempted to curb the exploitation of children in the cotton mills, forbidding the employment in them of juveniles below the age of nine and restricting to twelve hours the working day of boys and girls under the age of sixteen. As the task of supervising these requirements was placed upon the justices of the peace, the mill-owners could very easily evade them. A more comprehensive statute, which applied to many different types of mills and factories, was passed in 1833; it prohibited night-work for children under eighteen, and limited the working week for those under thirteen to forty-eight hours, and for those under eighteen to sixty-eight hours. Children under thirteen were only permitted to work for ten hours a day. Provision was also made for school attendance and the appointment of official factory inspectors.

Throughout the eighteenth century Parliament had endeavoured unsuccessfully to alleviate the problems of pauperism by the provision of more workhouses under the management of the parish authorities. In public thinking destitution and vagrancy were still closely interwoven. A statute in 1744, after reciting that 'the number of rogues, vagabonds, beggars and other disorderly persons daily increases', went on to define the various classes of vagrants, the vagrancy offences, and the prescribed penalties. The progress of the Industrial Revolution increased the incidence of poverty and caused the situation to deteriorate still further. Gilbert's Act in 1782 stated that owing to the inefficiency and misconduct of the parish overseers the money raised for the relief of the poor was frequently misapplied. A new body of salaried officials called the guardians of the poor was created and the destitute were divided into the 'able-bodied poor', who were to be found employment, and the 'impotent poor', who would be maintained in the workhouses. A statute in 1795 allowed for outside relief to be granted to the needy in their own homes.

A government commission was appointed in 1832 to study the whole Poor Law system. It reported two years later that there should be a rigid classification of the poor and that the various categories, such as the young and the old, should be kept in separate workhouses. The commission recommended the establishment of a central authority and the grouping of parishes together for the sake of more effectual control. These and other of the commission's proposals were incorporated in the Poor Law Amendment Act of 1834.

Part IX

THE VICTORIAN PERIOD

(1837–1901)

CHAPTER 19

THE ADVENT OF DEMOCRACY

By the commencement of the Victorian period the essential fabric of the British constitution had been wholly woven. There was a tripartite division of the powers of state between the Crown, Parliament and the courts, with the House of Commons as the predominant partner and with all the institutions of government constantly subjected to the omnipotent supremacy of the law.

'The principal motive force of the executive power in the British constitution', wrote Holdsworth, 'has always been the royal prerogative'. In 1837 when Victoria ascended the throne the personal dominion of the sovereign had considerably diminished, but the prerogative was still a vital factor in the ruling of the nation. This nebulous authority of a bygone age, closely controlled by legal convention, was exercised mainly by the Cabinet. In the field of foreign affairs it controlled the making of treaties, the declaration of peace or war, the appointment of ambassadors, and the granting of diplomatic immunity. In domestic matters it sanctioned the appointment of judges, magistrates, and a host of other officials, the creation of new titles, the implementation of decisions relating to the defence of the realm, the extradition of offenders, and a number of other incidents of daily administrative routine. It was by virtue of the prerogative that the Crown was established as a component of the legislature, with the right of affirming or rejecting any Bills which had been passed in both Houses, of nominating or dismissing the ministers of the Government, and in the last eventuality of dissolving Parliament and impelling a new election. A certain amount of prerogative authority was being gradually merged into various statutory powers, and from this fact, as from a complex system of checks and balances, the unwritten British constitution had derived an appeciable measure of endurance and stability.

Whenever the Cabinet acted under the royal prerogative they did so as servants of the Crown on behalf of their sovereign. During Victoria's reign many of the modern principles of cabinet government were becoming firmly established. It was accepted that the sovereign must choose as prime minister the leader of the largest party in the House of Commons, and that if his party should be defeated on an important issue the prime minister should offer to resign. The sovereign was bound to make appointments to the Cabinet in accordance with the wishes of the prime minister, and cabinet ministers formed the connecting links between legislature and the executive. Although the prime minister consulted the sovereign with regard to governmental policies, the Crown was supposed to be removed from active politics – a tenet with which Queen Victoria sometimes found it difficult to comply. In theory the sovereign was only justified in using a direct parliamentary initiative when no party had a clear majority in the Commons and it became necessary to offer the prime ministership to some statesman not commanding overall parliamentary support. Cabinet ministers were ordinarily selected from the ruling party and adopted a collective responsibility for their actions and decisions.

It has been seen that during the eighteenth century both the officials of the royal household and the senior ministers of state were paid by the sovereign out of a fund known as the civil list, which was acquired in part from excise duties and in part from hereditary revenues. The practice started by George III of surrendering most of the hereditary revenues in return for a fixed income had been followed by his successors to the throne. During the early years of the nineteenth century some state expenses were removed entirely from the civil list, and this process was continued during Victoria's reign until eventually the payments from the civil list were confined to the personal expenses of the queen and the costs of the royal household.

Burke had contended that a member of Parliament was elected as the representative of his constituents rather than as the propagator of their views. This was certainly the attitude of a large section of the humbler voters enfranchised by the Reform Act of 1832, who respected the superior education and intellect of their members and their greater experience in public and political affairs. As a consequence, the back-benchers in the early part of the Victorian period occupied a position of considerable independence and influence. Their basic allegiance to their leaders was seldom over-rigid and their critical opinions were usually treated with great respect. It is said that in the eighteenth and the early nineteenth centuries an individual speech could often sway the vote, but thereafter the growth of party ideology and discipline tended to narrow down the permissible discretion of members, thereby increasing the control of the prime minister and cabinet ministers in parliamentary debates.

The procedures in both Houses of Parliament altered very little in the years immediately after the Reform Act. A highly-paid and impartial Speaker was now a feature of the Commons, and the religious disqualifications from membership were gradually being removed: Roman Catholics had been eligible since 1829, Quakers were no longer debarred after 1833, and Jews after 1855. The property qualification for county members was also abolished about this time. The House of Commons was in complete financial control of the country owing to the convention that money Bills could neither be originated nor amended in the Lords. Apart from this limitation the House of Lords was an equal legislative partner. Both Houses habitually varied one another's Bills, but possibly because their membership was drawn predominantly from the same social class they were usually able to work together in an atmosphere of mutual deference and courtesy. It was generally felt that a second chamber was essential to the constitution, and also that a hereditary House should stand in an inferior position to a chamber which was chosen by popular election at the will of the people.

It was fortunate for Britain during the initial years of Victoria's reign that the two main political parties in Parliament were aware of the paramount need for adapting the law and the institutions of the British nation to the new conception of an industrialized democracy. Nevertheless, when Sir Robert Peel formed his second administration in 1841 the country was undergoing a serious depression, brought about by an epoch of diminishing trade and a succession of bad harvests. It was in that setting that the movement known as Chartism had emerged, drawing its main support from a segment of the working population which was entirely unrepresented in Parliament. Chartism really originated out of the total inability of the lowest-paid sections of the labouring poor to improve their basic conditions. At the start their claims were temperate and reasonable. They were seeking, so they said, the achievement of equal social and political rights for all classes of society. They embodied their demands in a 'People's Charter' published in the spring of 1838. They desired universal male suffrage, annual parliaments, an equating of the size of electoral districts, the payment of members, and a secret ballot. A great national petition was organized in support of their objectives. But towards the end of the year the movement was becoming more militant. Mass meetings and torchlight processions were organized throughout the country at which the speeches were both violent and revolutionary, and the moderate leaders were gradually supplanted by a coterie of dangerous and unprincipled agitators.

For a few years there were intermittent strikes, riots, woundings, and deaths as the Chartists pursued their cause. In 1842 they brought to the House of Commons a list of grievances bearing almost three and a half million signatures and demanding universal suffrage as an immediate antidote to the social injustices which were then prevailing. In the ensuing debate on this massive petition the leaders of both parties were opposed to any change in the electoral system and Lord Macaulay gave a solemn warning that universal suffrage, unless preceded by universal education, would be 'utterly incompatible with the very existence of civilization'.

The strikes, the rioting, and the vandalism continued unabated, causing disquiet amongst the movement's erstwhile supporters and nullifying any sympathy towards it which had existed amongst the middle classes. Another bad harvest, and a resultant economic depression, in 1845 rekindled the revolutionary ardour of the Chartists and enabled them to launch a new programme of violent agitation. Eventually in 1848 the Government clamped down. Troops were concentrated; emergency legislation was rushed through Parliament; there were warnings and arrests. And in the face of this show of resolution Chartism entirely collapsed. The reasons for its failure were manifold. The Chartist leaders were inefficient and uneducated and they had no unified objectives. Above all, the British people were in no mood for a popular rising. They had fashioned a polity appropriate to their national character and centuries of struggle and achievement had engrained in them a respect for authority and an obedience of the law.

In 1850 the question of enlarging the franchise was again raised in Parliament but little interest was aroused. There was a widespread feeling that a working-class electorate might choose to be represented in the Commons by members of their own fraternity and consequently that the time of the House would be endlessly diverted to debates on wages and the conditions of labour in general. Likewise the proposal that voting should be by ballot failed to awaken any widespread enthusiasm, the Liberal statesman Palmerston once remarking that it would be unworthy of the straightforward and honest English elector 'to go sneaking to the ballot-box' in order to record his vote.

When Palmerston's Government fell in 1858 it was succeeded by a Conservative administration headed by the Earl of Derby, with Disraeli as chancellor of the exchequer. Disraeli was a shrewd enough politician to have realized that a further measure of electoral reform was now inevitable, and rather than allowing the Liberals to gain the credit for introducing it he persuaded his colleagues to accept a limited extension of the county occupational franchise. However, this was never passed into law and in the summer of 1859 Palmerston returned to power, remaining as prime minister until his death in 1865. At the time of the 1865 general election only just under a fifth of the adult male population in England and Wales had been eligible to vote and the distribution of seats had borne no relationship to the size of the various constituencies. By now both parties were in agreement on the need for electoral reform. Earl Russell, who had taken over from Palmerston, brought forward some tentative suggestions, but whilst these were still being debated his ministry resigned and once again Derby took office with Disraeli combining the leadership of the House of Commons and his former position as chancellor of the exchequer.

Derby and Disraeli managed to pass their new Reform Act in 1867, adding 938,000 voters to an existing electorate of 1,057,000 in England and Wales. In the counties, where the occupation franchise was lowered to £12, the middle classes were still predominant; but in the boroughs, where the right to vote was now based on household suffrage, the working class were suddenly transformed into a position of absolute electoral power. The Act brought about a far more rational distribution of seats, set out a code for the fairer conduct of elections, and forbade certain corrupt electoral practices. It was also provided that the duration of Parliament should no longer be affected by the demise of the Crown. Supplementary Reform Acts were passed, applicable to Ireland and to Scotland.

In 1866 Gladstone had taken over the leadership of the Liberal party and in 1868 Disraeli became the leader of the Conservatives. For many years the unremitting duel between these two outstanding statesmen was to dominate British politics. One of the far-reaching results of the 1867 Act was to increase the importance of party organizations, with the result that members began to subscribe more to a party programme and less to an individual standpoint. In consequence of a report on the conduct of parliamentary and municipal elections Gladstone introduced a universal system of voting by ballot in 1872. Gladstone was also responsible for the democratization of the county franchise by the introduction of household suffrage. Since 1867, as has been seen, the householder in a borough had a right as such to vote, but this did not apply in the counties, due no doubt to the completely different structure of social life. The Franchise Bill of 1884, designed to remedy this inconsistency, had an easy passage through the Commons but met with stiff opposition from the Conservative peers in the House of Lords. In a moment of crisis a 'Peers against the People' controversy swept the country. In the end good sense prevailed and the statute, which redistributed a number of seats and increased the electorate from about three millions to about five millions, was passed into law.

During the eighteenth century a position in the Civil Service had still been regarded as a gift or reward from the king. Civil servants, in company with most officers of state, had been principally paid out of fees collected by them from the public, with a small additional supplement from the civil list. Their appointments had beeen at the pleasure of the Crown and had entirely lacked any element of permanence. During the first half of the nineteenth century the heads of department were allowed to allocate most of the posts in their own offices, and although this arrangement was subject to all the usual abuses of patronage, it seems that there was a general appreciation of the necessity for maintaining a reasonably competent system of administration.

The first two moves towards the establishment of a permanent and independent Civil Service, both taken towards the close of the Hanover period, had been the provision of retirement pensions for various classes of civil servants, and a fairly general regulation debarring them from sitting in the House of Commons. Civil servants at this time were growing in numbers and in importance. In 1848 the method of paying them by fees was abolished and thenceforth they received regular salaries, the amounts of which were approved by Parliament. Lord Macaulay had urged in 1833 that recruitment to the Civil Service ought to be by competitive examination. In 1853 a commission reported in favour of examinations for the higher grades and four years later this recommendation was partially implemented, the final selection of candidates being left to the discretion of the Civil Service commissioners. It was not until 1870 that a method of entry based purely on open competitive examinations was fully adopted. By the end of the Victorian period the Civil Service, with full freedom to recruit from the ablest graduates of the universities, had improved immeasurably and had started to build up a tradition of integrity, efficiency, and complete political impartiality.

During the eighteenth century the control exercised by the central executive over the various organs of local administration had been fairly lax. The nineteenth century was marked by the development of an organized and honest system of local government. Jeremy Bentham had always contended that local government should operate upon an identical structure to the central elective body and that, although it should possess a measure of autonomy, it should be subject to the constant supervision of the national Government. This view commanded wide support for, as Professor Dicey has said, the Victorian era was very much a period 'of Benthamism and individualism'. The Municipal Reform Act of 1835 had created a new statutory authority, the municipal corporation, which was empowered to take over from the improvement commissions such essential services as the paving, draining, cleansing, and lighting of the streets, the regulation of building, and the maintenance of public order. However, the 1835 Act was permissive and not mandatory and the majority of the local representative bodies chose to continue with their existing arrangements. In consequence, the civic responsibilities were divided between the municipal corporations, the improvement commissions, the local boards and, sometimes in London, the vestries. By the beginning of Victoria's reign the parish had lost most of its former significance as a unit of local government, but it remained as a unit of rate assessment until 1868 when parishes were finally deprived of their right to levy compulsory church rates.

In spite of an increasing civic sense – an embryonic community conscience – the lure of self-interest and the lust for parochial power were still dominant both in urban and country districts. It might have been due to this, as much as to what the Webbs have called 'the characteristic English preference for local over central administration', that any suggestions for the transfer of essential social services to a national control encountered such strenuous resistance. Nevertheless, the complexities of an industrialized society with the interdependence of its geographical segments, the growing professionalism of everyday life, and the special skills fostered by technical advancement, were numbering the days of the unpaid, amateur administrator.

A clear indication of the inability of the parishes to fulfil their ancient responsibilities was demonstrated in regard to the upkeep of the highways. In 1835 there were no less than 15,000 'highway parishes', individually responsible for the roads which passed through their areas. At that time the road system was totally inadequate to provide for the volume of traffic which was using it and the road surfaces were insufficient to stand up to the increasing weight of many of the vehicles. Improved methods of road construction were available but these were obviously beyond the financial resources of the parish surveyors. In an effort to improve the situation an Act was passed in 1862 giving justices power to group their parishes into highway districts governed by highway boards, but this statute was only permissive and many counties declined to adopt it. Even the turnpike trusts, which were operated on a commercial basis, were finding it impossible to meet their escalating expenditure and more and more of them were declining into bankruptcy. The end was inevitable. In 1878 the highways were removed altogether from the management of the parishes and placed under the general direction of the newly created Local Government Board. The last turnpike trust came to an end in 1895.

The Poor Law Amendment Act of 1834 had vested absolute control of the Poor Law in the hands of the central Government, acting through a body known as the Poor Law commissioners who succeeded within a matter of a few years in introducing a considerable measure of uniformity throughout the country. Workhouses were standardized in pattern and, although a lot depended on the masters or matrons in charge of them, were usually bleak and uncomfortable places operating under a rigid code of discipline. There was little segregation of the various classes of inmates and until 1842, when a degree of amelioration took place, the conditions resembled those of a prison more than a charitable institution. Married couples were separated, parents did not have any right to see their children, there were no facilities for exercise, meals were taken in silence, smoking and reading were forbidden, opportunities for receiving visits were strictly limited, and permission to leave the workhouse was seldom granted. In 1847 the Poor Law Commission was disbanded and its powers were transferred to the Poor Law Board. After that the conditions in workhouses gradually improved, particularly in the treatment of the sick, the elderly, and the young. An effort was made to educate the children – in 1848 there were between 40,000 and 50,000 children resident in workhouses – firstly at special poor-law schools and then by boarding them out to ordinary educational establishments.

Public health was another administrative field which was proving to be completely beyond the capabilities of the existing local authorities. The outbreaks of cholera in 1831–3 and again in 1847–8, at a time when medical knowledge was becoming more aware of the connection between dirt and disease and of the necessity for an adequate supply of pure water to large towns, resulted in the Public Health Act of 1848. This statute created a Board of Health, on similar lines to the Poor Law Board, which was empowered to make extensive regulations for preventing the spread of infectious diseases. The Act was only permissive, but the inhabitants of any district where the recent death-rate had exceeded a certain proportion of the population could petition for an enquiry from a Board of Health inspector and, if he thought fit, the area could be brought within the control of the Act. The Board of Health was extremely unpopular and it was disbanded in 1858, its duties being handed over to the Privy Council and the home secretary.

By the Sanitary Act of 1866, which was passed in the wake of another epidemic of cholera, the local authorities were compelled to provide sanitary inspectors for their respective areas. In 1868 Disraeli appointed a royal commission to carry out a full enquiry into the nation's sanitary conditions. In their subsequent report the commission attempted to enumerate the certain necessities 'for civilized life', mentioning in particular the need for a good water supply, a proper system of drainage, the regular inspection of the sale of food, and the removal of sources of infection. The report went on to advocate the creation of a single new government department which would control all the divers aspects of public health. In 1871 the responsibilities for hygiene which had been vested in the home secretary and the Privy Council since 1858 were transferred to the Local Government Board, and the Public Health Act of 1875, besides dividing Britain into urban and rural sanitary districts, imposed a number of statutory requirements for the maintenance of the health and well-being of the nation.

Early in the nineteenth century the British Government also began to take an interest in the education of the masses. It is difficult to say whether their initial motive was one of genuine philanthropy or was due to a belief that the intellectual and moral training of the young would serve in time to curtail the incidence of crime and to eradicate the violence of the mob. Certainly Lord Macaulay is on record as declaring, 'The gross ignorance of the common people is a principal cause of danger to our persons and our property'. In 1833 Parliament voted an annual grant of £20,000 in aid of the charitable education of the poor. The money was to be administered by two private societies, one representing the Church of England and the other the Non-conformists, and was to be used for the construction and upkeep of elementary schools. Six years later, in spite of considerable opposition, the grant was increased to £30,000, and its administration was taken over by an education committee of the Privy Council. In order to give the committee a more direct control, inspectors were appointed to supervise the management and teaching at all elementary schools, and in 1861 the receipt of a grant from the committee became dependent upon their satisfactory reports.

The education grant, which was also used for the training of teachers, was progressively increased and soon exceeded half a million pounds a year, but there were still very few persons in Britain who envisaged that schooling should be either free, compulsory, or non-secular. In fact by the middle of the century most young children were obtaining an education of some sort, those attending at elementary schools usually remaining there until the age of eleven with their parents paying less than a third of the total cost. The extension of the franchise brought about by the Reform Act of 1867, coupled with the realization that the British educational system was inferior to that of many of the countries on the Continent, eventually persuaded the politicians of the necessity for improvement. The Education Act of 1870, whilst not establishing a universal network of gratuitous schools, divided up the whole country into school districts and stipulated that the education department of the Privy Council should ensure that every district had sufficient places for its intending pupils. The statute further provided that all elementary schools should be granted complete religious freedom, and that parents who were unable to afford the modest scale of fees for their children's education might be excused from making any form of contribution. Accordingly 1870 may be regarded as the year in which Britain first accepted the proposition that the State is responsible for the education of its citizens. The element of compulsion was introduced in 1877 when another Act laid down a duty, subject to penalties, on every parent of children between the ages of five and fourteen to see that they received sufficient education in reading, writing, and arithmetic. The fees at elementary schools were abolished in 1891 and thereafter all pupils could attend them free of charge.

When household suffrage for the House of Commons became general in 1884 it seemed inevitable that the nation would also expect to be given the right of electing its own local rulers. By then the whole system of local government had become cumbersome and unco-ordinated with administrative powers being exercised separately both by the justices of the peace and by numerous *ad hoc* boards, all acting independently of each other. The Local Government Act of 1888 created a new unit of local government called the county council to take over all the varied responsibilities of county administration. County councils were to be elected by universal suffrage – women as well as men being allowed to vote but not to stand as candidates – the limits of their jurisdiction conforming to the boundaries of the ancient shires, and several large counties being divided up between two or more councils. A number of towns with populations of over 50,000 were granted their own councils and treated in all respects as though they had been separate counties.

The British preference for local over centralized control was never more manifest on any subject than on the management of the police. The hostility felt by Londoners towards the Metropolitan Police had not diminished. In the early days after the formation of the new force it was common enough for constables on duty to be subjected to unprovoked assaults and it is said that a number of carriage-owners encouraged their coachmen to lash out at police officers with their whips or even to drive their vehicles straight at them. In 1830 the police commissioners felt it necessary to issue a special instruction urging that despite the constant provocation, all policemen 'should do their duty with every possible moderation and forbearance'. The situation reached a climax in the spring of 1833 when a revolutionary society ignored a government ban and held a large open-air meeting in Coldbath Fields on the outskirts of London. When a few hundred police armed with batons attempted to break up the assembly, they were ferociously attacked by a mob wielding knives, cudgels, and stones. Not by any means for the last time, the heavily outnumbered police resisted valiantly. At the conclusion of the fighting few of them were uninjured, two were suffering from knife wounds, and one had been stabbed to death. It must be a reflection on the mood of the time that the coroner's jury, with the utmost cynicism, recorded a verdict that the deceased officer had been killed by an act of 'justifiable homicide'.

Nevertheless, even the most ardent opponents of the new police were soon forced to admit that they had achieved a dramatic decline in the crime-rate of the Metropolis. For the first time within living memory people could walk the streets in safety at night and could feel that their homes, their offices, and their shops were relatively secure from burglary. The Government were determined to bring all the police in London under the control of the commissioners and in 1839 the few remaining independent groups, including the Bow Street Runners, were disbanded. Britain was left with no detective force until 1842 when the home secretary authorized the appointment of twelve plain-clothes policemen to operate anywhere in the country. Shortly afterwards their number was increased to fifteen. It was not until 1869 that it was decided to create a detective branch in every police division, the commissioner at the time expressing considerable doubts about the practicality of the scheme which, he said, was 'viewed with the greatest suspicion and jealousy by the majority of Englishmen'.

In country districts the justices of the peace jealously guarded their direct control of the inefficient and amateur constabulary, whilst in the boroughs the Government's endeavours to improve the police system met with little response. In 1839 and 1840 the justices were empowered to recruit professional police forces and to replace their high constables with full-time officials to be known as chief constables. However, very few localities chose to avail themselves of these advantages and eventually by an Act of 1856 the creation of professional police forces throughout the country became mandatory. Home Office inspectors of police were appointed and if their reports upon any county or borough force were sufficiently satisfactory the State contributed a fixed proportion towards its maintenance. The office of high constable was officially abolished in 1869 and that of petty constable in 1872.

The numerical strength of the Metropolitan Police was growing steadily. In 1880 it numbered over ten thousand men. Even so, at times the resources of the professional police were stretched to breaking point, especially when they were given the task of combating mob violence. On one occasion, known as 'Bloody Sunday', in November 1887 they were unable to break up an illegal Irish Nationalist meeting in Trafalgar Square and guardsmen and cavalry had to come to their assistance. No shots were fired but both sides suffered heavy casualties and two of the crowd died later from their injuries.

CHAPTER 20

THE RECONSTRUCTION OF THE COURTS

It has been seen how the British judicial system grew up in a piecemeal manner, and during the early years of Victoria's reign there was a growing awareness, outside the more conservative elements of the lawyers themselves, that it would have to be drastically remoulded. The principal defects were obvious – the overlapping jurisdictions, the expense, the delays, the cumbersome procedures, the absence of a readily accessible appellate tribunal, and a host of anachronistic devices which had completely outlived both their relevance and their utility.

Around the middle of the nineteenth century the Government introduced some reforms which, although steps in the right direction, were far too half-hearted and insufficient. In 1848 a new court called the Court of Crown Cases Reserved was created by Act of Parliament with jurisdiction to quash or to confirm a criminal conviction when a point of law had been referred to it by the judge or the chairman of Quarter Sessions who had presided at the trial. In fact this measure only gave statutory authority to the existing practice of the judges to rule on the legal points in Serjeants' Inn. Another Act three years later strengthened the powers of the Exchequer Chamber in hearing appeals from the courts of Queen's Bench, Common Pleas and Exchequer. A number of obsolete formalities in litigation were abolished in 1852 along with some of the needless technicalities of civil pleading, and this process was carried further by the Common Law Procedure Act of 1854. Lord Cairns's Act in 1858 gave the courts of common law the right to administer certain equitable remedies and the Court of Chancery the ability to award some of the remedies which had formerly been exclusive to the courts of common law.

A commission appointed in 1850 recommended that matrimonial causes should be removed from the ecclesiastical courts and that a regular divorce court should be established. In spite of intense opposition, led by Gladstone and the leaders of the Anglican Church, an Act was passed by Parliament in 1857 providing that for the future 'all jurisdiction in matters matrimonial' should be exercised by a new court to be known as the Court for Divorce and Matrimonial Causes. Perhaps the most controversial part of the 1857 statute was the sections which related to the substantive law. Divorce *a mensa et thoro* was abolished and replaced by a decree of judicial separation. This could be granted, as it had been in the old ecclesiastical courts, on the grounds of cruelty or adultery, and in addition for desertion without reasonable cause for two years or more. The Divorce Court was also empowered to grant a complete divorce, a divorce *a vinculo matrimonii*, though here the grounds were different for both spouses, the husband being able to divorce his wife only for adultery and the wife being able to divorce her husband for incestuous adultery, rape, sodomy, bestiality, or adultery combined either with cruelty or with desertion for at least two years. The Act entitled a husband to claim damages against a co-respondent without the need for a separate action, and it laid down that decrees of divorce could not be made absolute until three months after the granting of decree nisi – this was increased to six months in 1866.

In 1857 too the ecclesiastical courts were divested of the power 'to grant or revoke probate of wills or letters of administration of the effects of deceased persons' and this jurisdiction was transferred to a new Court of Probate which, like the Divorce Court, was to have its own judge. Thereafter the jurisdiction of the ecclesiastical courts was strictly confined to the affairs of the Church.

A far more important reform of the judicial structure was brought about by the Judicature Act of 1873. This statute was introduced by Gladstone's first Government and was planned and largely drafted by the lord chancellor, Lord Selborne, though it received the wholehearted support of Lord Cairns who had served as lord chancellor in Disraeli's short-lived ministry in 1868. The preamble to the Judicature Act sets out its purpose as being the creation of a Supreme Court and the provision of a better administration of justice.

The Supreme Court was to consist of a High Court of Justice and a Court of Appeal, and the principles of equity and common law were to be fused so that every judge would apply them concurrently irrespective of the court in which he was sitting.

The High Court of Justice was to consist of the courts of Chancery, Queen's Bench, Common Pleas, Exchequer, Admiralty, Probate, and Divorce, and was also to include the London Court of Bankruptcy which had been formed in 1869. The Court of Appeal was constituted of five *ex officio* judges, the lord chancellor, the lord chief justice, the master of the rolls, the chief justice of common pleas and the chief baron of the exchequer, and these would sit in company with a few specially appointed appeal judges to be called lord justices of appeal. The Act provided that all the judges of the Supreme Court should hold office for life, subject to their removal in accordance with the Act of Settlement on an address to the sovereign presented by both Houses of Parliament. Only a barrister of at least ten years' standing might be appointed a Supreme Court judge and it was no longer necessary for him to have previously been a serjeant-at-law.

Lord Selborne had originally envisaged the new Court of Appeal as becoming the highest appellate tribunal in Britain and accordingly one of the sections in the Judicature Act abolished the appellate jurisdiction of the House of Lords. However, this provision caused the greatest consternation amongst the peers and, following the election of a Conservative Government, it was reversed in 1876 by the Appellate Jurisdiction Act which provided that appeals would lie to the Lords from the Court of Appeal in England and also from the appellate courts in Scotland and Ireland. Furthermore, it was stipulated that when the House of Lords was hearing an appeal the only members entitled to sit would be the lord chancellor, peers who had held high judicial office, and a new style of specially created judicial peer to be known as a lord of appeal in ordinary. On their appointment lords of appeal in ordinary would become barons for life.

In spite of the fusion of equity and common law under the Judicature Act the Chancery Division of the High Court of Justice retained a distinctive form with its own judges, its own bar, and its own type of case. Of the three common law divisions, Common Pleas and Exchequer were merged into the Queen's Bench in 1881 and thereafter the High Court functioned on a tripartite basis, the separate divisions being the Chancery, Queen's Bench, and the Admiralty, Probate and Divorce. Before 1884 the various courts had operated in different places in London, Queen's Bench in the Temple, Common Pleas and Chancery in Chancery Lane, the Exchequer in Lincoln's Inn, and Probate and Divorce in Westminster Hall. With the opening of new royal courts of justice in the Strand in 1884, all the branches of the Supreme Court were brought together in the same building.

At the beginning of Victoria's reign the public offices in the Metropolis, manned by police magistrates, were generally acclaimed as a vast improvement on the old justices' offices. In 1838 the House of Commons set up a committee, of which Robert Peel was a member, 'to recommend the amount of salaries to be paid to Police Magistrates'. In their report the committee suggested a substantial increase of salary in view of the 'difficult and most important duties' which police magistrates were called upon to perform: 'Judges' salaries', they commented, 'are, of all others, the least proper objects of rigid economy'. A further proposal that police magistrates singly should be able to exercise a jurisdiction which required two ordinary justices of the peace aroused bitter criticism, one speaker declaiming that it would be 'a blow at the existence of the unpaid magistracy, who have long been the boast of England'.

It was not altogether surprising that the 1838 committee should recommend that in future all new police magistrates should be appointed from practising barristers of at least seven years' standing. Again this evoked a measure of protest, especially from certain justices of the peace, but some more independent observers doubted whether even this qualification would be sufficient. A member of Parliament contended that a more appropriate qualification would be twelve years in practice, and *The Times* newspaper voiced a fear that these lawyer-magistrates might be 'gowned greenhorns suffering from the caprices and impetuosities of youth'. With the Metropolitan Police Courts Act of 1839 both increasing their salaries and making seven years' practice as a barrister an essential qualification for the appointment, the police magistrates became an official branch of the professional judiciary.

At the beginning of this period the absence of a universal system of local courts in which small civil actions could be speedily and cheaply settled was still a principal deficiency in the British legal system. It is true that the ancient County Courts, with their nondescript judges, could still try cases where the amount in dispute was £2 or less, but the decreasing value of money was reducing such a jurisdiction to almost trivial proportions. As for the Courts of Requests, apart from the fact that there were too few of them, they had been established in a random fashion according to little or no geographical design. In 1846 one of Jeremy Bentham's most ardent propositions was implemented when a statute was passed creating a network of new civil courts, 'for the more easy recovery of small debts and demands', with a jurisdiction limited to cases in which the debt or damage claimed did not exceed the value of £20 – this figure was raised to £50 in 1850. The 1846 Act divided the whole of England and Wales into five hundred districts on fifty-nine circuits. In general each circuit had its own judge and every district had a separate court which sat once a month. Although the courts were to be known as County Courts their areas bore no relationship to the actual county boundaries. The qualification for appointment as a County Court judge was to be similar to that fixed in 1839 for police magistrates, namely seven years' standing as a barrister, and the salaries were also to be identical for both officers. The old-style local courts had now completely outlived their usefulness; the Hundred Courts were formerly abolished in 1867 and the sheriffs' tourns in 1887.

Police magistrates and County Court judges continued to receive approximately the same salaries for the remainder of the nineteenth century. At one stage the remuneration of County Court judges drew slightly ahead and a controversy arose, which was remarkable for the interest it aroused, as to whether the differential was either merited or justified. A great deal of space was devoted to the discussion by the national Press and the glowing tributes were bestowed upon both sets of courts. *The Daily Telegraph* in an editorial referred to the esteem in which police magistrates were 'justly held by the public' and continued, 'It is not saying too much to state that in no other tribunal throughout the land is justice administered so fairly, rapidly, sensibly and, on the whole wisely as in a metropolitan police court.' The *Pall Mall Gazette* commented, 'The County Court judges and the Police Magistrates are in fact the most striking result of the introduction of modern common sense into the judicial department of affairs.'

It must have been quite obvious in that era of legal reform that the judicial function of the justices of the peace would have to be clarified and brought under stricter control. As far as their sittings at Quarter Sessions were concerned very little criticism could be made as most of these courts were well regulated and administered justice strictly in accordance with the law. They retained a very wide jurisdiction, although it was enacted in 1842 that no court of Quarter Sessions could try a charge of treason, murder, or any felony punishable with imprisonment for life. It was in regard to the exercise of their summary powers that the justices were most free from either direction or restraint, principally because Parliament had continually extended their authority whilst imposing only minimal requirements with regard to the manner in which it was exercised.

The whole of the judicial duties of the justices of the peace, outside their work at Quarter Sessions, was regularized by four Acts which were passed in 1848 and 1849. Justices were to be provided with proper courts in which to hold their Petty Sessions and any such court would be 'deemed an open and public place to which the public generally may have access'. The preliminary investigation held by them into an indictable offence became a formal court hearing which the defendant had a right to attend and in which the prosecution witnesses had to be examined and cross-examined in his presence. He himself was not obliged to answer any questions and if he was committed for trial he was entitled to receive a complete copy of the depositions. The purpose of the old preliminary enquiry, Stephen wrote, had been 'to expose and detect a man assumed to be guilty'. The reformed procedure, he said, was to be 'a full enquiry into his guilt or innocence'.

During the nineteenth century the judges were increasingly respected both for their judicial and for their intellectual qualities. Moreover, they had accentuated their detachment from any political or contentiously emotive issues. Their constitutional role was now accepted as being the interpretation of legislation rather than formulation of executive policy. As one judge remarked in the Court of Common Pleas in 1871, 'I would observe as to these Acts of Parliament, they are the law of the land; we do not sit here as a court of appeal for Parliament.' A major change took place in the degrees of the legal profession when serjeants lost their monopoly to practise in the Common Pleas, and with the abolition of the rule that a barrister must be a serjeant before he could become a judge. Before the end of the period the grade of serjeant had lost most of its former importance and the Serjeants' Inn had been closed down for good.

The Judicature Act of 1873 had confirmed the official status of solicitors by making them officers of the new Supreme Court. The solicitors' branch of the legal profession was in advance of the Bar in the matter of professional education as the Incorporated Law Society had established courses of lectures for solicitors' articled clerks in 1833. Three years later the judges ruled that before qualifying as a solicitor every candidate must pass an examination and in 1843 this became a statutory requirement. The position in respect of a barrister's training was quite different. In 1846 a select committee reported that there was no organized system of legal education either at the Inns of Court or at the universities. Having compared the position in Britain very unfavourably with that in some continental countries and in parts of the United States of America, the committee went on to recommend that the universities should start awarding degrees in law and that the Inns should arrange lectures and exams for every student prior to his being called to the Bar. The committee thought that there should be a preliminary examination for solicitor's clerks but they considered that it would not be advisable to fuse the education of the students of the two branches of the profession. In 1852 the benchers of the four Inns set up a Council of Legal Education to organize lectures for Bar students. Both preliminary and intermediate examinations became statutory requirements for intending solicitors in 1860, and in 1871 a joint committee of the four Inns jointly resolved that there should be a compulsory examination for call to the Bar. Law degrees were instituted by Oxford University in 1852 and by Cambridge University in 1855.

For most of Victoria's reign there was still no official in Britain with special powers or obligations in connection with the prosecution of criminal offenders. After the formation of the Metropolitan Police it had become customary for police magistrates to bind over police officers to prosecute in cases when a private prosecutor was not available or was unwilling to undertake the responsibility himself, or when the crime was serious or the prosecution complicated. For their part the police usually turned for assistance to the Home Office solicitor, or after that office was abolished to the Treasury solicitor. This situation was obviously unsatisfactory and in 1856 a committee suggested that there should be district agents to superintend all prosecutions on behalf of the State. No action was taken on this proposal but in 1879 an Act was passed setting up a director of public prosecutions to institute and to conduct prosecutions under the supervision of the attorney-general, and also to assist the police in the preparation of difficult charges.

A number of important developments occurred during this period in respect of criminal procedure, most of which continued to be to the advantage of the person accused. The burden on the prosecution to establish that a confession by the defendant had been made freely and voluntarily became extremely difficult to discharge. Stephen has said, 'At one time the courts were disposed to take almost any opportunity to exclude evidence of confessions, almost anything being treated as an inducement to confess.' After a leading case in 1852 the judges began to exercise their discretion more realistically. By the Criminal Evidence Act of 1898 it became possible for a defendant to give evidence on his own behalf if he wished to do so. He was protected from cross-examination as to his bad character, unless he had forfeited this protection in one of the ways enumerated in the statute – for instance, if he had adduced evidence of his good character or, by his defence, had attacked the reputations of one or more of the prosecution witnesses.

A major part of the criminal law had been codified by seven separate statutes, all passed in 1861. A new field of criminal legislation was opened up by the Food and Drugs Act of 1875 which was the first serious attempt by the Government to control the standards of purity of food and medicines, and to prevent the sale of any edible substance in such a state that it might be injurious to health. A large number of statutes followed laying down the conditions of sale of various particular foodstuffs. The Merchandise Marks Acts of 1862 and 1887 created various offences concerned with unscrupulous trading and unfair competition; these Acts applied particularly to the sale of goods under false descriptions.

There was a constant move throughout the nineteenth century towards the establishment of a standard system of practice in all the civil courts. This was greatly facilitated by the Judicature Act of 1873 which prescribed a uniform code of pleading and procedure for every division of the new Supreme Court. The rules of evidence were also being continually modified and improved. In 1851 the parties to a civil action became competent witnesses in their own cases, and this competency was extended to the husbands and wives of the parties two years later. The stipulation that all evidence must be given on oath was gradually relaxed and evidence on affirmation was allowed, firstly from members of certain religious faiths and then from anyone with a conscientious objection to taking the oath.

The Judicature Act made few changes to the substantive civil law, but various legislative enactments combined with the more enlightened outlook of the judiciary were tending to impart an added clarity and reason to civil proceedings generally. Before enforcing a contract the courts began to investigate the circumstances under which it had been made, and the objects of the parties when making it. The Sale of Goods Act in 1893 allowed a purchaser to return, and to claim repayment for the price of any article which did not correspond with the description given by the seller. Perhaps the most important measure in the field of tort was Lord Campbell's Act of 1846, resulting from the number of fatalities on the railways, which gave a right of action to the relatives of a person killed by the default or negligence of another. The legal status of married women was put on a far more just basis by the Married Women's Property Act of 1882 which granted complete emancipation of the wife's property from the husband's control; henceforth she was capable of holding or disposing of it as if she had been unmarried.

The progress of reform was neither so swift nor so certain in regard to methods of punishment. The number of offences carrying the penalty of death was gradually reduced until the 1870s when it was only applicable to the crimes of treason, murder, piracy with violence, and setting fire to dock-yards or arsenals. In fact from 1838 until Victoria's death no person in Britain was hanged for any offence except murder or, up to 1861, attempted murder. The campaign against public execution, maintained by several radical members of Parliament and supported by the novelists Charles Dickens and William Thackeray, and by Douglas Jerrold the editor of *Punch*, gathered momentum around the middle of the century. In 1856 the House of Commons accepted the recommendation of a select committee that future executions should be carried out in private, but the proposal was rejected by the House of Lords. A royal commission on capital punishment set up in 1864 again supported the abolition of the sordid spectacle of public hangings; another Bill was introduced to give effect to their findings and this time it passed successfully through both Houses. Public executions were abolished in Britain during the summer of 1868, the last public hanging having taken place outside Newgate Gaol in the City of London during the previous spring.

In 1842 the commissioners on the criminal law expressed their misgivings about the efficacy of flogging as a punishment for adult male offenders. Indeed the courts had started to sentence adults to corporal punishment far less frequently and in the codifying legislation of 1861 flogging was omitted altogether as a possibile penalty for persons over sixteen years of age. Nevertheless, in moments of public indignation the nation was still disposed to resort to the whip as a remedy for any prevalent species of serious crime. In 1842 after two psychopaths had levelled pistols at the queen it was intro-duced as a punishment for any man who had aimed a firearm at or near the sovereign. In 1863, following a wave of violent street robberies in London, it became a penalty for garrotters. And in 1898, in the wake of an outcry over white slave traffic, it was made a punishment for men who had lived on the earnings of prostitutes. The Whipping Act of 1862 provided that no person should be flogged more than once for a single offence and that all future floggings should be carried out in private. Corporal punsihment still remained as one of the principal punishments for youths and boys.

In the spring of 1840 the Government suspended all further transportation to New South Wales but retained a smaller, modified scheme for sending British convicts to the penal colony on Van Dieman's Land. Although some effort was made to teach the prisoners on this island 'the habits of industry and subordination', the project turned out to be as complete a failure as its predecessor and it was terminated in 1846. Thereafter a steadily decreasing stream of convicts was transported to Western Australia until that colony finally declined to take any more of them in 1867. After that the punishment of transportation disappeared from the British penal code.

The leading prison reformers were all agreed that the purposes of imprisonment should not be wholly confined to deterrence and retribution, but they differed in their opinions as to how a wider and more constructive factor might be assimilated into prison routine. Jeremy Bentham and James Mill favoured a process of 'reformation through industry', whilst Elizabeth Fry thought that a convict might best be reclaimed by a process of moral and religious instruction. The evils of indiscriminate association were manifest to all, and the Prison Act of 1839 provided that every prisoner should be separately confined 'during the whole or part of the period of his or her imprisonment'. This statute also laid down a standard code of prison regulations and gave the home secretary additional powers to control the design of prison buildings. Over the next seventeen years five new national prisons were opened, all constructed on the cellular principle, to accommodate men and women who had been sentenced to terms of penal servitude.

During the early 1860s the mood of the nation had hardened towards the law-breaker. In 1863 a select committee, headed by Lord Carnarvon, reported that penal servitude did not seem to be sufficiently dreaded 'either by those who have undergone it, or by the criminal class in general'. The committee felt that far more emphasis should be placed on the punitive aspect of a prison sentence. Separation should be rigidly enforced and the entire régime should be based upon solitude and toil. The Prison Act of 1865 embodied most of the recommendations of the Carnarvon committee and also gave the home secretary the power of withholding grants-in-aid to any prisons which were not complying with the new regulations. The sole redeeming feature of the years that followed was a statute in 1869 abolishing imprisonment for debt. In 1877 the control of all the prisons in Britain was vested in a body of five prison commissioners, appointed by and responsible to the home secretary.

The first chairman of the prison commissioners was an austere and insensitive autocrat under whose direction the prisons, though efficiently managed, became places of calculated misery, of solitude, discomfort, deprivation, and useless and exhausting labour. In 1894 a department committee was set up under Herbert Gladstone, youngest son of the statesman, to carry out a thorough enquiry into the prison system. In a humane and considered report the committee condemned both the 'terrible ordeal' of isolation and silence, and the penal drudgery of the crank and the tread-wheel. Prisoners, they said, had been treated too much 'as a hopeless and worthless element in the community' and they recommended a new system founded upon productive labour and education and designed to develop the prisoners' moral instincts and to teach them orderly and industrious habits. They stressed the importance of an efficient system of after-care for released prisoners, and they suggested that there should be juvenile-adult reformatories in Britain, similar to those which had been tried out effectively in the United States of America, for the training of young offenders.

There were other important developments in penal methods during Victoria's reign. A notable reform was brought about by the Summary Jurisdiction Act of 1879 which permitted a magistrate's court to allow defendants time in which to pay their fines instead of keeping them in prison until the amounts were satisfied in full. The origin of the probation service took place in 1876 when the Church of England Temperance Society appointed an agent, called a police court missionary, to attend at various metropolitan courts and to interview defendants if the magistrates required him to do so. This project was an immediate success and by the year 1900 there were no less then 112 police court missionaries, who were operating not only in London but in several large provincial towns as well.

CHAPTER 21

CAPITAL AND LABOUR

During the Industrial Revolution the levels of profits, prices, and wages had largely been controlled by the natural processes of supply and demand. The onsurge of mechanical development and the expansion of commercial enterprise had tended to impair the livelihood of the craftsman and the lesser proprietors. Throughout the Victorian period the manufacturing industries continued to enlarge, and agriculture to contract. Year by year the army of anonymous wage-earners was increasing and Britain was seeming to lose the easy fellowship of the small concern – the personal amity and the mutual respect which had formerly existed between employer and employed. The number of farm labourers was constantly falling and by 1901 over 77 per cent of the total population of England and Wales were living in the urban areas.

The introduction of the limited liability company in 1837, coupled with the growing wealth of the nation, gave rise to a flood of speculation, especially amongst a new class of small investors. Many of the companies floated during the ensuing years were either worthless or fraudulent, for Parliament had provided little protection against the false claims of the promoters. Two statutes were passed in 1844, the first of which allowed a company to register as such without the necessity of receiving a charter, but made it a term of registration that the promoters should supply certain information about their objects. It was also made compulsory for companies inviting investment in their shares to disclose to the public complete details of their present assets and of the identity of their directors. The second Act provided for an investigation into the affairs of any company which became insolvent. The shareholders of a company registered under the 1844 legislation remained fully liable for its debts.

There were, in fact, many economists and politicians who did not favour an extension of limited liability as they believed it would increase the possibilities of fraud. Nevertheless, a statute in 1855 made it possible for all registered companies to obtain limited liability for their shareholders providing they complied with various requirements. For instance, the name of the company had to include the word 'limited'; there had to be a minimum number of members each holding shares of a prescribed value; and at least three-quarters of the company's nominal value must have been subscribed. The Companies Act of 1862 created a new type of company limited by guarantee, altered the procedure for winding up, and transferred the jurisdiction over companies to the Court of Chancery. During the last thirty years of the nineteenth century the company system became the dominating factor in British industry, with control being exercised by boards of directors acting nominally on behalf of the shareholders.

In earlier generations wealth had implied the ownership of land, and the ownership of land had carried with it a tradition of service. The new investment wealth was nebulous and impersonal. Other factors had combined to attenuate the patriarchal image of English country life, not least of which were the series of statutes throughout Victoria's reign which had simplified the transfer of real estate and had broken down the prohibitions designed to maintain the great hereditary estates in the power of a single family.

Another type of property had now achieved general recognition – the property inherent in originality, in ideas, and in inventive creation. At the beginning of the Victorian period an inventor or his assignee could be granted a patent of an invention for a period not exceeding fourteen years, but the procedure was ponderous and expensive and beset with unnecessary formalities. An Act of Parliament in 1883 set up the Patents Office under an official known as the comptroller of patents. The comptroller could grant a patent for sixteen years for any new invention which was shown to be both original and useful, by a process which entailed the minimum of cost and delay. An author's copyright was more difficult to classify, for, as Lord Macaulay pointed out, if it was equated to property it was logical that it should continue in perpetuity. By the Copyright Act of 1842 the author of a book or his assignee was granted the copyright for his lifetime and for a further seven years after his death, but if the seven-year period expired earlier then forty-two years after the first publication, the copyright in the work endured for the full period of forty-two years. The Act also applied copyright to musical compositions.* In 1862 copyright was extended to original paintings, drawings, and photographs.

It was decided in 1842 that the inventor of a trademark possessed no right of property in it, owing to the difficulty of establishing an association between a dealer's or manufacturer's trademark and his particular brand of goods. A proposal was put forward in the House of Commons in 1862 that there should be an official register of trademarks. However, the majority of members thought that this would be impracticable and that the Merchandise Marks Act of that year, which provided remedies both in the civil and criminal courts for certain misrepresentations in regard to goods offered for sale, would sufficiently cover the matter. As has been seen, that Act was almost totally ineffective. In 1875 the principle of registration was adopted and the owner of a registered trademark was able to obtain statutory protection against its infringement.

In an era of speculation and monetary fluidity the moral and social stigma of insolvency was being gradually relaxed. Eight years before the ending of imprisonment for debt, the Bankruptcy Act of 1861 had stipulated that non-traders might become bankrupt in just the same manner as those engaged in commerce. In 1869 a new central Court of Bankruptcy was established which had no criminal jurisdiction, and the County Courts were formally constituted as local courts of bankruptcy.

Meanwhile the labour forces of Britain were seething with discontent. The desire for shorter working hours had been one of the foremost rallying cries of the Chartist movement and the agitation for a ten-hour day had slowly gathered momentum during Victoria's early years on the throne. The more enlightened manufacturers supported the principle

* By the Copyright Act 1911, the copyright of all literary, artistic, dramatic, and musical works persists for the life of the creator and for a period of fifty years after his death.

of shorter hours on humanitarian grounds: the more unyielding opposed it for the stark economic reason that it would probably increase the costs of production. There can be little doubt that the solid mass of workers who campaigned so tirelessly on behalf of the exploited women and children in their midst were fully aware that a curtailment in the working hours of one section of the labour-force would lead eventually to a general reduction all round.

In 1840 a report was published showing that working conditions in the silk and lace mills were as deplorable as ever. Another report two years later on conditions in the coal-mines stirred the public conscience by its appalling disclosures. In nearly every coal-mining district children of five or six, or even younger, were being employed underground in dragging trucks along tunnels which were too small to accommodate grown men, and in other solitary tasks requiring them to spend long periods in damp and unlit shafts. In certain areas women and girls too were taking part in drawing and carrying coal. Parliament reacted immediately by passing the Mines Act of 1842 which forbade the employment underground of women, girls, or boys of less than ten, and instituted an inspectorate to ensure that this regulation was obeyed.

It had become increasingly apparent that apart from the categories of child-labour which had received so much publicity, the exploitation of young children was being practised in many different industries. Consequently a general statute in 1844 prescribed a maximum six-and-a-half hour day for all children between the ages of eight and thirteen and a maximum twelve-hour day for all women and girls. Also, and of equal importance, the statute introduced stricter safety precautions, requiring machinery to be fenced off and properly maintained. A Bill prescribing a maximum ten-hour day for women and young persons passed through both Houses without appreciable opposition in 1847. The fact that men were excluded from this provision was principally due to a belief that it would be detrimental to hamper their freedom to negotiate on their own behalf; such a course, Palmerston once remarked, would be founded upon a 'vicious and wrong principle'.

Over the next few decades there were a succession of statutes affecting the working conditions of women, young people, and children, some of which were of general application and others referred to particular types of occupation. Agricultural workers, chimney-sweeps and bleach-field labourers each in their turn received consideration. Parliament also paid further attention to the health and safety of employees in the mines, the factories, and the workshops, and new regulations were made concerning fencing, ventilation, and the elimination of the more obvious dangers in the systems of operation.

This was the age when the trade unions were beginning to flex their muscles. Under the 1825 Act combinations of masters or men for fixing hours of work or rates of pay were no longer illegal, though combinations for other purposes, if they restricted trade, could still be indicted as criminal conspiracies. Even when a combination was for a permissible object the methods used to attain it were restricted, as the Act made it an offence, punishable with imprisonment, for a person to use violence, threats, molestation, intimidation, or obstruction. A great many cases came before the courts which entailed an interpretation of the words and meaning of the 1825 Act. Some trade unionists felt that the balance of judicial decision was biased against them, but it cannot be fairly said that the judges were doing otherwise than applying a law which was vague, unsatisfactory, and lacking in definition.

The failure of so many strikes in the years immediately following upon the legalization of the trade unions caused a certain despondency among trade union leaders and impelled a number of their members to transfer their allegiance to the Chartists. With the commercial boom in the early 1840s, however, the trade union movement gathered a fresh vigour. New associations of workers were formed and others were revived and expanded. Funds were increased, permanent officials were engaged, and organization was consolidated and strengthened. The trade unions wished to achieve respectability and acceptance: the employers wanted them to remain perpetually in the twilight of the law. The revolutionary outbreaks in Europe in 1848 had little or no repercussions amongst the British proletoriat. The unions at this stage were not really politically orientated, and in any case they had no co-ordinated policy as all attempts to form a general representative association of workers had been unsuccessful. The first constructive step towards coalescence was taken in 1851 when nearly all the branches of the engineering trade were fused in an Amalgamated Society of Engineers. This new union exercised its strength soon after its formation when it demanded the abolition of piecework and regular overtime. The employers' association responded by enforcing a lock-out. After a three-month struggle the union was forced to capitulate and the men returned to work on giving an undertaking to give up their union membership – a promise that few of them ever intended to keep.

The legal position of the trade unions was enigmatic in the extreme. In 1855 the Court of Exchequer Chamber held that even if a combination was pursuing a purpose permitted by the criminal law, any agreement made by the members which was in restraint of trade, and thereby contrary to public policy, was void. Between 1860 and 1870 the majority of the trade union leaders were acting in a far more responsible manner and preferring conciliation to strike action wherever possible. Nevertheless, the unions were still tarnished with a reputation for lawless agitation, an image fostered by a group of small unions which habitually indulged in terrorization and violence. Workmen felt a great deal of resentment at the fact that they could be brought before the justices and imprisoned if they were shown to have been in breach of a contract of employment. The law in this respect was modified by the Master and Servant Act of 1867 which provided that if the case against a workman was proved he would only be liable to pay a fine or a sum of compensation. The dissatisfaction among the workers remained, both because an essentially civil matter was still being tried in a magistrates' court and because of the discrepancy in treatment between employer and employed.

A further grievance of the trade unions related to the safeguarding of their rapidly accumulating resources. In a case in 1867 it was decided that a union, being an illegal combination, was debarred from registering as a friendly society and thereby acquiring the proprietary advantages and the fiscal benefits to which such an association was entitled.

Strikes were now occurring with increasing frequency, and as the strength and solidarity of the unions grew the employers responded with equal militancy, often using the lock-out against men who insisted in joining a union or who took part in any form of organized industrial action. Public antagonism towards the unions was being constantly enflamed by the inconvenience of strikes and by reports of the excesses and violence being perpetrated by the strikers. The so-called 'Sheffield and Manchester Outrages' in 1865 and 1866, when some of the local trade union officials were implicated in acts of terrorism, led to the appointment of a royal commission on trade unions. The majority report of the commission accepted that trade unions existed to protect their members 'against the undue advantage which the command of a large capital is supposed by them to give to the employers of labour'. It was suggested that henceforth no combination should be prosecuted for restraint of trade unless its action had involved breach of contract or a refusal to work with some particular person. 'The law should recognize the right of the labourer to dispose of his labour', the report went on, 'the capitalist of his capital, and the employer of his productive powers, in whatever manner each of them, acting either individually or in association with others, may desire for his own interest.' The majority of the members of the commission considered that picketing should be suppressed and that the existing law against molestation and obstruction should be retained. On the other hand, bona fide unions should be allowed to register as friendly societies.* The minority report of the commission was more favourable to the unions, proposing that no act by a combination should be regarded as criminal if it could lawfully have been done by a single person.

Gladstone's Liberal Government introduced two Acts in 1871 based upon the majority report of the royal commission. The first Act clarified the legal status of trade unions by providing that although their essential purpose was the restraint of trade, their members should not be liable to prosecution for conspiracy and their agreements should not be invalidated. The second, which was bitterly opposed by the union leaders, tightened the law regarding the use of violence, threats, and intimidation during the course of a trade dispute, and attempted to define such words as 'molestation' and 'obstruction' which had given rise to so many

* This proposal was implemented in 1869.

difficulties of interpretation ever since the statute of 1825. This second Act, the Webbs have said, 'deliberately struck a blow at the methods of all trade societies at all periods'. The unions held that the law was now so stringent that even the ordinary course of picketing might well be deemed a criminal offence. Their fervent agitation to have the statute repealed was successful in 1875 when a Conservative ministry under Disraeli passed the Conspiracy and Protection of Property Act, redefining all these emotive terms on a much narrower basis and exempting various acts when carried out 'in contemplation of furtherance of trade disputes' from normal criminal proceedings. The trade unions had now obtained for themselves a special legal status and a special exemption from the criminal law. 'Thus', Holdsworth wrote,

> not only did the state fail to control the formation and activities of these industrial associations in a manner similar to that in which it controlled the formation and activities of commercial associations, but it also began the process of giving them dangerous privileges – a process which in the following period the extension of the franchise and the growth of a labour party will so greatly extend that the peace of the state and the authority of the law will be gravely menaced.

Also in 1875 the County Courts were given a much wider jurisdiction over disputes between employers and workmen, and it was provided that proceedings before the magistrates for breach of contract would be classified as civil rather than as criminal matters. After this change Disraeli could comment, 'For the first time in the history of this country the employer and employed sit under equal laws.' Meanwhile, the trade unions were becoming politically conscious. The Trades Union Congress had met for the first time in 1868. At its third meeting in 1871 it had elected a 'parliamentary committee' which from then on became the political executive of the movement.

As the result of continual pressure from the unions hours of work were shortening and rates of pay were rising. Most branches of the textile trade had achieved a sixty-hour week by 1870 and the Saturday half-holiday was becoming commonplace. The average increase in the wages of the working-man between 1850 and 1870 was about 30 per cent.

Nevertheless, the risk of unemployment was still considerable as new machinery in the factories and workshops was constantly reducing the size of the essential labour-force. In 1891 the minimum age at which children could be employed in factories was put up to eleven, and the maximum working-day for a woman was fixed at twelve hours with time off for meals. Very soon after this a large proportion of manual labourers had established the principle of an eight-hour day.

Despite the continued improvement in labour conditions the closing years of the nineteenth century abounded in industrial strife. In 1889 the dockers struck for a standard wage of sixpence an hour. With public sympathy on their side they maintained their struggle until the employers were obliged to give way and grant their demand. This clear-cut victory was a great fillip for trade union morale. Up to this, strike action has been aimed solely at the striker's own employers but in 1893 the Miners Federation broke new ground when it endeavoured to close down all the pits in South Wales, whether they were affected by the prevailing dispute or not, and so indirectly to injure the community in general. The justification for this strike cannot be doubted as it was called in protest against certain mine-owners who were threatening to cut wages by 10 per cent and were imposing a lock-out on their men. The hauliers in South Wales supported the strike and the local miners' unions opposed it, which resulted in violent fighting between the rival groups, culminating in a pitched battle at Ebbw Vale when over 2,000 miners routed an equivalent number of men belonging to the hauliers' association. There were ugly scenes too in the Yorkshire coalfields where striking miners went out on the rampage, storming offices and collieries and smashing equipment. On one occasion they overpowered the police and had to be dispersed by a small body of troops who opened fire, killing two miners. After fifteen weeks both sides were brought together at the instigation of Gladstone, the veteran prime minister, and a compromise was arranged. The Amalgamated Society of Engineers called an all-out stoppage in the summer of 1897 but they were defeated after six months by the highly organized Engineering Employers' Federation. This time the settlement was negotiated by the president of the Board of Trade.

At the turn of the century the trade unions were going from strength to strength and were already beginning to exert themselves as the fourth estate in the realm. By 1900 their total membership had exceeded two million. At this time the courts were striving to interpret the new developments in the law of industrial relations. The leading case of *Allen* v. *Flood* in 1897 was regarded as a victory for the unions. The facts were that an official of the Boilermakers' Union had compelled an employer to sack two shipwrights for some inconsequential infringement of the union's regulations by threatening to call a strike if they were kept on. The two men brought an action for damages against the union official, but the House of Lords found in his favour on the grounds that he had been within his rights in inducing the employer to perform a lawful act, for legitimate behaviour could not constitute an actionable wrong to third parties who might have suffered incidental injury thereby. The *Taff Vale Railway Company* case in 1901, another important decision, went against the unions for it was held that persons acting in concert, as a trade union or as any other association, were as liable as an ordinary person for the damage they caused; and further, that a trade union could be sued in its registered name and would be liable to pay damages out of its common fund.

One of the standing grievances of the trade unions – and of the manual workers in general – was against the old common law doctrine of 'common employment', by which an employer was only liable to his servants for injuries they sustained by his own negligence, and not through the negligence of their fellow employees. The injustices occasioned by this doctrine in an era of mechanization and massive industrial production were all too apparent. The position was modified by the Employers' Liability Act in 1880, an unsatisfactory statute of very limited application. Common employment was virtually abolished in 1897 when employers became liable for the industrial injuries suffered by their servants even if these were totally due to the negligence of a fellow employee. An entirely new principle was initiated by the Workmen's Compensation Act of 1897 which gave to those employed in certain occupations a right to recover compensation for their injuries, whether or not these had been caused by the negligence of another. In effect, employers in the occupations concerned became the insurers of their employees against accidental injuries occurring at their place of work.

The failure of Chartism early in Victoria's reign dealt a blow to the propagation of socialist ideas in Britain, but the doctrines were revived in the last quarter of the nineteenth century by the study of Karl Marx, and by the formation of the Democratic Federation, the Socialist League, and the Fabian Society. The Independent Labour Party, a socialist propaganda organization, was founded in 1893 and from its origination a number of its members played a dominant role in the activities of the Trades Union Congress. In 1899 the trade unions called a conference 'to devise ways and means for securing an increased number of Labour members in the next Parliament'. As a result, a Labour Representative Committee was set up controlled by delegates from various socialist and trade union bodies, and it was decided to establish 'a distinct Labour Group in Parliament. who shall have their own Whips and agree upon their policy, which must embrace a readiness to co-operate with any party which for the time being may be engaged in promoting legislation in the direct interest of Labour.'

Queen Victoria died on 22 January 1901 and there could have been very few people in Britain who did not realize that with her death an age had drawn to a close and an epoch had passed away. The trends and the tendencies which had been stirring in her final years were to come to fruition during the ensuing period.

Part X

THE MODERN PERIOD

(1901–1974)

CHAPTER 22

A RADICAL IMPULSION

When Edward VII came to the throne in 1901 the constitutional function of a British monarch had been firmly settled. He could no longer direct his ministers, but as the authoritative Walter Bagehot had said, he had the right to be consulted, the right to encourage, and the right to warn. The power of government lay in the Cabinet – which still met informally with no records, no minutes, and no secretariat – acting under the continual sanction of a parliamentary majority.

The Conservative Government, which had been in office since 1895, passed two outstanding pieces of legislation during the early years of Edward's reign. One was an Act considerably improving certain aspects of the licensing laws, and the other a statute making county and county borough councils the local authorities responsible for secondary, technical, and elementary education. With regard to industrial law and labour relations generally, however, the Government were encountering a great deal of difficulty. The Conspiracy and Protection of Property Act of 1875 had virtually removed industrial relations from the ambit of the criminal law, but the doctrine of conspiracy had re-emerged in respect of civil actions arising out of labour disputes where employers had suffered damage through disruptive action by various unions. In the *Taff Vale Railway* case in 1901, which has already been noted, the Amalgamated Society of Railway Servants was ordered to pay a total amount of £32,000 by way of damages and costs. A short while later in *Quinn* v. *Leathem* a wholesale butcher succeeded in an action for 'combination to injure' against a trade union official who had threatened to call a strike at his own and his customers' premises unless he sacked some non-union workmen from his employment. It was held that 'coercion by threats, open or disguised, not only of bodily harm but of serious annoyance and damage' was an actionable wrong. Both the cases were decided on an eventual appeal to the House of Lords, and the leaders of the trade unions, disregarding the wholly judicial character of that tribunal, were convinced that the judgements had been tainted with class prejudice. In an effort to counteract the mounting disquiet amongst the union members, the Government set up a royal commission headed by Lord Dunedin in 1903 to investigate the state of industrial law.

Under the impetus of the new wave of regenerated discontent, the Labour Representative Committee more than doubled its numbers. What is more, it began to fight and to win by-elections and by the end of 1903 it had managed to get three very able men into the House of Commons. The Government decided to go to the country in 1906 and in the momentous general election which followed the Liberals were swept into power with a comfortable overall majority. The Labour Party managed to return fifty-three members, all of whom came from working-class backgrounds.

The Dunedin Commission reported in favour of safeguarding the unions from actions in similar circumstances to the *Taff Vale Railway* and *Quinn* v. *Leathem* cases. This proposal did not go nearly far enough for the trade union leaders who wished their members to be totally exempted from civil liability for their conduct in industrial disputes. The Trades Disputes Act of 1906 gave the trade unions a good deal of what they wanted by removing organized strikes from the law of civil conspiracy, in the same manner as the 1875 statute had removed them from the law of criminal conspiracy. Further, the Act provided that no one could be sued for damages because he had induced another to break his contract of employment, provided he had done so 'in contemplation or furtherance of a trade dispute'. An attempt was also made in the Act to define the vexed question of what amounted to lawful picketing, by providing that strike pickets could only be used for peaceful persuasion or for the peaceful transmission of information. It is worth noting, perhaps, that although this statute had been viewed with misgiving by the House of Lords, they had decided, rather than intensify the hostility of the working classes, to pass it without amendment.

In other respects the House of Lords were adament in their efforts to disrupt and destroy the radical legislation transmitted to them by the Liberal majority in the House of Commons. During 1906 and 1907 no less than six reformatory measures were passed through the Commons and either rejected or else deliberately mutilated beyond recognition by the peers. Amongst the worst examples of this were the Education Bill for which the Liberals had obtained a clear mandate from the electorate, and the Plural Voting Bill, which they were eventually forced to shelve, and which was designed to put an end to the inequitable franchise system whereby a man was granted a separate vote for all the premises he owned, whether they were residential or commercial. Finally, in the summer of 1907 Sir Henry Campbell-Bannerman, the prime minister, found it necessary to move a resolution in the House of Commons that 'in order to give effect to the will of the people as expressed by their elected representatives, the power of the other House to alter or reject Bills passed by this House must be so restricted by law as to secure that within the limits of a single Parliament the final decision of the Commons should prevail.' According to the prime minister's proposed scheme the Lords would only have been empowered to delay a Bill, and not to reject it out of hand.

The constitutional crisis between the Commons and the Lords came to a head in relation to the 1909 Budget. For several centuries it had been one of the precepts of parliamentary government in Britain that fiscal measures were entirely within the province of the House of Commons, but in 1909 the House of Lords, against the advice of the king and with a total disregard for constitutional precedent, rejected the Finance Bill by an overwhelming majority. Asquith, who had become prime minister on Campbell-Bannerman's retirement the previous year, promptly moved a resolution that the peers had committed 'a breach of the constitution and a usurpation of the rights of the Commons'.

Another general election was now inevitable. It was held at the beginning of 1910, and although the Liberals were returned in considerably reduced strength, they still managed to form a minority government. Before the constitutional deadlock had been resolved Edward VII died. He was succeeded by his son George V, who immediately persuaded the opposing political factions to meet at a round-table conference. This was held at 10 Downing Street, but after five months of protracted negotiations it became apparent that there was no hope of reaching a compromise. In November 1910 Asquith brought forward a Parliament Bill with three main provisions. Firstly, that any Money Bill would become law without the consent of the House of Lords; secondly, that other Bills might be delayed by the Lords for a maximum of two years but not be defeated by them; and thirdly, that the full term of a Parliament should be reduced from seven years to five years. The king had undertaken, if it became necessary, to create a sufficient number of new peers to force this measure through the House of Lords, but he had stipulated that a general election must be held beforehand so that the will of the people might be made known. The second 1910 election took place in December and it left the state of the parties almost unchanged. Again the Liberals formed a minority Government, and the prime minister introduced the Parliament Bill two months later. At first the House of Lords attempted to mutilate the measure by a series of amendments, but eventually in August 1911, when Asquith had prepared a proposed list of 250 new Liberal peers, they ended their confrontation and passed the Bill by a majority of seventeen votes.

During the early years of the twentieth century there were several important penalogical reforms in Britain. In 1902 the prison commissioners repeated the proposal made by the Gladstone Committee that there should be a special type of establishment to administer a combination of disciplinary and remedial training to young offenders. The same year Rochester Prison in the little Kent village of Borstal was taken over as an experiment on the lines suggested. The scheme proved so successful that by the Prevention of Crime Act in 1908 similar institutions were set up in other parts of the country and the courts were empowered to pass a specific sentence of 'Borstal training' upon any youth aged between sixteen and twenty-one instead of sending him to prison. Also in 1908, separate Juvenile Courts were created for children under sixteen, and it became the law that no boy or girl under fourteen could be sent to an ordinary prison. If children were aged between fourteen and sixteen they could only be imprisoned in particular circumstances. In 1907 the devoted and often inspired work of the police court missionaries – whose numbers had by then expanded to 144 – was placed on an official basis with the institution of a professional probation service. This enabled the courts to place defendants on probation for a period instead of punishing them. A minister who was at the Home Office at the time has written that the measure 'attracted little attention either in Parliament or outside and passed through all its stages in both Houses almost without discussion.' Each Petty Sessional Division was given complete discretion whether or not to appoint probation officers and the majority had declined to do so.* The right to order corporal punishment was curtailed by a statute in 1914, which provided that such a sentence would only be permissible when it had been expressly authorized by Act of Parliament. Until then, any male person convicted of a common law misdemeanour had been liable to be whipped.

One of the principal defects in the legal process was rectified in 1907 with the creation of a Court of Criminal Appeal to hear appeals both against conviction and against sentence. Hitherto a conviction had been final unless the trial judge had decided to reserve a point of law for the consideration of the Court of Crown Cases Reserved, or a defect appeared on the face of the record – a document which merely set out the arraignment, the plea, the issue, and the verdict. The Court of Criminal Appeal, however, could look at the evidence which had been given in a case and at the judge's summing-up to the jury. An appeal was possible whether it was based on law, on fact, or on both, and the new court was even given jurisdiction to quash a conviction if they felt that the jury's verdict had been an unreasonable one. Under certain circumstances a further appeal lay from the Court of Criminal Appeal to the House of Lords.† The provision of free legal aid for poor persons had been started in 1903 with the Poor Prisoners' Defence Act. The scope of this statute was extremely limited as it only applied to charges which were triable at Assizes or Quarter Sessions

* The appointment of probation officers was not made compulsory until 1925.

† The ancient privilege of peers to be tried for treason or felony by their fellow-peers in the House of Lords was abolished in 1948.

and the grant of legal assistance was conditional upon the defendant disclosing some adequate defence during the preliminary hearing before a magistrates' court.

The years immediately preceding the outbreak of the First World War were marred in Britain by a growing disregard for the established rule of law. The irresponsible conduct of the majority in the House of Lords was matched in cruder style by the calculated violence of the strikers and the fanatical fury of the suffragettes. But the Government of the day never wavered in their belief that the British system of law and order was generally capable of being maintained by an unarmed police force and by the ordinary powers of the courts.

There were two principal societies which conducted the militant activities of the suffragists, the Women's Social and Political Union, known as the WSPU, and the Woman's Freedom League. The pattern of their tactics was set in 1905 when two young girls forcibly interrupted a Liberal meeting and were imprisoned for refusing to pay their fines after they had been convicted of assault. From that time forward the suffragettes waged their campaign against the Liberal Party, although several of its leading members were openly in favour of women being granted the vote. At first the suffragettes confined their disorderliness to minor assaults and window breaking but later, when Mrs Pankhurst was conducting operations of the WSPU from an office in Paris, they reached a far more serious level with the arson of buildings, the destruction of telephone wires and pillarboxes, vandalism in museums and public galleries, and even the occasional exploding of bombs. When the women were arrested and sent to prison they habitually went on hunger strike, prompting the authorities to resort to the repellent process of forcible feeding and heightening the embittered anquish of the whole of the suffragist movement. It is a reasonable presumption that if the WSPU had adopted more lawful methods the completely unjustifiable exclusion of women from the franchise might well have been remedied during the period between 1906 and 1914. It was a meagre consolation for the militants that after 1907 women were permitted to sit as councillors, aldermen, mayors, or as the chairmen of county and borough councils.

The concessions made to strikers by the 1906 Act had no

immediate effect in quietening the prevalent industrial unrest; neither had the creation of labour exchanges for the unemployed, nor the new protective legislation forbidding excessive working hours. In 1907 a threatened rail strike was settled by Lloyd George, then president of the Board of Trade, and he again used his personal initiative to ward off a threatened strike of shipyard engineers in the following year. From 1910 to 1912 Britain was ravaged by strikes, some on a national and some on a local level. In November 1910 troops had to assist the police in quelling a rioting mob of miners at Ton-y-pandy. In 1911 there were simultaneous dock-strikes in London, Manchester, and Liverpool, often accompanied by fighting and bloodshed. During a riot in the Liverpool docks the troops had to open fire and two strikers were killed. The army was called in again a short while later to deal with disturbances instigated by striking railwaymen. At Llanelly, where there was sporadic looting of rail-wagons and shops, two more strikers were killed before the disorders were suppressed. It was only after a further dock-strike had collapsed in the summer of 1912 that the wave of strikes and industrial unrest eased off and eventually subsided.

Sixteen out of the fifty-three Labour members of Parliament who had been returned at the 1906 election were paid salaries by various trade unions, the necessary money being collected by a compulsory levy upon the members of the union concerned. In 1908 one of the London branches of the Society of Railway Servants challenged the legality of a compulsory levy for this purpose in the Chancery Division and the judge ruled it to be unlawful, a decision which was upheld by the Court of Appeal, and subsequently affirmed by the House of Lords. As a result the members of a number of other unions obtained similar injunctions to restrain their own committees from continuing to impose the levy. This was extremely infortunate because certain Labour members were deprived of their entire incomes. Moreover, it had occurred at a moment when the sinister philosophy of syndicalism was just beginning to permeate from France into the British trade union movement. Syndicalists believed in an ultimate and inevitable class-war: they rejected the notion that it could be conducted by democratic means – through a free parliament and the ballot-box – and insisted that it must be fought by sabotage, subversion, and massive co-ordinated strikes. Though the immediate grievances were resolved, as members of Parliament awarded themselves an annual salary of £400 in 1911, and in 1913 trade unions were empowered to exact political levies provided their members were given the opportunity to opt out of paying them, the doctrines of syndicalism were to be firmly embedded in trade union thinking for many years to come.

The savagery of 1914–18 war, the military crises, and the malign threat to Britain's cherished independence necessitated the imposition on her citizens of an assemblage of controls the like of which they had never encountered since the Protectorate of Oliver Cromwell. Censorship, restriction of movement, and conscription to the armed forces were accepted for the duration of the conflict, and the Defence of the Realm Acts furnished the Government with a host of other totalitarian powers. In the surge of patriotic sentiment which had dominated the country in 1914 the trade unions had declared that they would observe an industrial peace until the war was over. However, the shop stewards, the workers' representatives on the shop-floor, were by then a new force in the leadership of organized labour. Some shop stewards were revolutionary socialists who had little sympathy with the national effort or with the principles on which the war was being fought, and their influence was seldom used for the purposes of conciliation. The immoderate profits being made by a number of industrialists, especially in munitions, was a further continual irritant to the workers in the factories. Following the Communist revolution in Russia in 1917, the Independent Labour Party and the Marxist British Socialist Party formed a United Socialist Council. At that time Britain's fortunes were at a low ebb with military defeats, shipping losses, shortage of fuel and food, mounting casualties, general war weariness, and the defection of Russia from the struggle. During the summer of 1917 the United Socialist Council arranged a convention to inaugurate a British revolution and to draw Britain out of the war. Although this was attended by over a thousand delegates and mass resolutions were passed applauding the Russian example and calling for the creation of workers' and soldiers' soviets in Britain, the convention made little impression on the nation.

The Representation of the People Act, which became law in June 1918, greatly extended the electorate. The voting qualification for men of over twenty-one was to be attained by a six-months residence in a parliamentary constituency and was no longer dependent upon household franchise. Women also obtained the right to vote, but in their case they had to be over thirty years of age. Plural voting was brought to an end, with the only exception that a second vote could be cast either in a university constituency or for business premises.

To say that the Britain which had emerged after the Armistice in November 1918 was a totally different country from the Britain which had entered the war in 1914 would be stating the obvious. There were very few families which had not endured the death of at least one proximate relation as a total of some three-quarters of a million servicemen from the United Kingdom had been killed, and the mutuality of suffering had considerably lessened, though it had not removed, the ingrained barriers of class-distinction. The nation's economic situation was extremely grave as the financial losses, now reflected both in external and internal debts, had been enormous. But the discrepancies in individual wealth and living standards had also been reduced owing to the substantial increase in the level of wages and the mounting taxation of larger incomes. However, the basic inequality of opportunity still remained. Although after 1918 all children received compulsory, full-time education up to the age of fourteen, it was rare to find a child from a working-class family at a public school or a university, and the senior professions and higher grades in the government service were still recruited from a narrow segment of the community. Women had now overcome a great many of their former disabilities and were well on the way to achieving complete emancipation. Most of the professions had opened their doors to them and they had been granted an equal status with men at the leading universities.

One of the main social legacies of the First World War was an acceptance by the public in Britain that democratic liberty necessarily involved a certain control by the State over the absolute freedom of the individual. This was exemplified in the principle of rent restriction. During the war years the building of private homes had virtually ceased and by 1918 the shortage of private housing had become acute. To meet the possibility that some landlords might resort to profiteering and to wholesale evictions, the Government passed a series of statutes with regard to certain classes of lease, restricting all future increases in rents and granting security of tenure to tenants who continued to observe the covenants in their leases. This legislation affected a large proportion of the flats and houses throughout the country, and subsequent Acts extended the controls and created a vast new body of law which became, for the most part, the concern of the County Courts.

The industrial truce which the trade union leaders had promised for the duration of the war was broken by a succession of strikes during the summer of 1918, and labour unrest increased after the Armistice. The militant workers in Glasgow called for a general strike in 1919 in support of a forty-hour week and raised a red flag above the town hall as a symbol of their cause. In 1920, when trade union membership had risen to over eight million, the TUC decided to set up a permanent General Council in place of their Parliamentary Committee. The Council of the TUC from its initiation adopted a moderate and responsible attitude; however, there was in the unions at that time a powerful revolutionary movement inspired by the Communist Party which wished to emulate the example of Soviet Russia and to establish a dictatorship of the proletariat. In this atmosphere outline plans were formulated for the declaration of a general strike, but the militancy declined as the post-war boom ended, to be followed by increasing unemployment and falling wages. By 1922 industrial relations had become relatively peaceful.

At the general election in 1922 the Labour Party returned more members than the Liberals and became the second largest party in the House of Commons. Significantly, only 80 of their total of 142 MPs were trade unionists, the remainder being drawn from the middle or upper classes. At the next election in December 1923 they increased their strength to 191, and the following month they were able, with Liberal support, to form a minority Government. There were over a million unemployed in the country by that time, but any hopes that a Labour administration would be better able to handle this massive problem, or indeed to work more closely with the unions, were soon shattered. After a mere ten months in office the new Government felt obliged to go to the country again, and in November 1924 the Conservatives were swept back into power with a substantial overall majority.

Throughout 1925 the industrial scene in Britain was dominated by the grim shadow of unemployment and by the smouldering discontent among the miners. The coalfields had been nationalized during the war but had reverted to private ownership after the Armistice. Mine-owners were viewed with grave mistrust by their employees and when the coal industry entered a period of depression, due mainly to a surfeit of inexpensive German and Polish coal on the European market, this latent hostility came to a head. The owners had sought to remedy their diminishing sales with abrasive and unrealistic proposals of longer hours and lower wages and the miners, confident of the support of other workers, resolved to embark on a fight to the finish. The General Council of the TUC expressed their willingness to negotiate with the owners on the miners' behalf, but their offer only elicited a lukewarm response from the miners' union.

The miners refused to accept a notice terminating their existing agreement, and the owners threatened to stage a lock-out commencing on 31 July 1925 when the notice expired. At the last minute the Government stepped in and promised a subsidy to maintain the current level of the miners' wages for the next nine months, and they also set up a royal commission under the Liberal statesman Lord Samuel to consider the best methods of improving the efficiency of the coal industry. As a result of these moves, working conditions in the coal fields returned to normal. Nevertheless, the Government were pessimistic about the long-term prospects and they started to make their contingent preparations for meeting a general strike. The country was divided into ten districts, each of which was placed under the control of a civil commissioner, and emergency plans were devised for the operation of public transport and the distribution of food. The Samuel Commission published their report in March 1926. They proposed both a major reorganization of the coal industry which was utterly unacceptable to the owners, and an immediate reduction in wages which was equally unacceptable to the miners. The Government and the General Council of the TUC tried their best to bring about a negotiated settlement, but to no avail. On 1 May 1926 the provisional agreement in the coalfields came to an end and the owners imposed their threatened lock-out. The miners entrusted their cause to the General Council of the TUC which approved plans for a general strike to begin on 3 May at midnight.

The general strike in 1926 was notable for tolerance and restraint exhibited by both sides. Inevitably there were a number of ugly incidents, but these were isolated and localized. Outbreaks of violence occurred in the mining areas and the docks; buses manned by volunteer drivers were sometimes obstructed or damaged; there was a case of attempted sabotage on the railway; and all told some 4,000 people were prosecuted for acts of disorder. On the whole, however, the life of the country carried on fairly normally and the atmosphere never degenerated into outright hostility. Volunteers maintained the essential services, special constables were enrolled to preserve the law, and often the police and the strikers ended the day by playing football matches against each other. Meanwhile Lord Samuel was drafting further proposals for a settlement, and when these were announced, although they were rejected outright by the miners, they were agreed by the General Council of the TUC who called off the strike unconditionally on 12 May. After another six months the embittered miners accepted defeat and returned to work on terms dictated by the mine-owners.

Over the next decade the relationship between employers and employed in Britain appreciably improved. This was due to a partial change of attitude on both sides. The approach of the employers became more reasonable and understanding, and the outlook of unions, stimulated by the views of such exceptional leaders as Ernest Bevin and J. H. Thomas, became more conciliatory and realistic. In the aftermath of the general strike the Conservatives introduced a Bill in 1927 which amended the Trades Disputes Act of 1906 by making sympathetic strikes illegal if they were 'designed or calculated to coerce the Government'. The Bill also provided that before any union could collect political levys its members would have to 'contract in' by signing forms expressing their willingness to pay. Naturally enough, this measure was greatly resented in the trade union movement.

The 1924 Conservative Government remained in office for almost their full permissible period of five years. One of their last important measures was an Act in 1928 which belatedly removed the franchise distinction between men and women by giving the vote to every woman over twenty-one who had a six months' residential qualification. At the general election in the summer of 1929 Labour emerged for the first time as the largest party in the Commons, but still without an overall majority. Once again, as in January 1924, they formed a minority Government with Liberal support. It was an unenviable moment to take office, as Britain was on the threshold of a major economic depression. That winter British exports slumped catastrophically and some industries seemed to be grinding to a halt. By July 1930 there were two million unemployed, and by the end of the year this figure had risen to two and a half million.

During 1930 considerable improvements were made in the Poor Prisoners Defence scheme, which was extended to cover proceedings in the Magistrates' courts as well as those at Assizes and Quarter Sessions. The costs were to be paid out of local funds, and free legal aid was to be granted whenever it appeared to the trial court that 'by reason of the gravity of the charge or of exceptional circumstances' it was desirable for the defendant to be legally represented 'in the interests of justice'.

CHAPTER 23

THE FLOWERING OF THE RULE OF LAW

Britain's economic position had become so desperate and the pound was in such danger by the summer of 1931 that Ramsay MacDonald, the Labour prime minister, decided to form a broadly-based National Government with the Conservatives and the Liberals. The following autumn Parliament was dissolved and National Government candidates fought the new election on a single programme. They were returned to power in overwhelming strength under MacDonald's leadership, even though neither the official Labour or Liberal Parties accepted the concept of a coalition and both continued to put up candidates under their own party labels. The Labour leaders who had supported the National Government, such men as Ramsay MacDonald, J. H. Thomas, and Philip Snowden, were condemned as traitors by their own party and by an influential section of the TUC. From then on a marked cleavage was apparent between the executive committees of the various unions and the Parliamentary Labour Party – at any rate, in the field of strategy.

No endeavours and no resolve seemed capable of stemming the upsurge of unemployment with its debasement of the individual and its ultimate negation. The number of unemployed rose steadily throughout 1932 and reached a peak of just under three million by January 1933. The hated means test, the enquiries to ascertain whether the long-term unemployed were still eligible for relief, became symbolic of the insensible incapacity of the authorities to alleviate the problem, and the newly formed National Unemployed Workers Movement was moulded into an agency for the dissemination of Communist propaganda. However, the worst was over by the middle of 1933: during the second half of that year the long-awaited economic recovery gathered way, and as production expanded the unemployment figures began to fall.

On the whole, the 1930s formed a peaceful period in the domestic history of Britain. For the majority of the population the standards of living were rising; hours became shorter and the value of wages higher; labour-saving devices were finding their way into an increasing number of homes; and the mass-produced entertainment provided by the radio and the cinema was available to all at a fairly modest cost. Education, too, was improving and although the school-leaving age remained at fourteen, arrangements were in hand to raise it to fifteen in September 1939. Even during the commercial boom which followed hard on the great depression there was very little serious industrial unrest. This was due principally to the skill and wisdom of trade union leaders like Ernest Bevin and Walter Citrine. Indeed, the whole attitude of the unions had become more conciliatory and was often matched by far less obdurate behaviour on the part of the employers. Left-wing militancy had now shifted from the unions to the Parliamentary Labour Party, particularly amongst the Marxist intellectuals who had usually emanated from the more privileged sectors of society. At the Labour Party's annual conference in 1932 a resolution was passed pledging that, with or without an absolute majority, the next Labour Government would immediately introduce what was described as 'definite Socialist legislation'.

Sir Oswald Mosley formed the British Union of Fascists in 1932. Mosley, who had been a minister in the 1929 Labour Government and had been expelled from his party two years later, founded his movement on the model of Mussolini's Italian Blackshirts. The BUF, with their uniforms and their policy of calculated violence, were completely alien to British political life, and although their actual membership never exceeded 20,000, their marches, meetings, and rallys were on a sufficient scale to cause the gravest concern both to the authorities and to the public. In 1936 it was decided that this brand of planned intimidation had gone far enough and Parliament bought in a Public Order Act which, by banning the wearing of political uniforms and empowering the police to prohibit political processions, virtually terminated the activities of the British Fascists. The 1936 statute made it an offence for a person to take part in the control or management of an association which was organized and trained, or organized and equipped, 'for the purpose of enabling them to be employed for the use or display of physical force in promoting any political object'.

The Public Order Act of 1936 undoubtedly assisted the police in maintaining the peace, and the case of *Duncan* v. *Jones* in the same year strengthened their hand still further, for it decided that a police officer who 'reasonably apprehended' that the holding of a meeting would cause a disturbance could prevent it from taking place, and that anybody who ignored his directions would commit the offence of obstructing him in the execution of his duty. The exercise of a police officer's authority was still kept under very strict control; in fact the common law gave him very little more power than it gave to the private citizen. They could both arrest a person for felony or suspicion of felony, the only difference being that a private citizen's right of arrest was only lawful if a felony had actually been committed, whereas an arrest by a police officer was lawful whether a felony had been committed or not. Additionally, a police officer could arrest a person whom he saw committing a breach of the peace. In practice, of course, a private citizen would run a greater risk than a police officer of being sued in the civil courts for wrongful arrest. But in the past, as Maitland has observed, 'the ordinary man seems to have been expected to be very active in the pursuit of malefactors, and yet to act at his peril.'

Ramsay MacDonald relinquished the premiership in 1935 and was succeeded by the Conservative leader Stanley Baldwin, who went to the country at the end of the year. Once again the National Government was returned to power with a substantial, albeit a reduced, majority, but at this election the Labour Party managed to treble their representation compared with the figures in 1931. Although Baldwin had sought a mandate for rearmament, there were few people in Britain at that time who viewed at all seriously the prospect of another war with Germany, now aggressively re-emergent under their megalomaniac chancellor, Adolf Hitler. The era of prosperity still continued, and despite the massive unemployment in certain industrial districts the figures for export and production were breaking all records. This generated, perhaps, a totally delusive atmosphere of security.

George V died in January 1936 and his eldest son, who came to the throne as Edward VIII, formally abdicated eleven months later. The abdication crisis, which was never allowed to develop into a constitutional issue, revealed the changed position of the British monarchy and its ultimate subservience to the will of the Government. The new and immensely popular bachelor king had wished to marry a twice-divorced American 'commoner'. He was opposed in this desire by the prime minister, the majority of the Cabinet, and the leaders of the Anglican Church. A contention ensued which might well have become the subject of an impassioned debate in Parliament and an emotive dispute throughout the nation. In the event the king acted with prudence and with dignity. Having announced his abdication, he left the country forthwith and his younger brother George VI came to the throne in his place.

The style of parliamentary government in Britain had altered very little during the twentieth century, except that the strength of the party organizations and the influence of the party Whips had increased considerably. The other changes which occurred had tended to consolidate the settled practices of former generations. Under Lloyd George a proper secretariat had at last been formed for the Cabinet, and in 1937 a measure was introduced which seemed to envisage a perpetuation of the two-party system, as it provided for an official salary to be paid to the leader of the Opposition.

During the 1930s, which was a period of complacency rather than reform, the legal spectrum was not wholly bereft of development. In 1933 the superfluous grand jury system was abolished and thereafter a defendant could only be brought to trial at Assizes or Quarter Sessions on committal from a magistrates' court or, more rarely, on the preferment of a Voluntary Bill of Indictment authorized by a high court judge. The law of divorce was transformed by the Matrimonial Causes Act of 1937, introduced in the House of Commons by A. P. Herbert, the author and Independent member for Oxford University. Herbert's Act permitted decrees of divorce to be granted for cruelty, desertion for three years without cause, and for incurable unsoundness of mind. The grounds for judicial separation and nullity were also extended. In 1938 a departmental committee under the chairmanship of the Hon. Edward Cadogan recommended that the use of corporal punishment as a judicial penalty both for adults and for juveniles should be entirely abandoned. The Government was intending to implement this proposal in a new Criminal Justice Bill, but the measure was shelved on the outbreak of the Second World War.

Soon after the accession of George VI, Stanley Baldwin retired and Neville Chamberlain, then chancellor of the exchequer, became prime minister. After a humiliating effort to appease Hitler in the autumn of 1938 Chamberlain accepted the inevitability of another war and the Government set about a belated policy of rearmament. In July 1939 Britain's first ever peacetime conscripts reported to the colours for six month's military training. Events were now moving fast. On 23 August Soviet Russia and Nazi Germany signed a treaty whereby Russia undertook to remain neutral if Germany became involved in a war. Having secured his eastern flank, Hitler issued orders for the invasion of Poland and the German troops crossed the Polish frontier on 1 September. Britain issued an ultimatum which Hitler ignored, and on 3 September first the British and then the French declared war on Germany.

For the second time within a span of three decades the British people were called upon to renounce a large measure of their personal freedom in a desperate effort to preserve their cherished principles and their age-old heritage. Immediately on the outbreak of war a total black-out was enforced over the whole country, gas-masks were distributed to all civilians, and children were evacuated from areas which would be liable to air attack. German subjects and German sympathizers – including Sir Oswald Mosley and his wife – were hurriedly interned. Censorship was imposed on the Press. New ministries were created with special responsibilities for the control of economic warfare, shipping, information, and food rationing. In the interests of security all persons were issued with identity cards. During the following years governmental authority tightened still further, affecting the direction of labour, exchange control, the licensing of imports, and many other aspects of individual and communal existence. The Emergency Powers Act of 1940 gave the

Cabinet almost unlimited powers both over British citizens and their property and bestowed upon Winston Churchill, the great wartime prime minister, the widest and the most sweeping autocratic powers.

The devastation of the air bombardment and the ravages of the submarine blockade clutched in a stranglehold at Britain's economic life, and in this moment of jeopardy the trade unions were quick to respond by removing all restrictive practices on the factory-floor and permitting their members in vital industries to work a ten-hour day and a seven-day week if such was demanded of them. Ernest Bevin, who had become minister of labour when Churchill had formed his coalition Government in May 1940, played an outstanding role in alleviating the differences between workers and management and in securing the fullest co-peration from both sides. Throughout the early stages of the war the only effective political body in Britain which had opposed the national effort had been the Communist Party. Until the outbreak of hostilities the British Communists had been passionately anti-Hitler, a sentiment which they had not altered on the signing of the Nazi–Soviet pact in August 1939. During the following month, however, they had received a severe reprimand from Moscow as a result of which Harry Pollitt, the British Communist leader, was obliged to confess the error of thought which had led his party to support a capitalist war. Dialectic consistency was restored to the British Communists when the Germans invaded Soviet Russia in the summer of 1941 and the conflict once again became an ideological crusade. A further dissident voice was raised in 1940 by the members of the Independent Labour Party in the House of Commons who, in December of that year, brought forward a motion for a negotiated peace with Hitler. This was soundly defeated by 341 votes to 4. During the six years of the war only about 60,000 men and women applied for registration as conscientious objectors, and more than 40,000 of these were granted either conditional or unconditional exemption from service with the armed forces.

When at length in 1945 victory came to the Allies, Britain's economic plight was far worse than it had been at the time of the Armistice in 1918. She had lost about two-thirds of her export trade and about one-third of her merchant shipping fleet. In addition, she had expended most of her overseas assets and her overseas investments. It would be small exaggeration to say that the British had bled themselves white in the common struggle. The coalition Government had ended in May 1945 and Churchill had formed a Conservative Caretaker Government in its place. A general election was held the following July and the Labour Party, under the leadership of Clement Attlee, deputy prime minister in the wartime coalition, secured a substantial majority. One of the first measures introduced by the new Parliament had repealed the 1927 statute which had forbidden sympathetic strikes 'designed or calculated to coerce the Government' and had made the collection of political levys by unions dependent upon their members 'contracting in'. The Labour Government had gone on to carry out a major reform of the House of Commons by the Representation of the People Act of 1948, which abolished the second vote either for business premises or for university constituencies, and imposed a financial limit on the expenses incurred by candidates and their agents at any election. During the following year another statute amended the Parliament Act of 1911 by reducing the power of delay of the House of Lords from two years to one year. In 1969 when the age of majority in Britain was lowered from twenty-one to eighteen the ideal of parliamentary democracy seemed to have been fully achieved, with every adult exercising a single vote for the elective chamber and the ultimate powers of the non-elective chamber being reduced to a very minimum.

During the thirty years after the conclusion of the Second World War the sentencing powers of the British criminal courts were extensively developed and reformed. Corporal punishment was abolished by the Criminal Justice Act of 1948, which provided that no person should be sentenced by a court to a whipping and that any enactment which authorized such a sentence should cease to have effect. The abolition of capital punishment was a far more controversial issue and the majority opinion in the country at that time was probably in favour of its retention. However, the abolitionists had a powerful lobby and in 1957 Parliament passed the Homicide Act, a wholly unsatisfactory compromise measure which sought to divide murders into two categories, capital and non-capital. Five types of homicide, for instance those committed in the course of furtherance of theft and those committed by shooting or causing an explosion, were still capital and would be punished by hanging. All other sorts of murder became non-capital and would be punishable with imprisonment for life. It was soon apparent that this statute had created a host of inconsistencies and that a defendant's life might well depend upon some narrow construction of a complex point of law. Capital punishment was finally abolished eight years later by a Bill which was introduced in the House of Commons by a Labour backbencher, Mr Sydney Silverman, but which passed through Parliament as a non-party measure on a free vote. The first section of the Murder (Abolition of Death Penalty) Act of 1965 provided that 'No person shall suffer death for murder, and a person convicted of murder shall . . . be sentenced to imprisonment for life.' The death penalty still remained as the maximum sentence for the offences of piracy with violence and treason, but it seemed extremely doubtful if it would ever again be applied.

In the post-war years there was a general amelioration in the severity of sentencing. Probation orders and fines were used more frequently, and terms of imprisonment for ordinary offences became much shorter. In addition a far wider range of sentences was made available to the courts. In 1948 it became possible to discharge a defendant absolutely, without punishment, or to grant him a conditional discharge so that he would only be punished if he was convicted again within a stated period, which could be up to three years. After 1967 a court was enabled to pass a suspended sentence of imprisonment, which would never be served unless the defendant committed another offence, also punishable with imprisonment during the 'operational period'. A statute in 1972 introduced a new form of sentence, the community service order, which consisted of a spell of unpaid work of a civic character. The courts were also given the power to defer passing sentence on an offender for six months or less if there was a chance that greater leniency might be extended at a future time. By the same enactment a defendant could be ordered to compensate his victims and, in extreme circumstances, he might even be declared a 'criminal bankrupt'.

An offender under the age of seventeen could never be sent to prison, and those aged between seventeen and twenty-one could only be imprisoned if it was considered that no other method of dealing with them was appropriate. The medium-term custodial sentence for young persons of either sex was a period of Borstal training, but youths who required a shorter spell in custody could be sent to a detention centre instead. A great deal more care was being taken when sentencing defendants of all ages and increased attention was paid to the recommendations of probation officers, doctors, and psychiatrists. Special facilities were now provided for mentally-disordered offenders. There was also a parole scheme, by which a responsive prisoner might be released on licence, and a comprehensive system of prison after-care.

The people of Britain had learnt to accept that in the interests of a just society many of their dealings with each other must be subjected to legal restriction. The housing shortage had persisted and the statutory control over the majority of residential tenancies had become an institution of British life. The protection which the common law afforded to the public against the sale of injurious food and medicines was strengthened and augmented by a series of Food and Drugs Acts. The consumer was granted ever-increasing safeguards against deception or exaggerated claims; indeed, the Trades Descriptions Acts of 1968 and 1972 created a host of new offences which would be committed by a person 'in the course of a trade or business' who offered false or misleading information about his goods or his services.

For many years the divorce laws in Britain had been enmeshed in a tangled web of subterfuge and unreality, based on the fanciful principle that the petitioning party must be wholly, or almost wholly, free from matrimonial fault. All this was swept away by the Divorce Reform Act in 1970 which provided that thenceforth the sole ground for divorce or judicial separation would be that the marriage had broken down 'irretrievably'. The irretrievable breakdown could be proved by adultery, desertion, unreasonable behaviour, separation for five years, or even by separation for two years if the respondent consented to the decree of divorce being granted. The statute also made provision for an attempt at reconciliation, and abolished the rule that a decree could be refused if the petitioner had been in collusion with the respondent or had connived at or condoned the respondent's conduct. To emphasize the essentially domestic nature of the new matrimonial law, in 1970 the Probate, Divorce and Admiralty Division of the High Court was renamed the Family Division.* A considerable proportion of the time of the Family Division was to be spent in settling matters of the custody and welfare of the children of the marriage, and in sharing out the marital property between the ex-husband and ex-wife on a fair and equitable basis.

Although the post-war years were an era of prosperity and full employment they abounded in both official and unofficial strikes. Trade union membership reached gigantic proportions for in Britain, ever since 1824, every private employee and every public employee, except those in the police and the armed forces, had been entitled to join a union if they so desired. A royal commission on trade unions and employers' associations – usually known as the Donovan Commission – was set up by the Labour Government in 1965 and brought out an exhaustive report in 1968. One of their principal conclusions was that in conditions of full employment the power-centre amongst the workers in many industries had shifted from the union executives to groups of independent activists on the shop floor, who might or might not be led by their shop stewards.

In January 1969 Harold Wilson's Labour Government brought out a White Paper entitled *In Place of Strife* setting out their plans for an Industrial Relations Act, to be based substantially upon the findings of the Donovan Commission. They intended to establish a commission on industrial relations which would supervise collective bargaining, and an industrial board to have responsibility for matters of discipline. Amongst its powers the board would be able, in certain circumstances, to defer a strike by requiring those involved 'to return to work and to desist from industrial action for a period of twenty-eight days', or to require a union to ascertain the views of its members by a secret ballot before a strike was actually commenced. The board would also be empowered to settle conflicts between rival unions and to hear complaints against unions by any individuals who felt aggrieved by their actions. It would be authorized to

* The Admiralty work was in fact transferred to the Queens Bench Division (Admiralty Court).

impose 'financial penalties' on employers, unions and individual strikers, and such fines would be enforced through the County Courts. The White Paper aroused such a storm of indignation in the trade union movement that the Government decided to abandon the entire proposal.

The Conservatives came to power at the general election in 1970 with a specific mandate to introduce their own measure for the control of industrial disputes, to be founded again upon some of the recommendations of the Donovan Commission. The Industrial Relations Act of 1971 established an Industrial Relations Court with the status and powers of the High Court. A member of the higher judiciary would preside and would sit with persons who had 'special knowledge or experience of industrial relations'. Unions were required to give notice of intended strikes and the court had power to order a 'cooling-off period', or a secret ballot amongst the members of the union concerned. The court could make awards of compensation, enforceable as High Court judgements, and any persons who disobeyed its directions could be punished for contempt, which meant, in effect, that they might be sent to prison. The TUC and the majority of the unions, who had viewed the passage of the Industrial Relations Act with impassioned fury, set out to make its main provisions unworkable. They largely succeeded, and the Act was repealed by the Labour Government directly they were returned to power in 1974. Besides its concern with collective disputes, the Industrial Relations Court had had an extensive jurisdiction to investigate complaints of 'unfair dismissal', but amidst the acrimonious political controversies which surrounded its short existence this side of its work had attracted very little public attention.

The concept of unfair dismissal was another segment in the protective screen which Parliament was erecting to safeguard employees against harsh or arbitrary treatment. The Contracts of Employment Act in 1963 had provided that employers must give them written particulars of the terms of their employment, and had prescribed the minimum periods of notice. The Redundancy Payments Act in 1965 had ensured that an employee would receive adequate compensation on becoming redundant. The Race Relations Act in 1968 had forbidden employers to discriminate on the grounds of colour, race, or ethnic or national origin. And the Equal Pay Act in 1970, which would come into force in 1975, was to forbid any distinction in conditions of employment between men and women.

A vast increase in civil litigation resulted from the Legal Aid and Advice Act of 1949, which was designed to make the assistance of solicitors and counsel 'more readily available for persons of small or moderate means'. Nearly all forms of civil proceedings were included in the scheme and the legally-aided litigant was only liable to pay a maximum contribution in accordance with his means, the remainder of the expense being borne by the State. The provisions of the Poor Prisoners Defence regulations continued to apply to criminal cases until 1967 when a comprehensive legal aid scheme was introduced to cover every aspect of a criminal trial.

A royal commission on Assizes and Quarter Sessions, under the chairmanship of Lord Beeching, was appointed in 1966 to suggest reforms which might lead to 'the more convenient, economic and efficient disposal' by the courts of both civil and criminal cases. In their report, published in 1969, the Beeching Commission made a series of far-reaching proposals. They found that the general pattern of the court system 'was devised for circumstances which no longer exist', and that far too much had been retained only because it was traditional. Assizes were held too infrequently and often sat at inconvenient locations. The ancient geographical divisions which marked the jurisdictions of Assizes and Quarter Sessions had no relevance in present-day conditions; and the system whereby both sets of courts were administered by separate authorities was unnecessarily complicated. The report made no criticism of the County Courts, save that their jurisdiction was too limited. In a glowing tribute to the County Court judges the Commission expressed the view that their judicial talent appeared to be 'under-used' and that too few of them had been elevated to the High Court Bench.

The Courts Act in 1971 implemented most of the Beeching Commission's recommendations. Courts of Assize and Quarter Sessions were abolished and a new Supreme Court was established consisting of the Court of Appeal, the High Court, and the Crown Court. All the former criminal jurisdiction both of Assizes and of Quarter Sessions was to vest in the Crown Courts, which were newly created by the Act, and which would sit at convenient locations throughout the country. The jurisdiction and powers of the Crown Court would be exercised by a judge of the High Court, a circuit judge, or a recorder, each of whom might be assisted on occasion by not more than four justices of the peace. Circuit judges, who were also first created by the Act, would, like recorders, be appointed by the sovereign on the advice of the lord chancellor. They were to sit in the Crown Court, the County Court, and, if necessary, in any division of the High Court. Recorders were to act as part-time judges; they could be drawn from members of the barristers' or the solicitors' professions who had the necessary qualifications. In addition to barristers of at least ten years' standing, solicitors who had been recorders for five years were eligible for appointment as circuit judges. The office of County Court judge was ended, but existing County Court judges were transferred to the Circuit Bench. The entire administration and staffing of the unified court system was taken over by the lord chancellor.

The Beeching Commission had commented that the overloading of the criminal courts was not only due to the rise in crime but also to the extension of legal aid, one result of which had been to increase the proportion of fought cases which took 'about ten times as long to hear as pleas of guilty'. Those familiar with the work of the magistrates' courts were certain, too, that legal aid had caused a lot more defendants to claim trial by jury whenever they were entitled to do so. In 1967 the long-outmoded distinction between felonies and misdemeanors had been abolished, but the more meaningful division of offences into those which were summary, and only triable by the magistrates, and those which were indictable, and either could, or must be tried by a higher court, had remained. The view was widespread amongst lawyers that a defendant would have a greater chance of being acquitted by a jury than by magistrates, especially if his defence was a very flimsy one. It was believed that juries were inclined to be more credulous and more susceptible to the sway of emotion for, as Dostoyevsky once remarked, a juror's momentary impulse might always outweigh his civic responsibility. Two important developments had taken place with regard to the British jury. In 1967 it became possible for a jury which had been unable to reach a unanimous verdict after two hours' deliberation, to return a majority verdict of either eleven to one or ten to two. And in 1974 the minimum age for jurors was lowered to eighteen and every person on the electoral roll between the ages of eighteen and sixty-five became eligible for jury-service.

The social distinction between the barristers' and the solicitors' professions had long vanished, and many of the Bar's entrenched prerogatives were beginning to disappear. Solicitors could act as advocates in the magistrates' courts and the County Courts and they had now even been granted a limited right of audience in the Crown Courts. Further, since 1948 they could be appointed stipendiary magistrates, and by the Courts Act, as has been seen, they could become circuit judges. However, no matter how close the two branches of the legal profession had drawn together, a majority of the members of both felt that the interests of the law and the interests of the public would best be served if they were to retain their separate identities and their separate responsibilities. The senate of the four Inns of Court which was set up in 1966 had taken over all matters relating to legal education and professional discipline from the individual Inns, leaving the benchers to control their own constitutions, property and finances.

It had long been recognized that a strong, independent and reputable Bar was only second in importance to a strong, independent, and reputable Bench. The collegiate atmosphere of the Inns of Court, the smallness of the barristers' profession, and the decentralized community life in chambers had all helped to instil the traditions and to perpetuate the ethical standards of former generations. The independence of the Bar was exemplified by a convention that a barrister was bound to accept any brief, at a proper fee, in the courts in which he normally practised. That maxim had been enunciated as long ago as 1792 by the great forensic orator Thomas Erskine, who had himself been victimized from undertaking an unpopular defence, when he said that from the moment an advocate could be permitted to say that he would not stand between the Crown and the subject – from that moment the liberties in this country would be at an end. In the changing attitudes of the post-war world, the social convulsions and the altered sense of values, the image abroad of the British legal profession continued to stand high. An eminent American judge, chief justice of the United States, Warren E. Burger, commented in 1973, 'For twenty years I have watched advocates conduct trials in more than a dozen countries, and nowhere have I seen more ardent, more effective advocacy than in the courts of England.

British judges have always decided their cases according to the legal precedents laid down by their own or superior courts, the highest authority of all being vested in the House of Lords. Formerly the House of Lords was bound by its previous decisions however ancient, which tended to circumscribe both the flexibility and the free development of the law. This principle was changed in 1966 by a unanimous resolution of the lords of appeal in ordinary, in which they stated that although they still regarded the use of precedent as 'an indispensible foundation on which to decide what is the law and its application to individual cases', nevertheless they recognized the dangers which might arise from a too rigid adherence to this system. They therefore proposed to modify their existing practice and 'while treating former decisions of this House as normally binding, to depart from a previous decision when it appears right to do so'.

It is inevitable that a true respect for the Rule of Law should be partly dependent on a general acceptance of the wisdom, justice, and logicality of the regulations and the codes of conduct which govern the daily lives of the people. In recent years judges and lawyers have been called upon to play a prominent role on the permanent statutory committees, which have been instituted to keep the state of the law under continual review. The earliest of the committees, the Statute Law Committee, was started in 1868 and was mainly concerned with the modification of out-dated Acts of Parliament. The Criminal Law Revision Committee was set up in 1959 'to examine such aspects of the criminal law of England and Wales' as may be referred to it from time to time by the home secretary. And lastly, the most important body of all, the Law Commission, was created in 1965 to maintain a systematic survey over all branches of the existing law 'with a view to its simplification, consolidation and reform'. The Law Commission has now taken over the principal functions of the older Statute Law Committee.

CHAPTER 24

THE FRAILTY OF THE RULE OF LAW

Historians of the future will probably comment on the fact that around the middle of the twentieth century many people were beginning to doubt if the British constitutional system, founded as it was on the Rule of Law, would be capable of surviving for very much longer.

It was being remarked that the growing power of the large trade unions had undermined the sovereignty of Parliament – indeed the Trade Union Congress were demanding, and were sometimes obtaining, a right to be consulted by the Government of the day with regard both to general policies and to impending legislation. In the background, constantly menacing, was the grim shadow of industrial action. By this time strikes, for the most part, had ceased to be insulated struggles between employer and employed; it had been realized and amply proven that the most effective stoppages were those which could jeopardize the economy, the health, the safety, the comfort or the well-being of the nation as a whole. There were few who queried the right of the worker to withhold his labour: but there were equally few who remained oblivious of the fact that the strike-weapon, if ruthlessly applied, could prove the very negation of lawful, democratic process. Years earlier Professor A. V. Dicey, the eminent constitutional lawyer, had foreseen this basic conflict between the point of view of the striker and the point of view of the public at large. In the days when the trade union movement was still in its infancy he had written:

> The problem to be solved, either as a matter of theory or as a matter of practical necessity, is at bottom always and everywhere the same. How can the right of combined action be curtailed without depriving individual liberty of half its value; how can it be left unrestricted without destroying either the liberty of individual citizens, or the power of the Government?

Strikers were placing increasing reliance on the use of the picket. The legality of pickets was recognized by statute by the common law. During an industrial dispute the parties concerned were fully entitled to publicise their grievances against one another, and the employees were permitted to try to persuade their fellow-workers to join the strike. However, the scope of lawful picketing was limited to peacefully obtaining or communicating information and peacefully prevailing on a person to work or to refrain from working. It was forbidden for pickets to attend upon someone at or near his home, or to exercise any restriction, intimidation or constraint. The Donovan Committee had observed in 1968, 'it has not been easy for the courts to distinguish clearly the boundary between action by pickets which stays on the right side of the line and that which constitutes an invasion across the line on the rights of others'. It was generally felt during this period that prevalence of militancy and violent behaviour amongst pickets, who were often operating in considerable numbers, was a very far cry from the legal concept of peaceful picketing. Perhaps the worst example of this type of lawless conduct was demonstrated during a building strike in 1972 by the self-styled 'flying pickets' who travelled round in coaches, sometimes in parties numbering as many as 250, and visited various building sites which had remained at work wrecking the equipment there and molesting the employees who had chosen not to join the strike.

A new tactic in the employment of the picket had been successfully introduced by the National Union of Mineworkers during their strike in 1972, when they had blockaded the electricity power stations at which the employees were not on strike, and had soon brought about a situation where 800,000 of the working population had had to be laid off work and the national fuel stocks had been so reduced that they would only have been sufficient to maintain the country's electricity supplies for a further two weeks. A similar procedure had been adopted by the miners in their 1974 strike when they were opposing the Conservative administration's pay policy. Once again their blockade of the power stations had rapidly reduced the country to a state of industrial chaos, and had indirectly brought about the downfall of the Government. Shortly afterwards the Scottish mineworkers had produced a pamphlet in which they had surveyed the outcome of the strike and had commented, 'The real lesson is that in a capitalist society survival depends on using strength when you have it.' Nevertheless, many rational men and women had been left wondering how far this new employment of the picket could be carried. What would prevent any other group of workers, they asked, from pressing their claims by disrupting a vital commodity in national life and thereby strangling the community into submission?

Formerly the strength of the Rule of Law in Britain had emanated from its universal acceptance and from the ardent desire of the mass of the people to preserve it unblemished. Now, however, it had become apparent that certain well-organized political groups were intent on achieving its destruction.

One of the principal characteristics of the British way of life for almost a century and a half had been the unarmed police officers and the total absence of any specially-trained or para-military force for controlling riots or disturbances. In the late 1960s there had been three serious attempts to overcome the London police in carefully-prepared and ruthlessly-staged confrontations. The first of these had occurred in October 1967 when a large demonstration took place in Trafalgar Square to protest against the military operations of the United States in Vietnam. No doubt the bulk of the people who had attended had been peaceable and sincere, but after the meeting about 4,000 of the crowd, amongst whom about 250 Anarchists were said to be prominent, had endeavoured to attack the American Embassy in Grosvenor Square. Initially they had managed to burst through the police cordon and had forced their way into the Embassy garden before the cordon could be re-formed. The savage fighting had continued for several hours with the demonstrators using banners, sticks, bottles and stones as weapons. Out of the 350 police officers who had been present no less than 39 had had to receive treatment for their injuries.

The next confrontation had been organized by a movement known as the Vietnam Solidarity Campaign and had taken place in March 1968. This time there had been little doubt that the violence was premeditated as many of the posters advertising the meeting had been superimposed with the words 'come armed', and when coaches carrying demonstrators to London were stopped and searched by the police it had become apparent that the directive had often been obeyed. Once again the demonstration had centred around the storming of the American Embassy in Grosvenor Square, but the onslaught had been on a far larger scale than in the previous year; indeed it was estimated that at one time a mob of about 10,000 people had been trying to break through the cordons, while hurling smoke bombs, cans, ball-bearings and fireworks at the defenceless police officers. Attempts were also made, sometimes successfully, to bring down the horses of the mounted police by rolling marbles in front of them. At length the attack had been called off with the cordons still intact. Out of the 1,300 police on duty in the Square that day 117 had been injured, some slightly and some seriously.

Soon afterwards the Vietnam Solidarity Campaign had started to organize an even more massive trial of strength with the forces of authority. The planning of this third demonstration had been entrusted to a special committee, believed to have been dominated by Trotskyists. In October 1968 the students of the London School of Economics had occupied the School's buildings and had set them up as a haven and a first-aid post for the demonstrators. Two days later a vast crowd of about 25,000 people had assembled on the Victoria Embankment and marched across London to Speaker's Corner in Hyde Park where they had held a meeting. During the return march some 5,000 demonstrators, led by groups of Maoists and Anarchists, had broken away from the main procession to launch the customary attack on the American Embassy. During the fighting in Grosvenor Square 74 police officers had been injured, some being struck with steel scaffolding poles and others being hit by pieces of homemade bombs, but once again the cordons had stood firm.

It had been a period, too, of extensive student unrest and dissatisfaction, for the young had been over-ready to accept the intellectual leadership of anyone who was sufficiently persistent in advancing a radically-extremist or an anti-authoritarian philosophy. They had been unmindful of Edmund Burke's reflection, 'It is a general and popular error to imagine the loudest complainers for the public to be the most anxious for its welfare.' There had been more sinister elements on the student-scene as well. An official report in 1974 on some recent disturbances at Essex University had thrown the blame on a small minority of militant students, and had gone on to state;

> Their aims are clear. On any issue – and if there is none they will invent one – they wish to raise the temperature and create a situation in which the university authorities will be cornered and capitulate. For them university authorities are not only the tools of the capatalist state but the weakest link in that state, and to strike at them is to promote the destruction of that state and achieve the political objectives nearest to their hearts.

A cynical disbelief in the supremacy of the law had been encouraged by the attitude of certain leaders of public opinion and certain moulders of public ideas. Early in the 1970s the Apex Trust, a Home Office-supported agency for finding employment for recently-discharged prisoners, had reported the emergence of a new breed of social worker whose approach to their work was coloured by their political viewpoint. 'Many of them,' it was said, 'divided the laws of the land into those they were prepared to accept and those they had a moral right to break', and they were passing on this attitude to the ex-prisoners who were under their care. About the same time some more-influential voices were advancing a similar proposition. For instance, the General Secretary of the powerful Amalgamated Union of Engineering Workers had written in his union's journal, 'The law depends on people believing that the law is fair in its creation and fair in its application. When either of these conditions is not met, then no one is obliged to obey the so-called law.' And Mr Eric Heffer, MP, one of the leading figures in the Labour Party's left-wing Tribune group and a future Government Minister, had said in an article in the *Observer* newspaper, 'It is strongly argued that the law must be obeyed at all times and in all circumstances. As a general principle no one could disagree with that. But law is a product of society and Governments can and do introduce unjust class laws. . . . Such laws are bound to be broken by trade unions if they wish to maintain free collective bargaining. This is not anarchy, as some suggest, but a revolt against laws imposed on majorities in the interest of minorities.'

And then there had been the affair of the Clay Cross Councillors. The councillors in Clay Cross in Derbyshire, for political motives, had refused to implement the Conservative Government's Housing Finance Act, which in 1972 had passed quite properly through all its stages in Parliament. They had realized that by law they would make themselves personally liable for any lost revenue which had been occasioned by their default. In due course, under the procedure prescribed by the Local Government Act of 1933, the rebel councillors had been surcharged with the amount of the deficiency and had been disqualified from membership of any local council for a period of five years. They had appealed, first to the Divisional Court and then to the Court of Appeal, and in both instances after a full and careful examination of their legal arguments the appeals had been dismissed. The following year at the annual Labour Party Conference a resolution had been carried that 'upon the election of a Labour government all the penalties, financial or otherwise, should be removed retrospectively from councillors who have courageously refused to implement the Housing Act, 1972.' It might be said that a certain amount of latitude should be permitted even to the major political parties whilst they are in opposition, but unfortunately this particular resolution, so clearly an encouragement to the deliberate breaking of the law, had been actively supported from the platform by Mr Edward Short, then the Deputy Leader of the Labour Party. It should be added that when a Labour government had come into office very soon afterwards the Prime Minister, Mr Harold Wilson, had informed the House of Commons that there would in fact be no retrospective legislation to remove the financial penalties which had been imposed on the Clay Cross councillors. 'The law of the land,' he had said, 'however unfair, however divisive, must be obeyed until it is repealed.'

During the years 1974 and 1975 the British people had suddenly started to discuss quite openly the possibility of the collapse of parliamentary government and a breakdown in the established system of law and order. Various unofficial organizations had been set up throughout the country which were to be mobilized if the breakdown occurred and which would then take over from the official organs of control.

These organizations had no historical significance in themselves: what was historically significant was that they should have been formed at all. As *The Times* had commented in a leading article:

> They articulate the deepening anxieties of many of those who have a stake in the present order of society and want to be sure that changes, which are inevitable, are not of a kind to render it unrecognizable. . . .Their anxiety is whetted by the spectacle of authority, including the constitutionally-based civil administration, frequently and easily defeated by strikes at sensitive spots in the economic and social arrangements of the nation. They fear either the cumulative effects of government retreat before multiple sectional aggression, or widespread disorders ensuing upon a determined effort to oppose it.

During the 1980's Britain was subjected to a succession of inner-city riots. The first of these occurred at Brixton in the spring of 1981. Lord Scarman, who conducted an official enquiry into the disturbance, wrote in his report:

> During the weekend of 10–12 April (Friday, Saturday and Sunday) the British people watched with horror and incredulity an instant audio-visual presentation on their television sets of scenes of violence and disorder in their capital city; the like of which had not previously been seen in this century in Britain. In the centre of Brixton, a few hundred young people – most, but not all of them black – attacked the police on the streets with stones, bricks, iron bars, and petrol bombs, demonstrating to millions of their fellow citizens the fragile basis of the Queen's peace.

The rioting continued for two more days of aggression, looting and arson. Although the venom of the mob was principally directed at the police, the crews of ambulances and fire engines were also attacked; private cars were damaged or destroyed; and countless buildings were vandalised. During that weekend, Lord Scarman commented,

> "The police had undergone an experience til then unparalleled on the mainland of the United Kingdom. . . . They stood between our society and a total collapse of law and order in the streets of an important part of the capital."

Later in the year serious disorders occurred in Southall, Toxteth, Moss Side, and the West Midlands. The pattern was always similar – violent confrontations with the police, looting, arson, and the wanton destruction of private property.

A riot could erupt on the flimsiest pretext. In the Handsworth area of Birmingham in September 1985 a crowd assembled at the place where two black youths had just been arrested, and then proceeded to attack some firemen who were putting out a blaze in a disused bingo hall. When the police came on the scene in protective helmets and carrying shields they were assailed with petrol bombs and concrete blocks. A mob, estimated to number about two thousand men and women, then turned to looting and burning, the shops belonging to Asians suffering worst of all. A Times reporter described the scene:

> Some of the looters piled stolen goods into vans and cars. Others used supermarket trolleys. Parked vehicles in side streets were overturned, petrol tanks smashed, fuel lines cut and the pouring petrol set ablaze. The burning vehicles scattered at crazy angles across the streets were used as barricades against the police who tried to seal off the area.

During he night a frenzied mob virtually laid waste to the centre of Handsworth. Two Asian brothers were assaulted by black youths, and then were left to perish in the flames of their home. Police reinforcements were rushed to the area from surrounding localities and by dawn they had managed to restore order, but not without sustaining numerous casualties.

In his report to the Home Secretary, the Chief Constable of the West Midlands attributed the disorders principally to professional drug-dealers. The impulse behind them, he said, was hatred of the police; the aim had been to drive the police from the whole area.

After the suppression of the Handsworth riots there were ominous rumours that the same people who had instigated them had travelled to London to stir up more trouble. Police and community leaders in Brixton had begun to notice an atmosphere of increasing tension and growing militancy among the younger residents. A most unfortunate accident formed an ostensible motive for the outbreak of violence. The police had carried out a dawn raid on a house in which a dangerous, armed criminal was believed to be hiding, and one of the police officers had unintentionally shot and wounded the mother of the wanted man. In an effort to avert trouble the police immediately issued a public apology and promised a full investigation of the incident, but it was to no avail. A crowd of about 1500 black youths, many of whom were wearing balaclava helmets to conceal their faces, launched an attack on Brixton police station with petrol bombs and bricks. The disturbance spread rapidly. Shops were looted, houses burgled, parked cars were set on fire, and passing motorists were stopped and robbed. There were several cases of arson and firemen were prevented from putting out the flames.

A large force of police in protective clothing and carrying shields broke down the hastily-erected barricades and dispersed the mob. It was estimated that over two million pounds worth of damage had been done by the rioters. In addition, ninety-three police officers were injured and a 29-year-old journalist was killed.

A week later an even more savage riot broke out on the Broadwater Farm Estate in the London Borough of Tottenham. It was known that many of the younger people living there had a bitter hatred of the police, and police officers were frequently attacked when carrying out their duties on the Estate. Throughout the previous summer groups of youths had been seen assembling among the houses in masks and combat jackets. It had been noticed that empty bottles were disappearing and it was suspected that they were being collected for making petrol bombs.

The riot started after a woman on the Estate had collapsed and died while the police were carrying out a routine search of her house following the arrest of her son. There was no serious suggestion that any police officer had been to blame and at the subsequent inquest on the woman the coroner's jury had recorded a verdict of "accidental death".

The following evening a large crowd of black youths had emerged from the Broadwater Farm Estate armed with knives, machetes, and iron bars. They set up barricades of burning cars, and spent the next few hours looting shops, robbing pedestrians, and setting fire to houses and parked vehicles. The Police tried to subdue the mob, but were repulsed with showers of missiles, petrol bombs, and an occasional bullet from a rifle or revolver. Sometimes the road ahead of them was saturated with petrol which was ignited when they tried to advance.

The situation became so serious that the Metropolitan Police Commissioner authorised the use of plastic bullets and assigned some officers from the tactical firearms unit to be available in the riot area. In fact neither plastic bullets nor live ammunition were ever used.

At the height of the trouble one of the police officers, P. C. Blakelock, was brutally murdered. He had become separated from his colleagues and was surrounded by a gang of armed youths who stabbed him to death. One of the youths admitted later that an attempt had been made to cut off the dead constable's head so that it could be hoisted on a pole.

It was after midnight before the rioters were finally cleared from the streets. No less than 255 police officers had been injured, seven of them having sustained bullet wounds.

Some of the riots which had occurred quite recently in Britain have had only one motive – opposition to the enforcement of the law. In the autumn of 1986 the St. Pauls area of Bristol had become notorious for drug-trafficking and other criminal activities. On 11 September when the police were trying to carry out some arrests there, a large number of black youths took to the streets in protest, many of them with their faces concealed with scarves and hoods. Police with shields and batons took several hours to disperse them.

Very few latter-day disorders have emanated from political discontent. However, a politically-incited riot took place in the West End of London in 1990. On 31 March of that year a large demonstration against the government's unpopular community charge – widely known as the poll tax – was taken over by trouble-makers and hooligans. Underground stations were closed and traffic was brought to a standstill as a mob careered through the streets smashing windows and wrecking parked cars. Almost 350 people were arrested and scores of police officers were hurt before the riot was brought under control.

After the Brixton and the Tottenham riots Sir Kenneth Newman, the Metropolitan Police Commissioner at the time, ordered a full enquiry into strategy and tactics employed by the police in restoring order on both occasions. The conclusions reached by the officers who carried out the enquiry were published in 1986[1]. "Regrettably", they stated, "the traditional uniformed image of the 'British Bobby' is not compatible with that of an officer engaged in riot control." They went on to make recommendations for the greater protection of the police and for their increased effectiveness when dealing with hostile mobs. They should be provided with visored helmets and fireproof overalls. Two types of shield might be required; a long one designed for static defence, and one which was short and light, suitable for use in an advance or a charge. There were occasions when longer truncheons would be more practical than those with which police officers were normally equipped. There was a need for armoured personnel carriers, especially when firearms were being used by the rioters.

The government's reaction to the Review was commendably prompt. In the summer of 1986 Douglas Hurd, the Home Secretary, announced in the House of Commons that the Home Office was buying twenty-four bullet-proof landrovers and eighty protected personnel carriers for the use of the Metropolitan Police. There would also be a new type of long truncheon which would be issued to officers in situations of "extreme disorder". Similar equipment could also be acquired by police forces outside London.

The Public Order Act, 1986 gave the police a wide discretion in imposing conditions with regard to the numbers, the place, and the duration of any intended public assembly. In addition, the Act created the new offence of "violent disorder", which was defined in the following terms:

> Where three or more persons who are present together use or threaten unlawful violence, and the conduct of them (taken together) is such as would cause a person of reasonable firmness present at the scene to fear for his personal safety, each of the persons using or threatening unlawful violence is guilty of violent disorder.

In spite of these recent happenings, and the dastardly activities of the terrorist, it would be utterly fallacious to conclude that the Rule of Law will be in any real or

[1]Metropolitan Police, Public Order Review, Civil Disturbances 1981–1985.

immediate danger in Britain so long as leaders of the national life of the nation and the ordinary men and women in the street continue to retain their ardent passion for democratic freedom, and their infinite regard for constitutional government, which they have inherited from their forebears.

BIBLIOGRAPHY

The sources of information for this book have been many and various and I am only mentioning here the principal works which I have used.

In matters of legal history I have relied throughout upon W. S. Holdsworth's massive *A History of English Law*, 16 Volumes (London 1903–1966) and Sir James Stephen's equally comprehensive *A History of the Criminal Law of England*, 3 volumes (London, 1883). I have also referred to Sir Frederick Pollock and F. W. Maitland's *History of the English Law*, 2 Volumes (Cambridge, 1898), F. W. Maitland's *Justice and Police* (London, 1951), Sir William Blackstone's *Commentaries on the Laws of England* (London, 1876) and Leon Radzinowicz's *A History of the Criminal Law*, 3 volumes (London 1948–1956).

With regard to the general historical background I have made extensive use of the Oxford History of England, particularly the last six volumes of the series, *The Later Stuarts 1660–1714* by Sir George Clark (Oxford, 1934), *The Whig Supremacy 1714–1760* by Basil Williams (Oxford, 1939), *The Reign of George III 1760–1815* by J. Steven Watson (Oxford, 1960), *The Age of Reform 1815–1870* by Sir Llewellyn Woodward (Oxford, 1962), *England 1870–1914* by Sir Robert Ensor (Oxford, 1936) and *English History 1914–1945* by A. J. P. Taylor (Oxford, 1965). I have also been assisted by G. M. Trevelyan's *History of England in the Nineteenth Century and After* (London, 1922) and his *English Social History* (London, 1942), Macaulay's *History of England from the Accession of James II* (London, 1849) and Lecky's *A History of England in the Eighteenth Century* (London, 1887).

I have drawn a good deal of my material on the history of the British constitution from *The English Constitution* by Walter Bagehot (London, 1867), *Law and Custom of the Constitution* by Sir William Anson (Oxford, 1911) and *Introduction to the Study of the Law of the Constitution* by A. V. Dicey (London, 1924).

Out of the many authoritative studies of the history of the Justices of the Peace and the English police, I have found the following particularly useful, *English Local Government. The Parish and the County* by Beatrice and Sidney Webb (London, 1906), *Justices of the Peace 1361–1848* by Bertram Osborne (Shaftesbury, 1960) *A History of the Police in England* by W. L. Melville Lee (London, 1901), *A New Study of Police History* by Charles Reith (London, 1956) and *The English Policeman 1871–1935* by Alwyn Solmes (London, 1935. The history of Bow Street and the Bow Street police is well covered in *The History of the Bow Street Runners* by Gilbert Armitage (London, 1932) and *The Thief-Takers* by Patrick Pringle (London, 1958), as well as in Sir John Fielding's own work *An Account of Henry Fielding's Police* which he published in 1758. Some interesting material on Henry Fielding's activities at the Bow Street office is contained in *The History of Henry Fielding* by Wilbur L. Cross, 3 volumes (Yale University Press, 1918) and in *Henry Fielding (His Life, Work and Times)* by F. H. Dudden, 2 volumes (Oxford, 1952); a full description of Sir John Fielding's period at the office appears in *The Life and Work of Sir John Fielding* by R. Leslie-Melville (London, 1934).

In tracing the history of the British penal system I have again relied upon a number of books, more especially on *Imprisonment in Medieval England* by Ralph B. Pugh (Cambridge, 1968), *The British Penal System 1773–1950* by R. S. E. Hinde (London, 1951), *The English Prison and Borstal Systems* by Lionel W. Fox (London, 1952), *The Roots of Evil* by Christopher Hibbert (London, 1963) and *English Prisons under Local Government* by Sidney and Beatrice Webb (London, 1922).

For my account of the development of the Trade Union movement and labour relations generally I have used the standard work on the subject, *The History of Trade Unionism* by Sidney and Beatrice Webb (London, 1894). I have obtained additional facts from *The Legal History of Trade Unionism* by R. Y. Hedges and A. Winterbottom (London, 1930) and from the published collection of Otto Kahn-Freund's Hamlyn Lectures, *Labour and the Law* (London, 1972).

In writing the earlier sections of the book I have been assisted by two well-known works by Sir Henry Maine, his *Ancient Law* (London, 1920) and his *Dissertations on Early English Law and Custom* (London, 1891); also by H. F. Jolowicz's *Historical Introduction to the Study of Roman Law* (Cambridge, 1952). For a background to the English political scene in the eighteenth century I have gathered additional material from *The Parliamentary History of England* (London, 1811), and I have made use of both editions of *The Newgate Calendar*, that of G. T. Wilkinson (London, 1816) and that of A. Knapp and W. Baldwin (London, circa 1813) for the general setting of criminal life during the same period.

INDEX